C
M
G

SKI TOURING ROUTES:

Colorado's Front Range

ALAN R. APT and KAY TURNBAUGH

The Colorado Mountain Club Press

Golden, Colorado

Ski Touring Routes: Colorado's Front Range
© Alan R. Apt and Kay Turnbaugh 2020

Published by The Colorado Mountain Club Press
710 10th Street, Suite 200, Golden, CO 80401
303-996-2743
email: cmcpress@cmc.org
website: http://www.cmcpress.org

Founded in 1912, The Colorado Mountain Club is the largest outdoor recreation, education, and conservation organization in the Rocky Mountains. Look for our books at your local bookstore or outdoor retailer, or online at www.cmcpress.org.

CORRECTIONS: We greatly appreciate when readers alert us to errors or outdated information by emailing cmcpress@cmc.org.

Alan Apt and Kay Turnbaugh: authors, photographers, cartographers
Kay Turnbaugh: designer
Stephanie Vessely: copyeditor
Jeff Golden: publisher
Front cover photo: East Flattop Mountain, photo by Russ Brinkman
Back cover photo: Arapaho Lakes Trail, photo by Alan Apt

DISTRIBUTED TO THE BOOK TRADE BY:
Mountaineers Books, 1001 SW Klickitat Way, Suite 201, Seattle, WA 98134, 800-553-4453, www.mountaineersbooks.org

We gratefully acknowledge the financial support of the people of Colorado through the Scientific and Cultural Facilities District of greater metropolitan Denver for our publishing activities.

TOPOGRAPHIC MAPS created with CalTopo.com software.

ISBN 978-0-9671466-4-5

CONTENTS

North Central Colorado ··············

Northern Colorado ■■■■■■■■■■■■■■■■■

South Central Colorado ....

INTRODUCTION

Alan Apt moved to Colorado in 1973 and fell in love with mountain adventures almost immediately. He has skied many, many hundreds of miles, and of course, all the trails in this book, most multiple times. Kay Turnbaugh grew up in Colorado and has been skiing the backcountry for sixty years. She still revels in days spent on the trail.

Whether you're a seasoned Colorado resident or you just arrived here from the flatlands, this guidebook will provide a great deal of information about exciting places to enjoy and the equipment you'll want when you get there.

Topics

- Trails, most within easy driving distance from Front Range cities and towns.
- Information, including descriptions of the routes, length, and avalanche danger.
- Family-oriented, easy outings for beginners or youngsters.
- Intermediate and advanced trails for experienced skiers.
- Ski Tips. What kind of skis to use for each trail.
- Safety. Outdoor winter adventures need to be safe, and we'll talk about how that can be achieved.
- Gear and more gear. We'll talk about the ups and downs cross-country skis. (Hint—we advocate trying before buying. This book is intended to help you make informed equipment choices, but the final decisions must be your own.)

CROSS COUNTRY SKIING

The type of ski you will want to try, and possibly buy, depends on the type of back-country or cross-country skiing you want to do. Most skis require wax for grip on flat terrain and moderate uphills, and many now have climbing patterns on the bottoms so you don't have to apply wax for grip (they still need glide wax on the tips and tails for easy sliding). For very steep terrain you will want to rent or buy climbing skins.

Modern skis without metal edges turn more easily. Many have climbing patterns that vary in effectiveness, and waxable skis are usually not available for rent. Waxable skis climb better than pattern skis if the right wax is chosen for the temperature. They become challenging when the temperature changes while you are skiing; that's why many people ski on pattern skis.

There are different widths available as well. Narrower skis are generally more appropriate for experienced skiers who can negotiate downhills without edges and want more glide in their kick and glide, as well as a bit more speed. Wider skis with edges are better for beginners. Pattern skis are sometimes a bit slower than waxable skis, including on downhills, which is good for beginners. You won't want to use Alpine Touring (AT) or telemark skis on easy backcountry trails or in Nordic areas. They are awkward and heavier than you need for mellow, groomed trails.

GROOMED NORDIC AREAS

If you want to ski in groomed ski areas, then traditional, narrower skis (skinny skis) would be a good choice, with or without metal edges. Metal edges make it easier to turn on steep or icy runs, but add weight to the ski.

EASY BACKCOUNTRY TRAILS

If you want to try ungroomed forest trails that are not too challenging, you can use mid-width Nordic skis with metal edges, climbing patterns, or wax. They are usually still called cross-country skis rather than AT or telemark skis.

MODERATE TO CHALLENGING BACKCOUNTRY TRAILS

The general rule to apply is the more challenging the trail or the deeper the powder, the wider the ski. You can choose from wider AT or telemark skis with metal edges. AT and telemark skis can also be used at ski areas, so you can potentially get twice as much usage. If you are a downhill skier who is just starting to go "off-piste," the European term for ungroomed snow skiing, then take advantage of your parallel turning skills with AT skis. If you have never skied before, we suggest that you take either a downhill or telemark lesson at your local ski area, and then decide which style of skiing you want to learn.

Boots are almost all plastic or synthetic and are generally stiffer and much lighter than downhill boots and leather boots. The stiffness gives you more control of the skis.

HELMETS

When backcountry skiing, it is wise to use a helmet on steep downhill terrain where you will be dodging trees. It doesn't take long to determine that even skinny tree branches don't give way and can do damage to your noggin.

PACKS

On day trips, carry a day pack. You will want it for carrying the clothing layers you peel off so you don't overheat. You'll need a pack large enough for bulky winter clothing. You might also have to carry your skis over bare spots, and strapping them on a pack is easier than carrying them in your arms. Some packs include loops for carrying skis.

ALWAYS CARRY THE TEN ESSENTIALS:
1. Extra fleece or wool clothing
2. Extra food and water for one additional day in case of emergency
3. Sunglasses and goggles for strong winds and subzero windchill, and sunscreen (SPF 30 or more)

4.   Knife
5.   First-aid kit
6.   Fire starter (especially important in snowy terrain)
7.   Waterproof matches or lighter
8.   Flashlight or headlamp with spare batteries
9.   Map
10. Compass

Other safety gear to consider includes a whistle, a space blanket and/or tarp, and two black garbage bags for emergency shelter. Good additions for steep or avalanche-prone areas include a shovel (one per person), an avalanche beacon/locator (one per person), a snow probe (one per person), and an ice axe or ski poles. A GPS locating device is a worthwhile item (smartphones often do not work in remote areas).

There is some controversy about the use of cellular phones as a safety device because they are often not usable in high-mountain valleys, and cold weather can sap the batteries. Keeping your phone close to the heat of your body can extend battery life.

Pack your clothing around your water bottle to prevent your water from freezing. Start with warm water so it is less likely to freeze solid.

Be prepared! Bring hand and foot warmers (packets) if you tend to get cold easily. Bring a pair of prescription glasses if you wear contacts.

CLOTHING

As with most active outdoor backcountry winter sports, dress in layers. When you pack, imagine warm and sunny weather followed by driving snow and subzero wind. In other words, pack for all conceivable conditions using water-repellent or water-proofed gear and moisture-wicking clothing such as nylon, synthetics, or wool.

Begin your excursion dressed a bit lightly for the given day's conditions. You may be somewhat cold at first, but you will warm up as you begin skiing uphill. If you are dealing with extreme conditions, pay particular attention to what your body is telling you. Don't go too long before putting on warmer layers. Rest often rather than over-heating or, especially, breaking into a sweat and creating a potential chill situation later when you stop. When you break for lunch, you will want to put some layers back on, as you will cool off quickly. It is warmer to have an insulated pad to sit on.

Cotton is not recommended, including jeans. When cotton gets wet or damp, it does not dry out easily nor will it insulate you against the cold. On your average win-ter day, a pair of synthetic or merino wool long underwear is highly recommended. For the next layer, a wool sweater, fleece, or a lightweight down or synthetic-insulated jacket will work. Fleece is more effective than wool when wet, as it dries out more eas-ily. Your outer layer should be breathable and waterproof.

Headgear is especially important because you lose much of your body heat through your head and neck. Keep your head covered with a good wool or synthetic hat that covers your ears. A ski mask or balaclava is also a good idea in case it gets windy or starts to snow. Goggles are important for an enjoyable experience in wind or snow. Mittens are generally warmer than gloves, but either should be waterproof, and at least double-layered with insulating material. If you don't have waterproof mittens or gloves, you will want more than one pair of non-waterproof gloves. For skiing in comfort, refer to the following list before you head out:

- Long underwear tops and bottoms
- Turtleneck shirt or wool scarf to protect your neck
- Fleece or wool sweater
- Wind-proof and waterproof outer coat or shell
- Wool or very warm synthetic socks
- Warm mittens or gloves
- Warm cap
- Face or ski mask

FOOD AND WATER

Take the same sorts of food and drink when you go backcountry skiing that you would when hiking. Be practical, however, and consider what the cold will do to your hands if you are trying to peel an orange, for instance.

Bring easy-access snacks such as energy bars or trail mix. You will burn lots of energy and calories skiing—up to 1,000 calories per hour. Eating something with a bit of fat in it will help to keep you warm. Bring extra high-calorie food in case of an emergency, and ask your compatriots to bring enough so you won't have to feed them, too.

Much has been made of the new high-protein diets and foods designed as an adjunct to exercise. Although eating something that contains protein along with carbohydrates works well, carbohydrates are still the key ingredient for energy production. Exercising aerobically for longer than forty minutes will cause your body to use fat stores as energy. If you don't want to deplete your glycogen supply (the fuel your muscles use) and stay as fresh as possible, stop for a small snack about once an hour.

Carry water in something that will prevent it from freezing. A good general recommendation is to bring about a half liter of water per hour of moderate activity in moderate temperatures, but remember that cold weather dehydrates you more quickly. Don't wait until you feel thirsty to drink some water; drink regularly as you go. Don't eat snow as a substitute for drinking water—it will chill you to the bone, and there's the risk of pollutants.

You can add a sports drink or fruit-juice mixture to your water. Alcohol lowers your metabolic rate and can make you feel colder. A thermos of tea or hot chocolate is highly recommended.

Safe Winter Recreation

PICKING YOUR FIRST ADVENTURE

Be conservative your first time out. Pick a short, easy round-trip that will be an enjoyable half-day jaunt. That will give you a chance to see how your body reacts to skis and how you react to dealing with the equipment in the cold, snow, and altitude.

Snow conditions can vary drastically and unpredictably at any time of the season. Snow trails that are normally relatively easy can become very challenging in deep powder or on a crust that breaks under your feet.

SAFE SKIING TECHNIQUES

Look before you leap—study the terrain and plan where you will turn and stop. Ski uphill to stop or slow down. When skiing downhill, traverse to control your speed.

You will generally find the snow to be more powdery in or under the trees. Watch out for tree wells hidden by drifted snow: Don't get too close to tree trunks because sometimes a well of air or loose snow can form, and if you fall in, it is almost impossible to get out without assistance. They can collapse suddenly, and throw people into the tree, causing injury and suffocation.

Watch for trail markers and be very aware of your surroundings. Routefinding, even on marked trails, is more challenging in winter. Do not ski alone; go with a companion. Let others know where you are going and when you will be coming back. Sign in on trail registries.

Use extreme caution whenever you are crossing what appear to be frozen streams and lakes. They are often not frozen solid, especially around inlets and outlets, and falling through the ice can be fatal.

MANAGING RISK IN AVALANCHE COUNTRY

Colorado has the highest number of reported avalanches in the United States—there were 275 deaths from 1950 to 2016. The number of avalanche deaths has skyrocketed, roughly proportionate to the number of backcountry recreationists. **This section cannot take the place of an avalanche safety course or in-depth avalanche guidebooks.** If you haven't taken a course or attended a lecture, use the tutorial on avalanche.org, and check out the Colorado Avalanche Information Center website—avalanche.state. co.us.

The climate in Colorado's Front Range tends to produce light, dry, fluffy powder snow that skiers love, but it also tends to evolve into a highly unstable and dangerous snow underlayer that propagates avalanches. When such snow first falls, it is known as *surface hoar*. When these layers of powder snow are buried beneath subsequent layers of heavier snow, they are called *depth hoar*. The water content of this hoar snow is often only one-half that of snow in other regions; even Utah has much wetter snow.

The first question you need to ask yourself about avalanche danger is if you really want to risk traveling in avalanche terrain. If your answer is no, then pick a trail from the book that has low or no avalanche danger. In addition, you should know how to recognize avalanche terrain and practice good routefinding techniques to avoid it.

Most of the routes in this book are low-hazard routes. There is an avalanche rating for every trail option. You can avoid avalanche terrain completely if you plan your trip to do so. Check the rating of the trail, and then check conditions in the area you plan to visit at least a few days before. You can begin by visiting the CAIC website to get the mountain weather forecast and the avalanche forecast with snow stability information. You don't want to be surprised by local conditions upon arrival. Recent major snowfall or changing temperatures can enhance avalanche danger on steep slopes. On the morning of your trip, check the CAIC website again so you know current and predicted conditions, since forecasts can change overnight. CAIC usually posts their forecasts everyday by 7 a.m.

Colorado Avalanche Information Center (CAIC)

With the Center's mobile app you can get avalanche forecasts and upload your own observations about avalanche danger.
303-499-9650; avalanche.state.co.us

Most avalanches run on slopes that are 30 to 45 degrees. Avoid slopes that are above 20 degrees, and you will avoid most avalanches. To educate yourself about slope steepness, first learn how to read a topographic map so you can identify steep slopes for your potential route. Find a very short but steep slope and measure slope angle with an inclinometer or slope meter. If you don't have a slope meter, put two ski poles together to form a 90-degree angle. Look through your poles at 45 degrees in the center at the slope you are measuring to estimate the angle. Test slope angle on slopes of different steepness. Expert slopes in ski areas are rarely steeper than 30 degrees.

Learn about the parts of an avalanche path: the starting zone, the track, and the runout zone. If you are skiing below a steep slope, rather than on it, you might still be in the runout zone, meaning that the snow above you on a steep slope could slide down on to you. If you are above a steep slope, you might be in the starting zone. That means stay as high as possible on steep slopes and avoid crossing them if you can. If you must cross one, do so single-file and spread out so some self-rescue is possible if it does slide. Plan your route carefully before you start so you know you are avoiding potentially hazardous areas. Take a compass and a good topographic map with you and know how to use them. If you are planning winter mountaineering, rather than casual outings below treeline on safe trails, take an avalanche course.

Don't ski alone and stay away from steep terrain when avalanche danger is high. Even a small slide ten feet across and five feet deep can bury and smother a person. Carry a shovel and avalanche beacon and know how to use them. If you have any question about the safety of a proposed route, turn around and follow your own route back to a known safe destination.

If you choose to travel in avalanche terrain, you are not going to learn enough here to guarantee safe travel. Take an avalanche course that takes you into the snow, and read books and watch videos that show you how to understand the interaction between the terrain, the snowpack, and the weather. Only when you understand all three will you have the knowledge and the confidence to make good decisions, including the occasional decision to change your plans and stay safe.

AVOIDING AVALANCHES

Stay on marked trails when danger is high. A marked trail reduces but does not eliminate risk. Study your route in advance if it is not familiar to you.

- Avoid walking on, or below, steep slopes. Most avalanches occur on slopes of 30 to 45 degrees but also occur on slopes of 25 to 55 degrees. North-facing, leeward slopes are usually most dangerous in the winter months. They stabilize more slowly and are likely to have wind-drifted snow. Avoid north-facing, shaded slopes in the winter, especially after recent snow events and windstorms. South-facing slopes are most dangerous in the spring because of dramatic solar heating and melting. Open slopes are more likely to slide than those with tree cover or rocks that can anchor snow. However, avalanches can occur on tree-covered slopes as well.

- Stay high, on ridge lines if possible, but away from cornices. Cornices are masses of overhanging snow, blown by wind, which typically form along ridges. Don't ski or walk on or under cornices.

- Go straight up or down the edge of the slope if you have to descend or ascend a possible avalanche slope, and avoid the middle portion.

- Move across dangerous slopes one person at a time and as high as possible. Staying far apart provides for less weight stress on the underlying snow and enhances the opportunity for at least one person to be available to assist in a rescue effort.

- Avoid old avalanche chutes or slide zones. Don't walk below steep slopes that might be avalanche-starting zones. These could catch you in a run-out area.

- If you hear a whumping sound, alert your companions and make your way to trees or the edge of the slope. If it ever sounds as though the snow is collapsing beneath you, you are in a dangerous position and should take immediate precautions.

- Avoid areas with fracture lines in the snow. This indicates that a slab avalanche, the largest and most destructive kind, is likely to activate in the area.

- Beware of cold temperatures, high winds, and snowstorms with accumulations of more than six inches of snow or a rate of snowfall of one inch per hour or greater. Keep in mind that 90 percent of avalanches occur during or after snowstorms. Dry, powdery snow is more likely to avalanche than wet, heavy snow, unless the heavy snow is on top of the weak, powdery layer known as depth hoar.

- Never assume that an area is safe simply because others have safely used it.

- Avoid holes and gullies, not just steep slopes.

ALTITUDE

The best snow in Colorado is usually found in the mountains rather than the foothills, at higher elevations. The primary way to determine reliable snow cover is by the altitude of the trail. Generally, the higher the trail, the better the snow cover will be. Snowfall can be very localized, so checking the latest forecasts and calling the local

U.S. Forest Service, national park, or state park office is a good idea in order to assess trail conditions before leaving home.

A major Front Range upslope storm can often offer good early season, low-altitude cover. February, March, and April are usually Colorado's snowiest months. Trails that are 9,000 to 10,000 feet high are more reliable before February. Above 8,000 feet it can snow into May, but snow cover will likely be marginal or last only until the sun appears. You can often still ski above 10,000 feet into June. Tree-sheltered trails feature much more snow than trails exposed to sun and wind, regardless of elevation. Snow cover can vary greatly on the same trail, so be prepared to carry your skis over thin or windswept sections. Rocks are not good for skis.

If you rarely venture above 5,000 feet, recognize your and your party's potential limitations at higher elevations. Keep in mind the effects of altitude are unpredictable, especially for those who are visiting from sea level. If you or visitors have just arrived from a lower elevation, take at least one or two days to acclimate before venturing above 5,000 feet. If you live at or above 5,000 feet, less time is needed to adjust.

Drinking a lot of water before and during high-altitude exercise is a good, though not foolproof, preventive measure against altitude illness. Take along some headache medication (aspirin substitute, because aspirin can upset the stomach) and anti-nausea medication.

Altitude and elevation gain can certainly slow you down. Assume that you will travel one mile per hour or 1,000 feet of elevation gain per hour, at most, even if you are well-conditioned. Physical conditioning helps, but it doesn't prevent altitude illness.

ALTITUDE ILLNESS

Mild altitude illness is the most common manifestation of the high-elevation phenomenon called mountain sickness. Symptoms of altitude illness are severe headache, nausea, loss of appetite, a warm flushed face, lethargy, and insomnia or poor sleep with strange dreams. Altitude illness, also called Acute Mountain Sickness (AMS), can last several days. Resting, skiing at lower elevations, eating lightly, and drinking more non-alcoholic liquids can help. Avoid taking barbiturates such as sleeping pills because they can aggravate the illness. Some people, most often women, experience swelling of the face, hands, and feet.

Nosebleeds are more common at higher elevations because of the very dry air. Staying hydrated can help. The most effective way to stop a nosebleed is to gently pinch the nose shut for five minutes.

High Altitude Pulmonary Edema (HAPE) is a more severe form of mountain sickness and is a condition caused by fluid filling the lungs. Symptoms include difficulty breathing, a severe headache with incoherence, staggering, and a persistent hacking cough. This is a serious illness caused by altitude.

High Altitude Cerebral Edema (HACE) is a critical condition caused by swelling of the brain. Symptoms include persistent vomiting, severe and persistent headache, extreme fatigue, delirium or confusion, staggering, and/or coma. This is the most serious illness caused by altitude and can be fatal.

Though extremely rare in Colorado, if you or anyone in your party experiences the symptoms of either HAPE or HACE, go to a lower altitude immediately and get to a physician as soon as possible.

If you always suffer at altitude, ask your doctor about Diamox, a prescription drug used to prevent altitude sickness.

HYPOTHERMIA

Hypothermia is deadly. It is an acute traumatic event that occurs when your body's core temperature drops below 95 degrees. It does not take extremely low temperatures to get into trouble—people have died from hypothermia with air temperatures in the 40s and 50s. Core temperature loss can easily happen if someone falls into a lake or stream and is not able to get warm and dry right away. It can also happen if you are simply not dressed adequately when temperatures drop, the wind picks up, or it snows or rains on you.

You can avoid hypothermia by taking along the right kinds of clothing. Preventing hypothermia is much wiser than waiting until the situation becomes life threatening. Some symptoms of hypothermia are uncontrollable shivering, slurred or slow speech, fuzzy thinking, poor memory, incoherence, lack of coordination causing stumbling or vertigo, and extreme fatigue or sleepiness.

If you observe any of these symptoms in yourself or another person, take immediate action to warm the individual experiencing the problem. Stop and use your emergency supplies to make a fire and provide warm liquids, or wrap the individual in additional warm clothing and urge him or her to move around enough to warm up. A backpacking stove is ideal for heating up liquids or providing warmth.

Weather in the mountains can change dramatically in a matter of minutes. Early fall or late spring blizzards are especially sneaky. Pay attention to weather forecasts: pack extra gear, and when the weather is in doubt, head back! Zero-visibility snow conditions, known as whiteouts, can be deadly. If you study the histories of winter disasters, you will find that most of them could have been prevented by better preparation and by knowing when to retreat from difficult conditions.

FROSTBITE

Prevent frostbite by keeping your hands, feet, face (especially the tip of your nose), and ears well protected. Early signs are tingling and numbing sensations, or a numb, pale patch of skin, or skin that feels hard or looks waxy. Mild frostbite, also called frostnip, can be treated with first aid. Warm your hands by tucking them into your armpits. Cover your face, nose, or ears with dry, gloved hands, and don't rub the affected area. Once you're out of the cold gently warm frostbitten areas. More serious frostbite requires medical attention.

SUN PROTECTION

The sun's rays are much stronger at higher elevations. With the added effect of reflection off the snow, even on a cloudy day you can end up with a severe burn. The harmful effects of the sun are magnified at high altitudes, so covering up and avoiding direct sunlight is the best strategy, especially between the hours of 10 a.m. and 2 p.m.

Sunscreen is essential at high altitude. Use one that is at least SPF 30 to avoid sun damage and reapply throughout the day. Excess sun also adversely affects the immune system. Your dermatologist will tell you that there is no such thing as a healthy tan.

Sunglasses or goggles are also essential to avoid sun damage to the eyes. If you do not protect your eyes you might become temporarily snowblind, which is very painful and makes travel difficult.

MOUNTAIN WATER—A CAUTION

You need to drink plenty of water, but don't drink from mountain streams and lakes without treating it. Though they look crystal clear and inviting, they are not creature-free. Cold does not purify mountain water, and a nasty parasite called *Giardia lamblia* actually thrives in cold water and can cause giardiasis, or diarrheal disease. If you want to drink from streams and lakes, bring water-purifying tablets, use filtering equipment, or boil your water. Filtering water in the winter can be a challenge.

RENTAL YURTS, CABINS, AND HUTS

See the Appendix for some sources for renting overnight accommodations in the backcountry.

SKI TRIPS

The following organizations host ski outings that you may enjoy: Colorado Mountain Club, Rocky Mountain Sierra Club, Rocky Mountain National Park Nature Association, and the staff of Rocky Mountain National Park. Contact information is listed in the Appendix. Check their websites for detailed information.

VOLUNTEERING

If you want even more enjoyment in the outdoors, please consider volunteering to lead or support outings and activities. You can take advantage of these rewarding opportunities with the following organizations: Ignite Adaptive Sports at Eldora Mountain Resort, Colorado Special Olympics, the National Sports Center for the Disabled at Winter Park, Rocky Mountain Sierra Club, Colorado Mountain Club, and any local, state, or national parks.

WILDERNESS ETHICS

"We aren't inheriting the Earth from our fathers, we are stealing it from our children."
— David Brower, *Let the Mountains Talk, Let the Rivers Run*

Public land is not government land. It is land that we, the public, own. Our national forests are valuable land that is protected and maintained for us by government employees. This ownership comes not only with the opportunity for recreation—for "re-creation" of the body and soul—but also with the responsibility to care for and respect our land. Many of the areas described in this book are wilderness areas that require extra precautions to prevent deterioration of the wilderness experience and wildlife habitat for present and future generations. We should all try to apply the Leave No Trace philosophy to the use of public lands. The things that move us to go into the wilderness are what make it one of our most cherished national treasures.

PLAN AHEAD

Know the risks and regulations of the area you are visiting.

To minimize your impact on the land, visit the backcountry in small groups and carpool or take public transportation if possible. Try to avoid popular areas in times of high use.

To minimize your visual impact on others, use naturally hued clothing and equipment. Although, note that some winter recreationists will wear bright-colored clothing as a safety measure—in the event of avalanche or rescue, bright colors are easier to spot.

To minimize garbage, repackage food into reusable containers that won't leak.

LEAVE NO TRACE

The Leave No Trace Center for Outdoor Ethics (LNC.org) provides a framework of seven principles for leaving minimal impact during your visit outdoors.

• Camp at least 200 feet from trails, water sources and muddy areas, and wildlife forage or watering areas. Animals are stressed in winter and your activities could reduce their chance of survival.

• Avoid building a fire. Bring a lightweight stove and extra clothing for cooking and warmth. Open fires are illegal in wilderness areas. On overnight stays, enjoy a candle instead of a fire. Where fires are permitted, use them only for emergencies and do not scar large rocks, overhangs, or trees with the flame from your fire. Use only downed or dead wood and do not snap branches off live trees. If you burn garbage, burn only paper; remove all unburnable and unburned trash and bury ashes.

• Pack out whatever you pack in.

• Dismantle snow structures and cover snow pits.

• Use backcountry toilets whenever they are available. Get as far off the trail as possible when you have to answer nature's call—at least 50 feet for a urination stop—and camouflage soiled snow. Use bare ground for burial or pack out human waste; don't bury it in the snow. Dispose of solid waste at least 200 feet from trails or water sources.

• Pets are allowed in most national forests and state parks, but not on trails in national parks. If possible, leave your pets at home; they will love you for it. Snow and ice often cause painful paw injuries, and dog booties rarely work properly. If you do bring a pet, control it at all times. Beware that dogs have been seriously injured by the sharp edges of skis; skiers can't always turn or stop quickly when descending narrow trails. Camouflage soiled snow from your dog's urination. Carry out dog feces.

• Leave what you find. Do not remove trees, plants, rocks, or historical artifacts—they belong to everyone.

HOW TO USE THIS BOOK

The routes in this book range from family adventures to winter mountaineering treks.

Most of the easy out-and-backs are suitable for families with young children. Included are some trails specifically for young children or less ambitious family outings with visitors from lower elevations. There are many trails suitable for the intermediate skier who is looking for a fun and scenic day trip, and there also are a few more challenging trails that require mountaineering and advanced skiing skills.

Routes are grouped according to geographic regions and further segmented into chapters covering local areas. Each route begins with an information summary with highlights that enable you to judge whether that trip is appropriate for you. This is followed by more specific driving directions to the trailhead and a detailed description of the trail itself. The accompanying maps are not intended to be used for routefinding, but to assist you in visualizing the route and locating it on a topographic map.

DISTANCE

The distance for each route, whether an out-and-back (termed "round-trip"), a loop, or one way, is given in miles.

DIFFICULTY

For many of the routes, the difficulty rating is given as a range because you can always opt for traveling only a portion of the trail and thereby turn a moderate or challenging trek into an easier one. Many of the routes offer more than one option because even a short out-and-back can be a nice outdoor experience with pleasing scenery.

The difficulty ratings in this book are generally on a par with those given by the U.S. Forest Service. **EASY** routes are appropriate for beginners or novices; the number of steep sections and the overall elevation gain are limited. **MODERATE** routes include several steep sections and require a longer, more sustained effort that is appropriate for intermediate skiers. **CHALLENGING** routes have many steep sections and likely include a sustained climb.

These ratings assume that people using this book are reasonably fit and physically active, or have been medically cleared for physical activity at altitudes above 7,000 feet. If you have been leading a sedentary lifestyle, check with your health care provider before engaging in strenuous outdoor activity.

SKILL LEVEL

NOVICE: Novices have never used skis or have used them only once or twice. The alpine skiing equivalent would be a Green Beginner Run in a downhill ski area. To truly enjoy one of these treks, novices should be physically active and exercise at least two times per week for at least twenty minutes per session; they should also be able to handle an elevated heart rate and lack of oxygen at higher elevations. Novices probably won't attempt the entire route, but will cover a section of it and then turn around before they become exhausted. As a novice, decide how long you want to be out before you go, and then time your outbound trip, frequently estimating how long it will take to return to the trailhead. This way, you won't accidentally exceed your limits.

INTERMEDIATE: Intermediate skiers have used skis several times. The alpine skiing equivalent would be a Blue Intermediate Run in a downhill ski area. They enjoy routes rated as moderate if they have a somewhat higher level of fitness. This doesn't mean they have to be serious athletes. It just means they are physically active and exercise at least three times per week for twenty to forty minutes per session.

EXPERT: Expert skiers have been using skis for a year or more and have a high level of fitness. The alpine skiing equivalent would be a Black More Difficult Run in a downhill ski area. They have the experience to survive rapidly changing weather and snow conditions. Experts should be exercising almost daily, have good routefinding skills, and always carry a topographic map and compass or GPS with the knowledge of how to use them.

HIGH POINT AND ELEVATION GAIN

These two entries tell you the highest elevation reached on the ski, and the elevation difference between it and the trailhead. These are both given in feet.

AVALANCHE HAZARD RATINGS

Call or visit the Colorado Avalanche Information Center online for up-to-date reports (see the Appendix).

LOW: On steep, snow-covered gullies and open slopes, avalanches are unlikely and snow is mostly stable except in isolated pockets. Natural and human-triggered avalanches are unlikely. Backcountry travel is generally safe.

MODERATE: Areas of unstable snow and slabs make avalanches very possible on steep, snow-covered gullies and open slopes. Human-triggered avalanches are possible. Backcountry travelers should use caution.

CONSIDERABLE: Unstable slabs make human-triggered avalanches probable. Naturally triggered avalanches are possible. Backcountry travelers should use extreme caution.

HIGH: Mostly unstable snow on a variety of aspects and slopes makes natural and human-triggered avalanches likely. Avalanches are likely on steep, snow-covered gullies and open slopes. Backcountry travel is not recommended.

EXTREME: Widespread areas of unstable snow on a variety of aspects and slopes make natural and human-triggered avalanches a certainty on steep, snow-covered gullies and open slopes. Large, destructive avalanches are possible. Backcountry travel should be avoided.

MAPS

The relevant topographic map or maps for the area of each route are included. New maps are published often, and they may not be listed here.

WHO TO CONTACT

This entry lists the land-managing agency to contact for more information; phone numbers are also listed in the Appendix under Contact Information.

Rocky Mountain National Park

Chapter 1

ROCKY MOUNTAIN NATIONAL PARK— NORTHEAST

"Beyond the wall of the unreal city, beyond the asphalt belting of superhighways, there is another world waiting for you. It is the old true world of the deserts, the mountains, the forests, the islands, the shores, the open plains. Go there. Be there. Walk gently and quietly deep within it."

—Edward Abbey, *Beyond the Wall: Essays from the Outside*

One of the gems of the national park system, perhaps even the crown jewel, Rocky Mountain National Park features some of North America's most spectacular scenery. Its winter landscape casts an almost mystical spell. Rocky Mountain National Park is truly "beyond the wall." There are few places that encompass so much natural beauty in such limited geography. From the craggy peaks of the Continental Divide to the gentle beauty of the glacial moraines and meadows, or the cascading frozen streams, it is a captivating environment that makes you want to stay.

Moraine Park's ever-changing mountain weather and light make it a magical place where elk roam freely and birds of prey soar overhead. This stunning setting features one of the most scenically impressive glacial moraines in the Rockies. Glacier Gorge is an entry point to massive rock, frozen waterfalls of hanging ice, Black Lake, and the Loch. The majestic cliffs of Mount Lady Washington and Longs Peak soar to the south, with views of the Mummy Range gracing the horizon to the north. The spectacular beauty of the Bear Lake and Hallet Peak area with its easy accessibility, wide variety of trails, and reliable snow conditions make it one of the most popular areas in the park year-round. The majestic backdrops of frozen Bear, Bierstadt, Dream, Emerald and Jewell lakes are almost mystical, as spindrift and filtered winter light float down from the summits. You can also explore the shoulders and summits of Flattop and Hallet's Peak or, if you are very ambitious, attempt their summits.

To get to Rocky Mountain National Park from Denver, take I-25 north 40 miles and exit at Loveland/US 34. Take US 34 west through Big Thompson Canyon 40 miles to

Estes Park. Allow at least one hour and 30 minutes. Other routes from Denver include US 36 northwest through Boulder and Lyons for 60 miles to Estes Park; and I-25 north for 30 miles to Highway 66, west on Highway 66 for 15 miles to Lyons, and northwest on US 36 for 20 miles to Estes Park. Once in Estes Park, follow the signs to the park entrance.

Skiers on the slopes of the former Hidden Valley ski area in Rocky Mountain National Park.

1. North Fork Trail

ROUND TRIP	13 miles to Lost Falls; 16.2 miles to Lost Lake
DIFFICULTY	Easy to challenging
SKILL LEVEL	Novice
HIGH POINT	9,900 feet
ELEVATION GAIN	2,000 feet
AVALANCHE DANGER	None to low
MAP	Trails Illustrated #200, Rocky Mountain National Park
CONTACT	Rocky Mountain National Park, nps.gov/romo Canyon Lakes Ranger District, 970-295-6700

COMMENT: This lesser-known trail (also known as the Dunraven Trail or Lost Lake Trail) features varied topography in a beautiful riparian area and winds its way through the short forested canyon of the North Fork of the Big Thompson River, with its striking rock outcrops and meadows. The trail goes through a narrow portion of the Comanche Peak Wilderness before entering Rocky Mountain National Park. It climbs through a backcountry campground in the Comanche Peak Wilderness, more broad meadows, and eventually ventures above treeline and to Lost Lake. Because of the low elevation at the start, this trail is only reliable if there has been a major Front Range snowstorm. However, if you are willing to unstrap your skis and possibly hike for a mile or two, it can still be a great way to spend a day in a beautiful pine-forested valley. After the initial descent, the trail is level for a considerable distance, making it a good choice for family excursions or mellow outings. Nordic skinny skis are the best choice for this route. The initial descent is the only major hill.

GETTING THERE: From Denver, take I-25 north 40 miles and exit at Loveland/US 34. Take US 34 west through Big Thompson Canyon to Drake. In Drake, turn right onto CR 43 toward Glen Haven and drive northwest 6 miles. Turn right on Dunraven Glade Road/CR 51B. Drive northwest for 2.4 miles on the well-maintained dirt or snow-packed road to its end, where you will find the Dunraven Trailhead.

THE ROUTE: From the parking lot you can see the well-marked trailhead. Proceed to the right of the privy and up a slight hill. The trail then descends about 0.5 mile to the North Fork of the Big Thompson River, losing 200 feet of elevation. At the bottom is a wonder world of pretty brook-side winter settings, with tall pines and a meandering, babbling or frozen brook. There are a few very narrow, potentially icy or wet spots in the first mile. The snow conditions can vary widely depending on sun exposure, and the first mile is likely to be snow-free.

View to the south from the North Fork (also called Dunraven or Lost Lake) trailhead.

After 0.5 mile you will pass next to the private Cheley Camp. Though you are in a thick forest, the trees are tall so there are good views all the way. In the first 2 miles you go through open areas and a large meadow. There is a good bridge for a stream crossing. At this point the snow might be questionable for a while until you enter the trees again, but you are steadily gaining elevation, so odds of better snow are good as you proceed.

The trail to the first Comanche Peak Wilderness backcountry campsite is 2.1 miles from the trailhead, and other campsites are between 2.7 and 3.4 miles from the trailhead. The trail then climbs significantly before you enter Rocky Mountain National Park just before 4 miles, but then levels again. You reach park campsites about 4.25 miles from the trailhead.

At about 4.5 miles there is a trail junction. To the left is the North Boundary Trail. Stay straight/right. As you travel the next 2 miles along the river, there are meadows and more backcountry campsites as the trees thin and the trail opens up. You reach Lost Falls at about 6.5 miles, where there is another trail junction. To the right is Stormy Peaks Trail (Route #8, p. 37); stay straight/left.

WARNING: Going all the way to Lost Lake means traveling below a high ridge just beyond Lost Falls. If you plan to go that far, check with the National Park Service or the Arapaho-Roosevelt National Forest office to see if there is avalanche danger, and proceed accordingly. Up to that point, about 7 miles from the trailhead, there are no avalanche hazards.

The last mile to the lake goes through Lost Meadow, finally reaching the stark beauty of the glacial cirque at 8.1 miles. You can decide to turn around at any point depending on the conditions and your ambitions.

NORTH FORK TRAIL

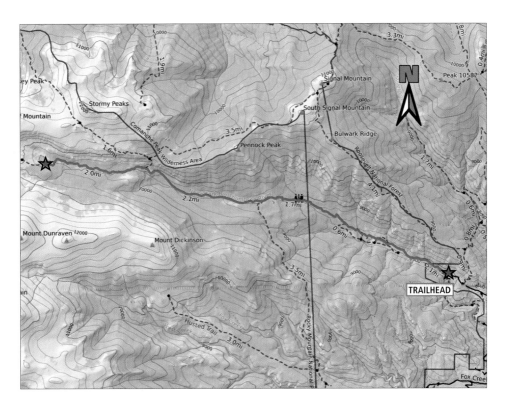

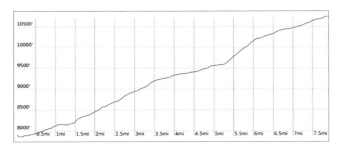

2. Hidden Valley

ROUND TRIP	2 miles to Trail Ridge Road; 3 miles to top of Tombstone Ridge
DIFFICULTY	Moderate to challenging
SKILL LEVEL	Intermediate
HIGH POINT	11,500 feet at top of Tombstone Ridge; 10,500 feet at Trail Ridge Road
ELEVATION GAIN	1,200 feet to Trail Ridge Road; 2,200 feet to top of Tombstone Ridge
AVALANCHE DANGER	Low to moderate
MAP	Trails Illustrated #200, Rocky Mountain National Park
CONTACT	Rocky Mountain National Park, nps.gov/romo

COMMENT: This winter playground is a former small alpine ski area that is now great for snowshoeing, tubing, and cross-country and telemark skiing. The park has installed a warming hut and heated restrooms and expanded the parking lot. The ski runs are still well-defined, making it impossible to get lost. Go out as far as you like, and turn around when you have gained enough elevation to enjoy the views of the Mummy Range. If you continue on for an additional trek on Trail Ridge Road you will have even better views of the Mummies. AT or telemark skis are the best choice for this area.

GETTING THERE: From the Beaver Meadows entrance to Rocky Mountain National Park, do not take the Bear Lake Road turnoff on the left. Instead, stay straight/right and drive 4 miles northwest to Deer Ridge Junction. Continue straight through the intersection toward Trail Ridge Road. After 2.25 miles, you will round a sharp hairpin turn and the Hidden Valley parking lot will be on the left/west side of the road.

THE ROUTE: The area offers an initially uphill, out-and-back option, as well as a potential car shuttle. From the warming hut, travel uphill past the tubing area on the left/south side. You will see two potential uphill routes that are former ski runs. They are unmarked and unnamed. They will appear on the northwest/right side of the trail. You can take either run uphill. The trails get gradually steeper as you climb, so go as far as you like before turning around.

If you continue for 1 mile, you will climb more steeply to intersect Trail Ridge Road, which is closed from October through May. If you turn around at the road, you will have a 2-mile round-trip and around a 1,000-foot gain. If you want more exertion,

Hidden Valley from Trail Ridge Road.

and even more impressive views, you can cross the road and climb much more steeply up near the crest of Tombstone Ridge, the top of the old ski area. That is another 1,000 feet of climbing in just over 0.5 mile, a very vertical stretch. This section is steep enough to avalanche, so don't climb it unless you know the snow is very stable, or you can dig a snow pit to check it. If you don't want steeper climbing, but do want a longer trek, take Trail Ridge Road east from the road closure or west from the top of the ski runs. You can still do this as an out-and-back trip, and return to the base area. If you turn west, you will go uphill.

Another easier option is a car shuttle, though you would need two cars. Leave a car at the road closure and then drive back to the base area. Climb up and across Trail Ridge Road and back to the car at the closure. After ascending to Trail Ridge Road, turn left/east on the road. It is 2.75 miles to the road closure and your vehicle. The road descends gradually downhill to the closure, losing around 600 feet. Your one-way trip will be around 4 miles. You can also do it the other way around.

HIDDEN VALLEY

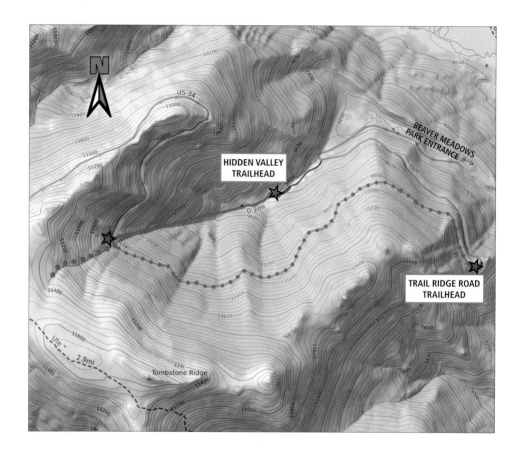

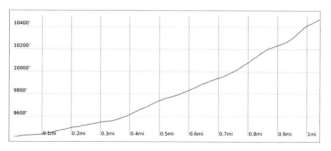

3. **Trail Ridge Road**

ROUND TRIP	5.5 miles
DIFFICULTY	Easy to moderate
SKILL LEVEL	Intermediate to expert
HIGH POINT	10,484 feet
ELEVATION GAIN	700 feet from road closure; 1,000 feet from base area
AVALANCHE DANGER	Low to considerable
MAP	Trails Illustrated #200, Rocky Mountain National Park
CONTACT	Rocky Mountain National Park, nps.gov/romo

COMMENT: This road goes all the way over the Continental Divide to Grand Lake. In the summer, Trail Ridge Road is jammed with traffic. In the winter, it is a quiet, windswept route to spectacular scenery, especially the views of the Mummy Range—Chapin, Chiquita, Ypsilon, and Mummy mountains, to name a few. Experienced skiers can use any style of ski on this route if you aren't skiing the steep sections.

With a car shuttle you can ski the road to the top of the former ski area and descend a trail to Hidden Valley. Or ski down and skin back up to the road. For that kind of adventure, you will need AT or telemark skis and advanced skills. If you are just going out and back on the road from the closure, skinny skis and beginner skills will be sufficient.

GETTING THERE: From Denver, take I-25 north 40 miles and exit at Loveland/US 34. Take US 34 west through Big Thompson Canyon 40 miles to Estes Park. Allow at least one hour and 30 minutes. Other routes from Denver include US 36 northwest through Boulder and Lyons for 60 miles to Estes Park; and I-25 north for 30 miles to Highway 66, west on Highway 66 for 15 miles to Lyons, and northwest on US 36 for 20 miles to Estes Park. When you reach Estes Park, continue west to the third traffic light, where you will see a sign for Rocky Mountain National Park. Turn left at the sign and go up a hill, bear right at the stop sign, and then bear right at the intersection 0.5 mile after the next traffic light. You will see signs for the Beaver Meadows Visitor Center.

From the Beaver Meadows entrance it is 8.3 miles to the Trail Ridge Road closure. At the Bear Lake Road turnoff on the left, stay straight/right and drive 4 miles northwest to Deer Ridge Junction. Continue straight through the intersection up Trail Ridge Road. You will round a sharp hairpin turn and pass the Hidden Valley park-

Alan Stark on Trail Ridge Road.

ing lot on the right/west side of the road. Continue about 2 miles to the road closure, unless you plan a loop with a car shuttle. There is a plowed parking area at the closure.

THE ROUTE: This is another option in Rocky Mountain National Park where the route is easy to follow and you can't get lost. The only downside is that the wind can be fierce at times and blow snow from sections of the road. You will have to be prepared to take off and put on your skis because of the wind scouring. The views are non-stop and there is a sense of adventure as you wind your way up the road, which tops out at 12,000 feet. It is much more peaceful to enjoy the route without vehicles.

There are several adventure options: you can ski out and back from the road closure or from the warming hut, or you can do a loop route with a car shuttle if you want to start from the road closure and then descend via the former Hidden Valley ski runs down to the Hidden Valley recreation area warming hut. You can climb up from the warming hut to Trail Ridge Road and back, or continue to the road closure after you have climbed up. You should allow an entire day for this most challenging option.

One other option is less safe: starting at the warming hut and going straight up to the top of Tombstone Ridge from Trail Ridge Road. The top of the former ski area offers spectacular views, but also avalanche danger and a very steep additional 1,000-foot climb. Check with the rangers about avalanche danger before climbing or skinning to the top. It is fairly safe in late spring when the snow has consolidated and is not known to frequently avalanche.

If you start from the road closure you will get the best sustained views, although probably the least consistent snow. As you travel northwest on Trail Ridge Road you will be viewing the Mummy Range across the valley. After less than a mile, you will see the former ski area and the route from the bottom to Trail Ridge Road. You will be climbing steadily but gradually as you follow the road toward the top of the ski area, where shuttle buses used to drop off skiers. You can turn around at any time after you have had your fill of the sweeping mountaintop scenery, or ski down if you have solid intermediate to advanced skills.

If you wait until spring and the opening of Trail Ridge Road, you can drive to a turnout 0.5 mile east of the Ute Trailhead. You can traverse to the top of the former Hidden Valley ski runs, but be prepared to hike snow-free areas.

SNOW CONDITIONS

Snow conditions can vary widely, from easy hard-pack to deep powder to collapsing crust or ice. It isn't unusual to dig in, or post-hole, even on skis, on steep slopes or lightly used trails. When you're the first to ski a trail after a snowstorm, take turns doing the hard work of breaking trail. If the snow conditions are especially challenging, it can be wise to revise your goals and only ski as far as is enjoyable.

TRAIL RIDGE ROAD

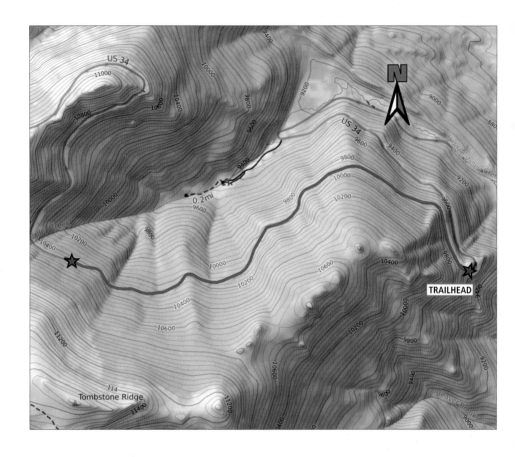

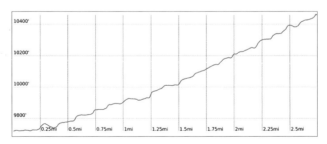

4. Cub Lake

ROUND TRIP	4 miles
DIFFICULTY	Easy to moderate
SKILL LEVEL	Novice
HIGH POINT	8,600 feet
ELEVATION GAIN	500 feet
AVALANCHE DANGER	None
MAP	Trails Illustrated #200, Rocky Mountain National Park
CONTACT	Rocky Mountain National Park, nps.gov/romo

COMMENT: On this pleasant out-and-back trail it is not unusual to encounter elk. It is a popular trail for elk viewing in late September and early October, before there is enough snow for skiing. Because the trail starts and ends at relatively low elevations and includes several sections of rock, wait until there is good snow cover. Even then, you might have to take off your skis to get over the rocky sections and pick your way carefully around and over the rocks. You can do the route as a loop and return on the Fern Lake Trail, but you will have 0.7 mile of road walking back to the Cub Lake trailhead and another 0.2 mile to the winter parking area. You can ski the trail with skinny cross-country skis because of its gentle gradient.

GETTING THERE: From Denver, take I-25 north 40 miles and exit at Loveland/US 34. Take US 34 west through Big Thompson Canyon 40 miles to Estes Park. Allow at least one hour and 30 minutes. Other routes from Denver include US 36 northwest through Boulder and Lyons for 60 miles to Estes Park; and I-25 north for 30 miles to Highway 66, west on Highway 66 for 15 miles to Lyons, and northwest on US 36 for 20 miles to Estes Park. When you reach Estes Park, continue west to the third traffic light, where you will see a sign for the Rocky Mountain National Park. Turn left at the sign and go up a hill, bear right at the stop sign, and then bear right at the intersection 0.5 mile after the next traffic light. You will see signs for the Beaver Meadows Visitor Center.

From the Beaver Meadows entrance, take the first left at 0.25 mile, onto Bear Lake Road. After 0.5 mile there is a hairpin S-turn and a sign for Moraine Park. Take the next right, and then, at the next junction, bear left and continue 1 mile to the Cub Lake Trailhead. (If you continue straight, you go into the Moraine Park Campground, which remains open in the winter.)

THE ROUTE: At the start, the Cub Lake Trail goes south to cross two streams over wooden bridges. It might be advisable to wait until you cross before putting on your skis. You encounter the first rock crossing in about 0.5 mile; go to the left around the rocks. The trail turns west and climbs slowly, and you encounter another rocky section after another 0.25 mile. It then parallels a marshy area as the tree cover thickens and it starts its gentle climb. The first mile or so borders the open expanses of Moraine Park and offers nice views back to the east and south. You will have views of the ridge line that separates you from the Sprague Lake and Bear Lake area.

Eventually you enter a beautiful tree tunnel and then, as you get within 0.5 mile of the lake, at 1.5 miles, the trail opens up and climbs steeply to the edge of the lake. This is the steepest section of the trail, but it isn't a very long climb.

CUB LAKE

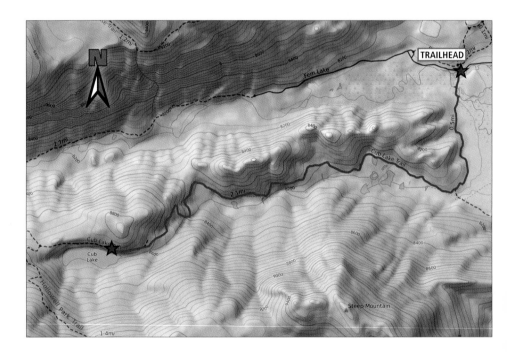

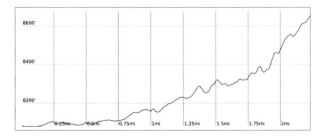

5. Hollowell Park & Mill Creek Basin

ROUND TRIP	5 miles to overlook
DIFFICULTY	Easy to moderate
SKILL LEVEL	Intermediate
HIGH POINT	9,200 feet
ELEVATION GAIN	800 feet
AVALANCHE DANGER	None
MAP	Trails Illustrated #200, Rocky Mountain National Park
CONTACT	Rocky Mountain National Park, nps.gov/romo

COMMENT: Hollowell Park is an expansive, classic high-mountain meadow rimmed by stately pine trees interspersed with aspen. As you head south on Bear Lake Road, this is the first trailhead after Moraine Park. It is a fairly gradual climb. The snow might not be very good in the meadow, but it improves dramatically as you gain elevation. The trail can be turned into an out-and-back of any length and also offers a very nice view of Cub Lake from above. This trail can be used for a steeper 1-mile trek up to Bierstadt Lake from Mill Creek Basin or as the beginning of a 6.4-mile loop back to the Cub Lake trailhead. Check for excellent snow conditions before skiing. Skinny or mid-width Nordic skis are appropriate.

GETTING THERE: From Denver, take I-25 north 40 miles and exit at Loveland/US 34. Take US 34 west through Big Thompson Canyon 40 miles to Estes Park. Allow at least one hour and 30 minutes. Other routes from Denver include US 36 northwest through Boulder and Lyons for 60 miles to Estes Park; and I-25 north for 30 miles to Highway 66, west on Highway 66 for 15 miles to Lyons, and northwest on US 36 for 20 miles to Estes Park. When you reach Estes Park, continue west to the third traffic light, where you will see a sign for the park. Turn left at the sign and go up a hill, bear right at the stop sign, and then bear right at the intersection 0.5 mile after the next traffic light. You will see signs for the Beaver Meadows Visitor Center.

From the Beaver Meadows entrance, take the first left onto Bear Lake Road. After a hairpin S-turn, the road travels downhill past the Moraine Park Campground and Discovery Center and then goes uphill through a pine forest that is adjacent to the YMCA camp. When you emerge from the trees, you are looking at Hollowell Park straight ahead. Just as the road reaches the turnoff approximately 3.5 miles from the

View of Longs Peak from Hollowell Park.

Beaver Meadows entrance, it makes a hairpin turn to the left; bear right into the parking area.

THE ROUTE: Take the trail west across the meadow and bear left at the first intersection in 0.25 mile. Go up a gradual hill into the trees. You will soon be next to pretty, frozen—or babbling—Mill Creek, lined with pine and aspen trees. At the next intersection, at 1.25 miles, the trail to the left climbs steeply up to Bierstadt Lake; go straight (west) for the overview of Cub Lake. If this sign is completely covered by snow, just bear right or go straight; don't take the first stream crossing to the left (southwest).

The trail climbs gradually through the trees. At 1.7 miles, reach another junction where you stay right (the trail to the left goes to Bear Lake). Soon the trail opens up to a couple of nice small meadows in Mill Creek Basin. It then winds back into the trees, alternating with steeper and flatter sections until it opens up into a great view back up the moraine onto Cub Lake at about 2.5 miles. This is a good place to turn around because the trail descends steeply to Cub Lake.

Retrace your steps—with caution—for the return to the trailhead.

HOLLOWELL PARK & MILL CREEK BASIN

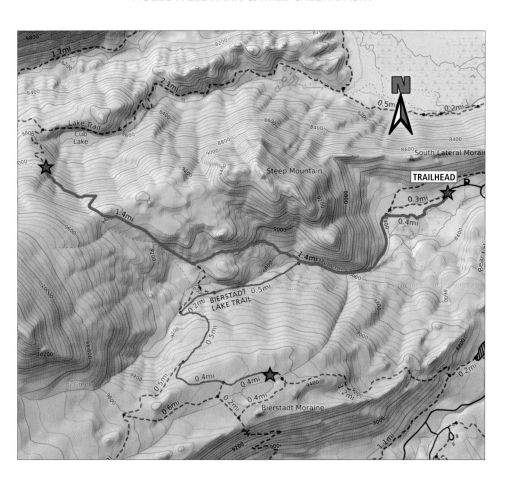

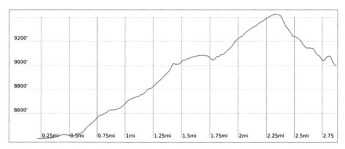

6. **Sprague Lake Trails**

ROUND TRIP	3.3 miles
DIFFICULTY	Easy to moderate
SKILL LEVEL	Novice
HIGH POINT	8,900 feet
ELEVATION GAIN	200 feet
AVALANCHE DANGER	None
MAP	Trails Illustrated #200, Rocky Mountain National Park
CONTACT	Rocky Mountain National Park, nps.gov/romo

COMMENT: The Sprague Lake area offers a couple of nice, easy loops for beginners or intermediate skiers, as well as trailheads for more ambitious adventures, such as the Boulder Brook and Storm Pass Trails. The easiest trip is simply around the lake itself, which is only 0.5 mile with no elevation gain. You can start the easy longer loop at either Glacier Basin Campground (closed during winter) or Sprague Lake. The best views are at Sprague Lake or at the campground, with some nice views through the heavy tree cover along the way. This has been a popular network of easy to moderate trails for skinny skis. Experienced skiers can use any style of ski on this route, but skinny skis are adequate. If you're skiing the Boulder Brook section, wider skis would make navigating the steep, narrow sections easier.

GETTING THERE: From Estes Park, continue west to the third traffic light, where you will see a sign for Rocky Mountain National Park. Turn left at the sign and go up a hill, bear right at the stop sign, and then bear right at the intersection 0.5 mile after the next traffic light. You will see signs for the Beaver Meadows Visitor Center.

From the Beaver Meadows entrance, take the first left at 0.25 mile onto Bear Lake Road. In 5.25 miles, approximately 1 mile after Hollowell Park, the Glacier Basin Campground is on the left. Parking is on the right/north side of road, and the trailhead is on the south side of the campground. Approximately 0.5 mile from the Glacier Basin Campground parking lot is the turnoff for the Sprague Lake picnic area and parking lot on the left/south side of the road. When you enter the Sprague Lake parking area, you follow a one-way road to the right; at around 10 o'clock on the road loop you will see the small picnic area and the trailhead.

THE ROUTE: The longer 3-mile loop can be planned to end on either a long downhill or a gradual uphill. To start and end your trek on uphill sections, start at the Sprague

The view of Hallett Peak–Flattop Mountain ridge from Sprague Lake.

Lake picnic area and follow the route counterclockwise. After ascending a steep hill for 200 yards, you level out to an easy climb and enter the lodgepole pine forest. The trail is marked with orange markers on tree limbs. After about 0.5 mile you reach a trail junction (the trail to the right goes out to Bear Lake Road). The trail entering from the left has a sign that says "Glacier Gorge/Bear Lake." Turn left onto this trail and continue to climb a short distance to another trail intersection. This is where the trail intersects the Boulder Brook Trail (straight ahead) and Glacier Gorge Trail (to the right). Follow the sign to the left to the Glacier Basin Campground.

The trail goes downhill and over Boulder Brook twice, rolling somewhat before beginning another short climb. At the crest of the hill you intersect the Storm Pass Trail on the right at about 1 mile. Stay to the left and continue downhill toward the campground. Enjoy the views across to the Beirstadt Lake ridge and Mount Wuh and into some glades of aspen and pine. At about 2.25 miles, the trail breaks out of the trees for the best view of the route, with the Mummy Range in the distance to the north and Flattop Mountain and Hallet Peak to the west. If the wind isn't blowing, this is a nice sunny spot for a snack or photo break.

Reach a junction at the end of the switchback in about 0.25 mile. The trail to the right returns to the picnic area along the creek: go to the left to reach the lake. Once you reach Sprague Lake at about 3 miles, there is another spectacular view to the west, and another trail junction. Either option is a short hop around the lake back to the picnic area. To the left is a wheelchair-accessible trail to a picnic area. The picnic tables are in the shade, but the nice glade below is a windbreak. To complete the loop, take the trail to the right.

SPRAGUE LAKE TRAILS

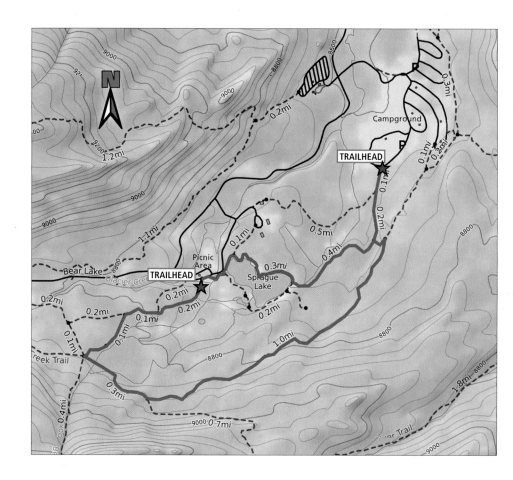

7. Alberta Falls & The Loch

ROUND TRIP	1.2 miles to Alberta Falls; 5.4 miles to The Loch
DIFFICULTY	Easy to moderate
SKILL LEVEL	Intermediate
HIGH POINT	9,400 feet at falls; 10,180 feet at lake
ELEVATION GAIN	160 feet to falls; 940 feet to lake
AVALANCHE DANGER	None
MAP	Trails Illustrated #200, Rocky Mountain National Park
CONTACT	Rocky Mountain National Park, nps.gov/romo

COMMENT: The trip to Alberta Falls is a beginner family excursion if you have small children or people very reluctant to participate. The trail is usually quite safe because of the hard snowpack. You'll have to take off your skis if you want to walk on the rock, which is not a good idea with small children because it can be slick and ice-coated. Alberta Falls is a short, easy round-trip that can be extended. The trail continues on up to The Loch on one of the prettiest treks in the park. As you climb away from Alberta Falls and Prospect Canyon, you enjoy ever better views of the canyon and the Mummy Range behind you. There is rarely snow good enough for skiing to the falls, but it improves dramatically beyond that point. Check the snow conditions before skiing since the trail can be rocky with thin cover. Experienced skiers can use any style of ski on this route, though AT or telemark skis are probably overkill.

GETTING THERE: From Estes Park, continue west to the third traffic light, where you will see a sign for the park. Turn left at the sign and go up a hill, bear right at the stop sign, and then bear right at the intersection 0.5 mile after the next traffic light. You will see signs for the Beaver Meadows Visitor Center.

From the Beaver Meadows entrance, take the first left at 0.25 mile onto Bear Lake Road. Drive 8.2 miles (0.8 mile short of the Bear Lake parking lot) to the Glacier Gorge parking lot. Bear Lake Road makes a major curve around the parking lot, which fills up early—summer or winter. If it is full, park in the Bear Lake lot and walk back on the road or, preferably, on the trail connecting the two, which is a pleasant, short jaunt of about 0.4 mile. The Glacier Gorge lot is impossible to miss, 1.2 miles before you reach the Bear Lake lot.

THE ROUTE: The trail travels west from the parking lot above the small gorge, and then descends and crosses a bridge and begins a steady but not very steep climb. It

The lovely Loch in spectacular Glacier Gorge.

eventually climbs next to a small gorge carved out by a stream that can boil for a short time during the spring runoff. In the winter its rock shoulders are snow-covered, and the color contrasts among the rock, trees, snow, and ice can be striking. In 0.6 mile you reach the frozen Alberta Falls, which can take on a wide variety of shapes and makes for some interesting photography.

After you reach the falls, if all is well, try venturing farther up the trail, because with every step the views get better. If you go high enough, you have a spectacular vista of the Mummy Range in the distance and the cliffs of the Bierstadt Moraine across Prospect Canyon.

The trail climbs steadily through loose switchbacks to the intersection with the North Longs Peak Trail (Route #9, p. 41) to the left at 1.1 miles; go right. The trail then climbs around one of the Glacier Knobs on the north side of the Icy Brook drainage, which is icy and rocky. At 1.5 miles you will reach an intersection with the Black Lake Trail to the left (up this way about 0.25 mile is Glacier Falls) and the Dream Lake Trail to the right; continue straight ahead.

The scenery gets even more interesting as you near the entrance of the Loch Vale (valley). After about 0.5 mile the switchbacks level out and you enter between steep, canyon-like walls. Then, after winding your way 0.5 mile through the canyon, you will reach your destination. The Loch, Scottish for "lake," is in a magnificent setting surrounded by Otis, Taylor, and Powell peaks, offering great photographic opportunities.

ALBERTA FALLS & THE LOCH

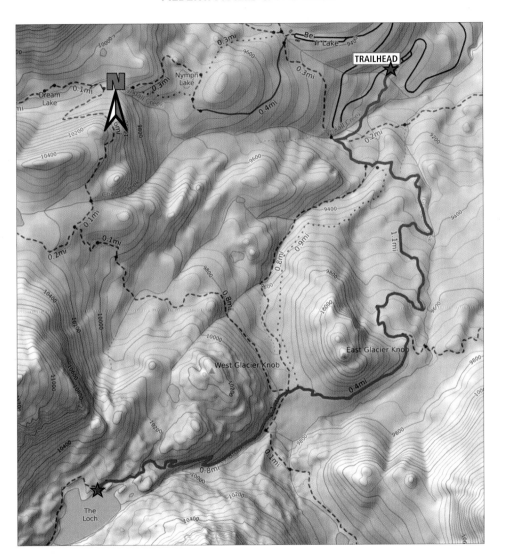

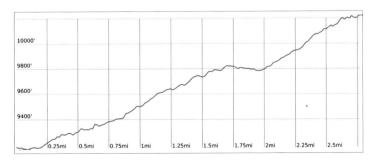

8. Mills Lake, Jewel Lake, & Black Lake

ROUND TRIP	4 miles to Mills Lake; 5 miles to Jewel lake; 8 miles to Black Lake
DIFFICULTY	Moderate to challenging
SKILL LEVEL	Novice to expert depending on distance skied
HIGH POINT	9,940 feet at Mills Lake; 9,950 feet at Jewel Lake; 10,620 feet at Black Lake
ELEVATION GAIN	700 feet to Mills Lake; 710 feet to Jewel Lake; 1,380 feet to Black Lake
AVALANCHE DANGER	None to low; last hill moderate to high
MAP	Trails Illustrated #200, Rocky Mountain National Park
CONTACT	Rocky Mountain National Park, nps.gov/romo

COMMENT: If you want a superb winter adventure, Black Lake Trail is one of Rocky Mountain National Park's better offerings short of climbing a peak. As with many of these destinations, it takes on an almost mystical quality in the winter that is not quite as profound on a nice summer's day. The trail visits three spectacular frozen lakes. The journey to the first two can be nice day trips in themselves. Venturing all the way to Black Lake in the winter can make for a very satisfying day for the experienced and very fit. It can be challenging for anyone, depending on conditions that often vary between bare rock and deep powder. You can usually expect to take your skis off and on at different points during the trip, even if snow conditions are generally good.

Do not attempt this route unless snow conditions in the park are very good, because after about 3 miles it is usually necessary to cross rocky, windswept stretches of trail that are only snow-covered after mid-January (if at all). Check with the park's backcountry office. There are some rocky wind-swept sections that could make skiing more challenging. This is a good trail for skinny or mid-width skis.

GETTING THERE: From Estes Park, continue west to the third traffic light, where you will see a sign for the park. Turn left at the sign and go up a hill, bear right at the stop sign, and then bear right at the intersection 0.5 mile after the next traffic light. You will see signs for the Beaver Meadows Visitor Center.

From the Beaver Meadows entrance, take the first left at 0.25 mile onto Bear Lake Road. Drive approximately 8 miles to the Glacier Gorge parking lot. If it is full, park in the Bear Lake lot and walk back on the trail connecting the two, which is a pleasant, short jaunt of about 0.4 mile.

Early season view of Black Lake.

THE ROUTE: The trail travels west along the small gorge for 0.25 mile and then crosses the creek on a footbridge to the south. The next 1.5 miles of this route follows the Alberta Falls Trail. Once you get beyond Alberta Falls, you continue winding back and forth over Glacier Creek next to a small gorge that gives you more than one photo opportunity. Eventually the gorge opens up, with cliffs soaring above.

At 1.1 miles you come to the North Longs Peak Trail on the left, which goes toward Granite Pass. Take the right branch toward Mills Lake and Loch Vale. The trail steepens here, and there are views of The Arrowhead and Chiefs Head Peak straight ahead with Glacier Gorge on your left.

The trail then goes downhill for a short distance and eventually returns to the trees. At 1.5 miles, you reach the next trail intersection. To the right is the trail to Dream Lake; straight ahead is the trail to The Loch. Take the left branch, the Black Lake Trail, and you soon encounter a stream crossing that uses a log as a bridge. There is a second stream crossing in a relatively short distance that features wooden steps and rocks, which should be snow-covered. Exposed rocks and cairns as well as bare wooden steps might make it necessary to take off your skis temporarily. At 1.75 miles you reach Glacier Falls.

There are at least two good routes to Mills Lake. Pick your way through the best snow or take off your skis and scramble over the large rock formations. You are 0.25 mile from the lake at this point, so it is well worth the trouble of surmounting the rocks and taking a circuitous route through the trees to stay in the snow. Once you reach the north shore of Mills Lake at 2 miles, you can see the Keyboard of the Winds on Longs Peak. This is a great place for photos or a snack break. Mills Lake is a good place to turn around if you find the mixture of snow and rocks annoying.

From the north end of Mills Lake you are 1 mile from the Glacier Gorge backcountry campsites and 2 miles from Black Lake. The varied trail continues with lots of interesting options over, under, and around large outcroppings and trees. Don't fret too much about staying on the trail; don't wander too far upslope to the left (east), and stay relatively close to the shores of Mills Lake and Jewel Lake, and you will be safe. Jewel Lake's south end is 0.5 mile beyond the north end of Mills Lake, and is barely distinguishable as a separate body of water. It can be a very long 0.5 mile under windy conditions. If the lakes are solidly frozen you can use the surface to avoid obstacles.

At 3 miles you'll pass backcountry campsites. In another 0.5 mile the main trail wanders away from the shore of Glacier Creek, reaching an open meadow with great views of Stone Man Pass, The Arrowhead, Chiefs Head Peak, and McHenrys Peak. You are 200 yards from the very steep stretch that takes you 0.5 mile up to the edge of Black Lake. The standard trail is to the left, but sometimes it is easier to get off the trail because the snow cover is better on the steeper slope. Avoid running water and ice. Shortly after you reach Black Lake at 4 miles, Ribbon Falls should be a frozen spectacle.

MILLS LAKE, JEWEL LAKE, & BLACK LAKE

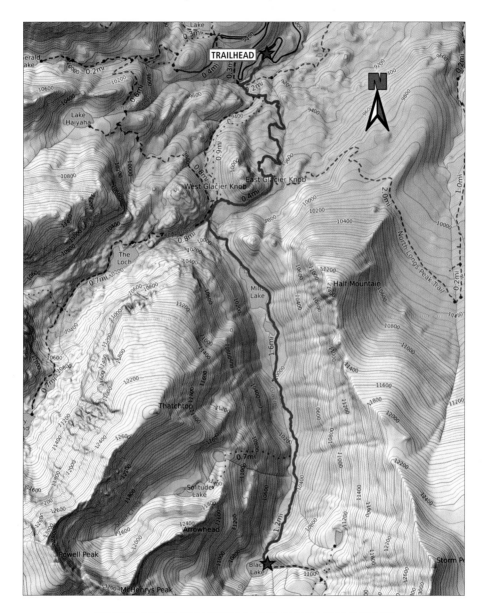

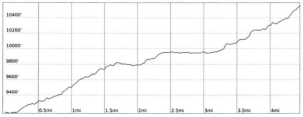

9. North Longs Peak Trail

ROUND TRIP	12.4 miles to Granite Pass
DIFFICULTY	Moderate to challenging
SKILL LEVEL	Intermediate
HIGH POINT	12,080 feet
ELEVATION GAIN	2,840 feet
AVALANCHE DANGER	None to high
MAP	Trails Illustrated #200, Rocky Mountain National Park
CONTACT	Rocky Mountain National Park, nps.gov/romo

COMMENT: This trail is a rarity because of its beautiful views and relatively low use. Few people take it in the winter. The first 3 miles or so to the Boulder Brook Trail intersection have low to no avalanche danger most of the year. On the return, it offers superb views of Glacier Gorge, Flattop Mountain, Hallett Peak, the Mummy Range, and the entire valley. This can be a fun ski on skinny or mid-width skis.

GETTING THERE: From Estes Park, continue west to the third traffic light, where you will see a sign for Rocky Mountain National Park. Turn left at the sign and go up a hill, bear right at the stop sign, and then bear right at the intersection 0.5 mile after the next traffic light. You will see signs for the Beaver Meadows Visitor Center.

From the Beaver Meadows entrance, take the first left at 0.25 mile onto Bear Lake Road. Drive approximately 8 miles to the Glacier Gorge parking lot. If this lot is full, park in the Bear Lake lot and walk back on the trail connecting the two, which is a pleasant, short jaunt of about 0.4 mile.

THE ROUTE: The trail travels west from the parking lot above the small gorge and then descends and crosses a bridge. It is about a 400-foot gradual gain past Alberta Falls to the intersection with the North Longs Peak Trail in 1.1 miles. Here The Loch Trail continues straight ahead, but you turn left. From this intersection it is 5.1 miles one way, or a total of 6.2 miles one way, to Granite Pass—an ambitious winter or summer round-trip.

The trail goes downhill from the intersection for approximately 100 to 200 feet and you are immediately greeted by great views of the Mummy Range and valley as well as Glacier Gorge. This part of the trail is very open to sun and wind and can have sections that are in need of snow. Don't be dismayed, because you will soon be on a north-facing portion. Climb back out of the draw after crossing Glacier Creek. The

The Mummy Range from North Longs Peak Trail.

trail levels out for a bit and enters a short new-growth forest of lodgepole and spruce. After another 0.25 mile or so you round the bend into the Boulder Brook drainage where you can get an impressive view of the summit of Longs Peak. You can also see the north shoulder of the mountain's massif soaring above and daring you to make the climb above treeline to Granite Pass.

At about 1.5 miles from the trailhead you will enter a more mature forest of taller trees; this is a reasonable turnaround point because the view is obscured until you near treeline. About 2.25 miles, the trail reaches approximately 10,000 feet. Going higher above treeline is only advisable if avalanche danger is minimal. It is safer in the late spring when the snow has consolidated. From here it is another 1 mile or so to a small stream crossing and the intersection with the Boulder Brook Trail on the left. This also makes a good turnaround point for a great round-trip trek of approximately 6.6 miles.

To continue on to Granite Pass, go straight/right. At about 3.5 miles, you cross Boulder Brook and begin climbing. This requires steep switchbacking about 1.5 miles through an avalanche zone that should only be crossed if avalanche danger is low. The switchbacks can be tricky in winter and require a map, compass, GPS, and good routefinding skills. After you emerge above treeline the route can be windswept, with scarce snow.

The trail levels out at about 5 miles and climbs much more slowly for the next 0.25 mile before steepening again on the shoulder of Battle Mountain. At about 5.5 miles, the ascent eases for the last 0.7 mile or so. The view from Granite Pass is a 360-degree wonder, but don't risk life or limb getting there. Turn around if avalanche conditions are dicey.

NORTH LONGS PEAK TRAIL

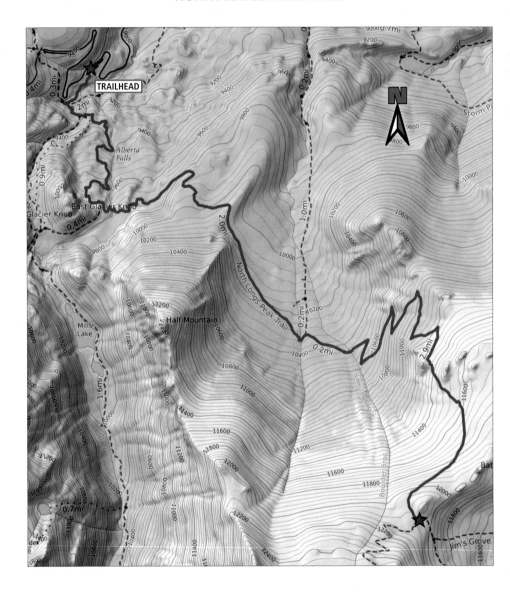

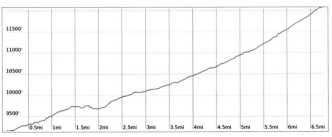

10. Nymph Lake, Dream Lake, & Emerald Lake

ROUND TRIP	1 mile to Nymph Lake; 2.2 miles to Dream Lake; 3.6 miles to Emerald Lake
DIFFICULTY	Easy to moderate
SKILL LEVEL	Intermediate
HIGH POINT	9,700 feet at Nymph Lake; 9,900 feet at Dream Lake; 10,100 feet at Emerald Lake
ELEVATION GAIN	225 feet to Nymph lake; 425 feet to Dream Lake; 625 feet to Emerald Lake
AVALANCHE DANGER	Low to moderate
MAP	Trails Illustrated #200, Rocky Mountain National Park
CONTACT	Rocky Mountain National Park, nps.gov/romo

COMMENT: The trail to Nymph, Dream, and Emerald lakes features some of the most beautiful scenery in Rocky Mountain National Park. Because the trail is relatively short and easy to navigate, it is not difficult to understand why the lakes are also among the most popular in the park. From the parking lot, it is only 0.5 mile to Nymph Lake, so it is not a difficult trek. Arriving early after a major snowstorm is best for skiing and not as important for snowshoeing if you don't mind lots of company on weekends.

Experienced skiers can use any style of ski on this route, but skinny skis are adequate. The challenge for skiers is the hard-pack on the last mile due to the number of snowshoers packing it down. It can be icy.

GETTING THERE: From Estes Park, continue west to the third traffic light, where you will see a sign for the park. Turn left at the sign and go up a hill, bear right at the stop sign, and then bear right at the intersection 0.5 mile after the next traffic light. You will see signs for the Beaver Meadows Visitor Center.

From the Beaver Meadows entrance, turn left/south in 0.25 mile onto Bear Lake Road and follow it 9 miles to its terminus to reach the Bear Lake parking lot.

THE ROUTE: The trail heads south and then curves west and north 0.5 mile to Nymph Lake. It is usually frozen solid and safe to cross at the height of winter, but err on the side of caution. You can loop around the lake to the right in or very near the trees to enjoy views of Hallet Peak, Thatchtop, and Flattop Mountain. Turning around at

Peaks soar over the Nymph Lake, Dream Lake, and Emerald Lake Trail.

Nymph Lake is a nice, short family outing that can be combined with some off-trail walking on the way back to Bear Lake.

From the north side of Nymph Lake the trail continues uphill to the left. It requires a traverse over steep terrain, which can be trying after a heavy, fresh snowfall. Once you emerge from the trees, if the snow is deep, the trail can be hard to find. Don't be drawn straight uphill to the right. That is a route that will probably lead you into avalanche danger. Bear left and stay at a fairly low angle. Stay above the picturesque valley spreading out on the left, and below the impressive rock cliffs looming on the right. A steady climb uphill is what you want, though there is more than one route to Dream Lake. The various paths eventually merge at the top, but bearing to the right after the initial slope is the most common route. On the return trip, the hillside that will be on the right is a nice place to run and jump through powder.

The trek from Nymph to Dream Lake is eye candy. Stately evergreens climb the mountainsides with branches and needles that seem etched in the crystal high-altitude atmosphere. You will soon have a striking view of Longs Peak. Just before you reach Dream Lake there is an intersection with the trail to Lake Haiyaha on the left; continue straight/right. In 0.6 mile from Nymph, moderate switchbacking gets you to the sleepy shoreline of Dream Lake. Weave your way through a few rocks, climb the last hillock, and enter the stunning setting of Dream Lake. This is a terrific photo opportunity because of the exquisite surroundings: towering mountains and cliffs, scruffy wind-sculpted trees with gnarled roots, and the mists, clouds, and blowing and drifting snow of the high country in winter.

The remaining 0.7-mile trail to Emerald Lake is straightforward. Track around the north side of Dream Lake and climb steadily over the rolling terrain with views on all sides. This can be a challenging section of trail in deep, untracked powder as you continue up Tyndall Gorge. At Emerald Lake the shoulder and cliffs of Flattop Mountain soar on the north, while Hallet Peak and Tyndall Glacier complete the panorama.

NYMPH LAKE, DREAM LAKE, & EMERALD LAKE TRAIL

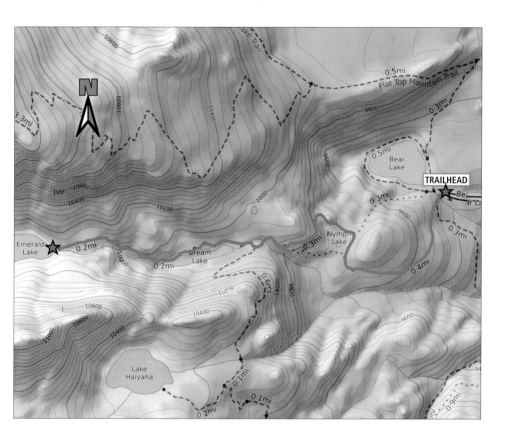

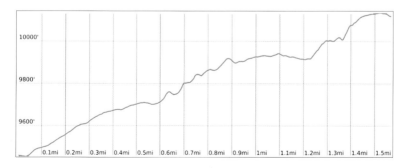

11. Flattop Mountain

ROUND TRIP	8 miles
DIFFICULTY	Moderate to challenging, depending on distance
SKILL LEVEL	Intermediate to expert
HIGH POINT	12,324 feet
ELEVATION GAIN	2,849 feet
AVALANCHE DANGER	Low to considerable on north-facing slopes; check with Rocky Mountain National Park
MAP	Trails Illustrated #200, Rocky Mountain National Park
CONTACT	Rocky Mountain National Park, nps.gov/romo

COMMENT: This challenging summer hike is best suited for the very physically fit and more experienced adventurers in the winter. The trail offers views of Bear Lake and the tops of Glacier Gorge and Longs Peak. If you get an early start and get lucky with the weather, summiting is a distinct possibility. You need to be an advanced ski mountaineer to summit. This mountain has several popular ski routes aside from the main trail. You will want AT or telemark skis for this route. The first mile can be very hard-packed and icy, requiring you to carry skis uphill and downhill. It is best skied after a major snowstorm.

GETTING THERE: From Estes Park, continue west to the third traffic light, where you will see a sign for Rocky Mountain National Park. Turn left at the sign and go up a hill, bear right at the stop sign, and then bear right at the intersection 0.5 mile after the next traffic light. You will see signs for the Beaver Meadows Visitor Center.

From the Beaver Meadows entrance, turn left/south in 0.25 mile onto Bear Lake Road and follow it 9 miles to its terminus to reach the Bear Lake parking lot.

THE ROUTE: Starting from the parking lot, walk to the right toward the lake. When you reach the shoreline you can see the impressive massif of Hallett Peak and the unimpressive summit of Flattop behind. Go to the right and watch for the sign that takes you gradually uphill through the pretty aspen that frame both the lake and Hallett Peak. At the first intersection, after about 0.2 mile, the trail to the left continues around Bear Lake; stay to the right. At the first major switchback, at 0.4 mile, you come to the Bierstadt Lake Trail straight ahead; take a left to stay on the Flattop Mountain Trail.

Flattop Mountain from Bear Lake.

The next steep stretch parallels Bear Lake, affording you some of the best views of Longs Peak, Bear Lake, Glacier Gorge, and the glacier-carved U-shaped valleys. It's a perfect place for photographs because it will be a while until you break into the clear again. In about 0.25 mile, the trail veers north into Engelmann spruce trees and you can see east into Mill Creek Basin. Overall, you climb steadily for approximately 0.8 mile to reach the intersection with the Fern-Odessa Lake Trail. The rangers try to keep the trail sign uncovered, but deep snow can obscure most of it.

Going this far is a nice, quick trip for a family with kids. You could turn around and go back to circle Bear Lake, having enjoyed some spectacular views and elevated your heart rate. Though the time will vary, making it this far and circling Bear Lake could easily be an hour-plus family jaunt with small children.

At the trail intersection, the Odessa Lake Trail goes straight ahead; stay to the left on the Flattop Mountain Trail, which switchbacks up. The trail climbs steadily, mostly in fir and spruce trees, until you reach the Dream Lake overlook, which is not obvious or well marked. Here once again are great views of both Longs and Hallett peaks. Depending on the depth of the snow, just getting to treeline can easily take a couple of hours or more if you stop frequently for breaks and have to break trail through very deep powder. If you are determined, very fit, and on the move, and the snow isn't too powdery, you can make treeline in an hour or so, which is approximately 2.5 miles from the Bear Lake trailhead. When you reach treeline you likely will encounter wind, and possibly severe windchill. This is a good time to have a snack and decide if discretion is the better part of valor. The wind can blow some of the trail clear; however, you can usually pick your way through to find more snow.

If the snow is good above treeline, track toward the northeast slope and ski down as far as the Fern Lake Trail. Going below that trail will take you into thick trees and willows, and it is easy to get lost. From treeline you still have another 1.5 miles of very steep hiking to make the summit. Unless there has been a recent storm, the snow from treeline to the summit is often wind-blown and sun-crusted. If there has been a recent powder event with little wind, enjoy the rare ski to the top.

How long it takes from treeline to the summit is dependent on the conditions. If it is snowing or if whiteouts are possible, turning around is highly recommended. The views are nonstop above treeline. As you near the summit there are breathtaking views of Bear Lake valley and the pointy false summit and actual summit of Hallett Peak. You can also see the Tyndall Glacier. On the flat, windswept summit that is your destination, you can see over the Continental Divide into the west side of the park and the trails that lead into the Grand Lake and Colorado River drainage.

Some people ski from the top toward Hallett Peak and then down the glacier, but this route has avalanched and caused fatalities.

Photo by Chris Case

DAY PACK

Taking along a day pack is always a good idea. It allows you more flexibility in what you wear so you can adjust to changing weather. Choose a pack that can carry the essentials, plus extra clothing, and that will accommodate what you might take off when you heat up. Some packs have straps to carry your skis, which can be handy on trails with sections where you don't need your skis.

FLATTOP MOUNTAIN

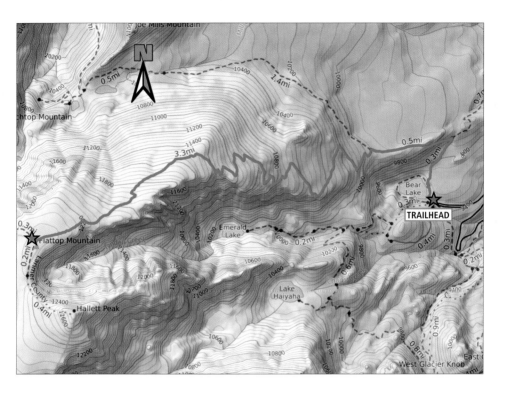

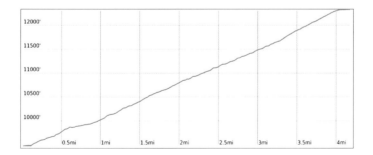

12. Lake Helene

ROUND TRIP	6 miles
DIFFICULTY	Moderate
SKILL LEVEL	Intermediate
HIGH POINT	10,620 feet
ELEVATION GAIN	1,145 feet
AVALANCHE DANGER	Low to moderate; check with Rocky Mountain National Park
MAP	Trails Illustrated #200, Rocky Mountain National Park
CONTACT	Rocky Mountain National Park, nps.gov/romo

COMMENT: This trail isn't for the fainthearted in the winter after heavy snow, but it is a spectacular route. It branches off from the Flattop Mountain Trail about 0.8 mile from Bear Lake. As with all of the routes in this book, you can bite off a smaller morsel to savor rather than attempting the whole route and still have a great time. There is a good approach for skiing the northeast slope of Flattop Mountain about 0.5 mile above the Flattop Mountain Trail turnoff on the west side. The slope is less than 25 degrees, so not extremely hazardous for avalanches. Experienced skiers can use any ski, but mid-width or wider skis would be more fun.

GETTING THERE: From Estes Park, continue west to the third traffic light, where you will see a sign for Rocky Mountain National Park. Turn left at the sign and go up a hill, bear right at the stop sign, and then bear right at the intersection 0.5 mile after the next traffic light. You will see signs for the Beaver Meadows Visitor Center.

From the Beaver Meadows entrance, turn left/south in 0.25 mile onto Bear Lake Road and follow it 9 miles to its terminus to reach the Bear Lake parking lot.

THE ROUTE: Start at Bear Lake and follow the signs for Flattop Mountain or Odessa Lake. It is a fairly steady and somewhat steep climb before the trail eventually levels a bit. At about 0.2 mile the Bear Lake Trail goes left; stay right. At 0.4 mile there is a trail junction (the Bierstadt Lake Trail continues straight/northeast); take a sharp left (west) to stay on the Flattop Mountain/Odessa Lake Trail as it heads uphill.

There are great views as you climb above Bear Lake and look out across the valley at Glacier Gorge and Longs Peak. The trail travels more northwesterly, leveling out and climbing at a slower rate. You then climb to the second trail junction at 0.8 mile. The Flattop Mountain Trail switchbacks sharply left/west and uphill; continue straight ahead to the right/northwest on the Odessa Lake Trail.

A traverse on Lake Helene Trail.

Though the trail is not steep, the slope it is carved into is. In fact, it becomes a moderate avalanche area after a heavy snowfall because its gradient approaches 30 degrees. The trail is usually well traveled and obvious, but might become obscured by deep snow and be somewhat difficult to negotiate if you are the first one on it. It is not well-marked beyond this point, but remember that it climbs steadily to the northwest and does not descend northeast as some errant tracks might indicate. Nor does it climb high up on the shoulder of Flattop Mountain. You can generally follow tracks another mile until you reach treeline at about 1.8 miles. At that point the summer trail is hard to find and you need good routefinding skills to angle your way west and then southwest; first west up to Two Rivers Lake, and then southwest to Lake Helene.

You definitely want to have a compass and a topographic map when you break out of the trees. You do not want to climb the steep, open slopes of Joe Mills Mountain. In winter, the route can seem much steeper than in summer if there are several feet of deep, fresh powder. Ask the rangers at Bear Lake for the status and proceed cautiously beyond Lake Helene because there is potential avalanche danger. The trail steadily climbs in and out of the more sporadic and wind-twisted trees for approximately the next 2 miles and 600-plus feet of elevation gain. It crosses Mill Creek at about 2.3 miles, and winds past the small Two Rivers Lake and Lake Helene at about 3.5 miles.

Farther on, the trail reaches the impressive Tourmaline Gorge after you round a bend to the left at just over 4 miles. There are majestic, windswept winter visages of Notchtop (12,129 feet), Knobtop (12,331 feet), and the Little Matterhorn (11,586 feet). Their snow-covered slopes make what seems like a rather casual jaunt in the summer much more of an achievement and wilderness experience in winter. It is a long 0.5 mile of hazardous travel to reach the northern shore of Odessa Lake. It is safer and much easier to approach Odessa from the Fern Lake Trail. If you do get off track, it is fairly easy to keep Mill Creek Basin on your left and go south until you reach the Bear Lake Basin and the cliff band.

LAKE HELENE

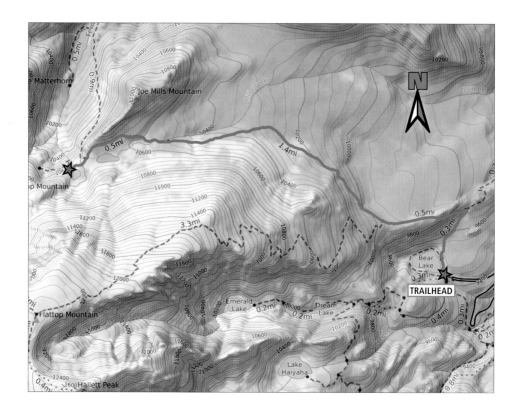

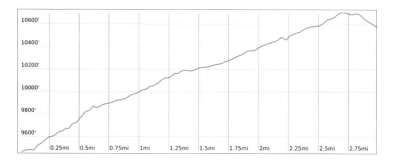

Chapter 2

ROCKY MOUNTAIN NATIONAL PARK— SOUTHEAST

"If you know wilderness in the way you know love, you would be unwilling to let it go...This is the story of our past and it will be the story of our future."

—Terry Tempest Williams

South of Estes Park is the Longs Peak Trailhead. The peak was considered unclimbable from the time of its discovery by Stephen Long in 1820 until fearless, one-armed Grand Canyon navigator John Wesley Powell summited it in 1868 from the south side. His approach was especially remarkable because his party had to climb all the way up and over the Continental Divide through uncharted terrain from Grand Lake before attempting the summit. However, it is likely that Native Americans climbed the peak before him.

Longs Peak is one of those places you never tire of, no matter how many times you have visited, summited, or attempted to summit it. Many an expert climber has spent an unplanned bivouac among its frigid granite cliffs praying for dawn. The towering northeast face of Longs Peak, known as The Diamond, is one of the most challenging technical climbs in North America. It requires superb high-altitude rock climbing skills in radically variable weather between 11,000 and 14,000 feet.

The true beauty of Longs Peak is the wide variety of trails that crisscross its massive expanse and which make it possible for trekkers of all skill levels to partake of its high-altitude glory. Winter months are less crowded because making the summit is impossible for all but a very select set of winter mountaineers. Another bonus is that even when there is little snow in Estes Park, this trailhead generally offers good snow because of its elevation of 9,500 feet. The trails also have excellent tree coverage that protects the snow below tree line. If it is late or early in the season, you might have to do some intermittent hiking between skiing.

The embrace of Wild Basin is unique and intimate as you ski next to frozen waterfalls or make your way above tree line, where you can see 13,900-foot Mount Meeker and its soaring neighbors. You can venture as far as the Continental Divide, or savor the icy lakes that are nestled below. You can also venture onto the flanks of Longs Peak up to the frozen, snow-covered tundra, where it wraps its arms around Chasm Lake. The options and sights are limitless in this winter wonderland. If you are lucky, you will be accompanied by elk, deer, moose, stellar jays, or mountain goats. Enjoy.

An entrance fee is now charged for the Wild Basin part of Rocky Mountain National Park.

Nancy Olsen on the Nymph Lake, Dream Lake, and Emerald Lake Trail.

13. Estes Cone

ROUND TRIP	6 miles
DIFFICULTY	Moderate
SKILL LEVEL	Novice
HIGH POINT	11,000 feet
ELEVATION GAIN	1,600 feet
AVALANCHE DANGER	Low
MAP	Trails Illustrated #200, Rocky Mountain National Park
CONTACT	Rocky Mountain National Park, nps.gov/romo

COMMENT: This pleasant trek to Estes Cone offers striking views of Longs Peak and Mount Meeker, as well as the Twin Sisters Peaks to the east. You can reach Estes Cone from either the Longs Peak Trailhead or Lily Lake Trailhead. The Longs Peak Trailhead is shorter, higher, and easier to ski, with more reliable snow because you will be starting at an elevation of 9,400 feet. Experienced skiers can use any kind of ski. The final climb to the summit is not recommended for young children or on skis.

GETTING THERE: From Estes Park, take Highway 7, the Peak to Peak Highway, south 7.5 miles to the turnoff on the right/west side of the road for the Longs Peak Campground and trailhead. Go up the hill about a mile to the intersection with the campground road, and bear left into the trailhead parking lot.

From Denver, take I-25 north 40 miles and exit at Loveland/US 34. Take US 34 west through Big Thompson Canyon 40 miles to Estes Park. Allow at least one hour and 30 minutes. Other routes from Denver include US 36 northwest through Boulder and Lyons for 60 miles to Estes Park; and I-25 north for 30 miles to Highway 66, west on Highway 66 for 15 miles to Lyons.

From Lyons, take a left on Highway 7 and drive west 14 miles then north 10 miles to the Longs Peak Campground road on the left. From Denver the route through Lyons is the best.

THE ROUTE: The trail begins at the Longs Peak Ranger Station, which is generally closed during winter months. The route starts on the Longs Peak Trail for about 0.5 mile of gradual uphill through the lodgepole pine forest. At the junction, trail signs say it is 2.7 miles to Estes Cone (the Longs Peak Trail goes left/south to Chasm Lake in 3.7 miles according to the trail sign). Turn right/north. You arrive shortly at another junction. The trail to the right goes down into Tahosa Valley. Continue straight/

View of snowy Estes Cone.

left. At around 1 mile the trail veers to the northwest and levels off somewhat before climbing gradually to Inn Brook at 1.25 miles. Just after crossing the brook, you reach the site of Eugenia Mine, where some aspen trees are mixed in with the pine. This is a good place for a snack and water break.

The trail then travels northeast downhill into Moore Park, reaching a trail junction at 1.7 miles. The trail to the right goes down into Tahosa Valley. Turn left to join the Storm Pass Trail. It goes northwest, gradually climbing to Storm Pass at 2.4 miles, where the trees begin to thin out and there is another trail junction. To the left, the Storm Pass Trail continues down to Sprague Lake; turn right/northeast to reach the rock summit of Estes Cone. Here the trail switchbacks more steeply uphill. The most challenging section is the last long switchback section because it climbs the last 1,000 feet in approximately 0.6 mile. This rocky part of the trail will reward you with the best views of Longs Peak and Mount Meeker.

WARNING: If you make it to the summit area at 2.8 miles, you will have to shed your skis and climb very carefully on the sometimes slick, wet, and icy rocks to reach the the summit. You can still have a very enjoyable outing by going as far as Storm Pass and walking up enough of the switchbacks to catch a few photo ops, or to the bottom of the summit rocks, then turning around. If you are fortunate, you will catch a sunny day or fresh snow.

ESTES CONE

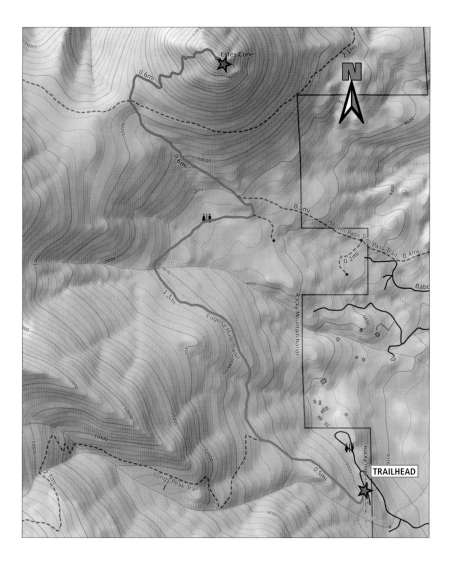

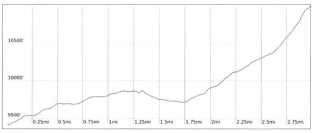

14. Chasm Lake

ROUND TRIP	8.4 miles
DIFFICULTY	Challenging
SKILL LEVEL	Intermediate to expert
HIGH POINT	11,800 feet
ELEVATION GAIN	2,400 feet
AVALANCHE DANGER	Low to considerable, can be avoided; check with Rocky Mountain National Park and Colorado Avalanche Information Center
MAP	Trails Illustrated #200, Rocky Mountain National Park
CONTACT	Rocky Mountain National Park, nps.gov/romo

COMMENT: This spectacular trek offers striking views of Longs Peak and Mount Meeker as well as the Twin Sisters Peaks to the east. The entire trail should be attempted only by those experienced in mid-winter travel above treeline. You have to cross one avalanche chute that could avalanche in high conditions. Check for avalanche conditions in the area before attempting the route and consider digging a snow pit if danger is moderate. It is usually safe, but the trail is easy to lose if it is not already broken, and even then people tend to blaze their own paths in the snow cover of winter when the standard route gets obliterated by drifts. It is a skiable route with AT or telemark skis and advanced ski skills. You can ski the route toward Jim's Grove instead of toward the lake itself for more open, easier conditions. Since the area above treeline is sun-exposed and wind-scoured, conditions can vary dramatically. If the snow is old and the cover thin, the descent will be tricky.

GETTING THERE: From Estes Park, take Highway 7, the Peak to Peak Highway, south 7.5 miles to the turnoff on the right/west side of the road for the Longs Peak Campground and trailhead. Go up the hill about a mile to the intersection with the campground road and bear left into the trailhead parking lot.

From Denver, take I-25 north 40 miles and exit at Loveland/US 34. Take US 34 west through Big Thompson Canyon 40 miles to Estes Park. Allow at least one hour and 30 minutes. Other routes from Denver include US 36 northwest through Boulder and Lyons for 60 miles to Estes Park; and I-25 north for 30 miles to Highway 66, west on Highway 66 for 15 miles to Lyons.

A soggy spring day on the way to Chasm Lake.

ALPINE TUNDRA: THE LAND OF KRUMMHOLZ

Alpine tundra is the magic land above tree line (11,500 feet) where trees generally cannot grow because of the severe wind and snow. Krummholz (German for crooked) fir and spruce trees twisted and shaped by the wind often mark this transition zone. Some of the krummholz firs are thousands of years old. Winds at this elevation can exceed 170 miles per hour and windchills and temperatures can plummet to 40 degrees Fahrenheit below zero. Damage to tundra can take centuries to repair, so take off your skis when you reach snow-free areas. Average annual precipitation up high is often only 25 inches, so snow-free areas high on mountainsides are not unusual. Few animals can survive on tundra year-round: pikas stash plants for winter, marmots hibernate, and ptarmigans, the only birds in the alpine zone that remain there during winter instead of migrating, grow feathers on their feet and toenail "teeth" for their own snowshoes.

From Lyons, take a left on Highway 7 and drive west 14 miles, then north 10 miles to the Longs Peak Campground road on the left. From Denver the route through Lyons is the best.

THE ROUTE: The trail starts with 0.5 mile of gradual uphill through the lodgepole pine forest to an intersection where trail signs say it is 3.7 miles to Chasm Lake. In another mile, the Storm Pass Trail splits off to the right/north; continue straight/left (southwest). After the trail splits it climbs more steeply with occasional short switchbacks. Unfortunately, one of the steepest sections of the trail is at the beginning when you aren't sufficiently warmed up to enjoy it. It climbs 500 feet to an elevation of 10,000 feet fairly quickly in thick tree cover and in a little less than 1 mile. It then levels a bit and climbs more gradually for the next 0.4 mile as the trees thin out, allowing you to enjoy views of the summit of Longs Peak looking down from on high, daring you to climb it. On a clear day you will enjoy an impressive view of The Diamond on Longs Peak.

As the trail starts to climb and switchback, it turns more due south, edging its way up past Goblin's Forest. You cross Larkspur Creek and then have to cross one potential avalanche chute to reach the small footbridge that crosses Alpine Brook. Don't dawdle.

In a good-to-average snow year the trail can be difficult to follow from this point on, as it traverses south and then climbs steeply west up to 11,000 feet. Sometimes the snow is very old and hard-packed, so don't hesitate to turn around if conditions become challenging. The trail down might not be as straightforward as you remember; allow extra time for slower members of your party.

If you continue toward Chasm Lake, you will soon see stunted trees that reveal a spectacular view of the slope all the way to treeline at 11,000 feet where you have a panoramic view in all directions. In a thin snow year you might have to take off your skis and hike because the intense sun can melt the snow off the very rocky ridge. Always keep an eye on the weather.

Once above treeline you gradually make your way to a ridge and somewhat steep snowfield which you have to traverse to the south to reach the final stretch up Mills Moraine. Here, at about 2.8 miles, stay straight/left and veer to the south toward Chasm Lake.

Follow the ridge about a mile to 11,600 feet, then walk around a corner and be stunned by the views of Longs Peak and Mount Meeker, with Peacock Pool almost 600 feet below. It can be a bit of a difficult and precarious ridge walk for a short 0.4 mile across another sometimes vertical snowfield, and then across Roaring Fork. Here a Rocky Mountain National Park hut was recently swept away in a major avalanche. It is then another 200 feet up to Chasm Lake, which is surrounded by soaring Mount Meeker and Longs Peak.

CHASM LAKE

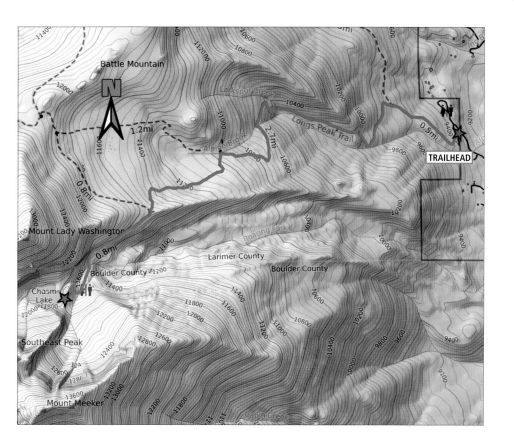

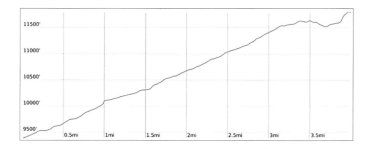

15. Copeland Falls, Calypso Cascades, & Ouzel Falls

ROUND TRIP	3.8 miles to Copeland Falls; 6 miles to Calypso Cascades; 7.4 miles to Ouzel Falls
DIFFICULTY	Easy to moderate
SKILL LEVEL	Intermediate
HIGH POINT	8,515 feet at Copeland Falls; 9,200 feet at Calypso Cascades; 9,450 feet at Ouzel Falls
ELEVATION GAIN	195 feet to Copeland Falls; 880 feet to Calypso Cascades; 1,130 feet to Ouzel Falls
AVALANCHE DANGER	None
MAP	Trails Illustrated #200, Rocky Mountain National Park
CONTACT	Rocky Mountain National Park, 970-586-1206

COMMENT: If you have young children who are not very ambitious, the short ski from the road closure near Copeland Lake to Copeland Falls might be enough adventure for one day. For those ready for a little more distance and climbing, continue to Calypso Cascades and Ouzel Falls, one of the most popular winter treks in Wild Basin. The trail features the subtle beauty of a frozen stream with snow-covered ice sculptures that can be enjoyed by adventurers of all ages and abilities. This area is fairly low in elevation so wait for a major Front Range storm or mid-season conditions for good snow. Call Rocky Mountain National Park for snow conditions in Wild Basin.

This trail can be skied with skinny or mid-width skis. If you want to ski all the way to Ouzel or Thunder lakes, you will have challenging steep descents on skinny skis. Experienced skiers can use any style of ski on this route.

GETTING THERE: From Lyons, travel west and north on Highway 7 to Allenspark. Wild Basin is between the small towns of Allenspark on the south and Meeker Park on the north. From Highway 7, drive west on the Wild Basin road; proceed past the lodge to Copeland Lake and around the lake to the left. The road narrows to almost single-car width. The road is closed near Copeland Lake (8,320 feet).

THE ROUTE: From the parking area, go about 1.5 miles, either on the flat road or the adjacent horse trail on the left side of the road, to the summer trailhead at Wild Basin Ranger Station (8,500 feet; closed in winter). The trail, which is a bit more pleasant and interesting than the road, rolls gently and gains approximately 200 feet to the ranger station.

From the ranger station, proceed to the left through the parking lot to a route map and sign. Bear left and take the trail across the bridge. Take the well-marked side trail 0.4 mile from the ranger station to see Copeland Falls. The multi-level, subtle beauty of the frozen falling water is worth exploring with young children and camera in hand.

The trail continues up North Saint Vrain Creek, offering a lot of variety as it winds, rolls, and steadily climbs through a pretty mixed forest of aspen and a variety of evergreens. Parts of the trail are next to the beautiful frozen waterfalls and ice of the creek; however, at times you move some distance from it. At about 2.5 miles there is a trail junction; continue straight/left.

Shortly, you come to the bridge that crosses the creek about 0.4 mile below Calypso Cascades. This is a good spot for a snack break. It usually offers nice photo opportunities of the hillocks of snow and ice crystals that dress the creek. After another

Ouzel Falls in Wild Basin.

0.25-mile climb, you will reach the intersection of North Saint Vrain Creek and Coney Creek. Just a bit farther at the 3-mile mark is the magic of the Calypso Cascades.

At the cascades, the Allenspark Trail is on the left; bear to the right, and cross Coney Creek over two more bridges. Above the bridges are countless frozen-water cascades. At this point the trail levels for a bit and then steepens as it switchbacks straight uphill. From Calypso Cascades it is another steep 0.7 mile to Ouzel Falls. If you do not plan to go all the way to Ouzel Falls, it is worth going another 200 yards—even if it takes some gentle persuasion—to enjoy the views of the west slopes of Longs Peak and Mount Meeker that open up.

Once you get beyond the steep switchbacks you will soon cross Ouzel Creek and see Ouzel Falls in the near distance. In another 100 yards you reach an overlook at 3.7 miles, with spectacular views of Longs Peak, Mount Meeker to the northwest, Meadow Mountain to the southeast, and Wild Basin and the North Saint Vrain Creek below to the north. The peaks are the primary attraction here.

COPELAND FALLS, CALYPSO CASCADES, & OUZEL FALLS

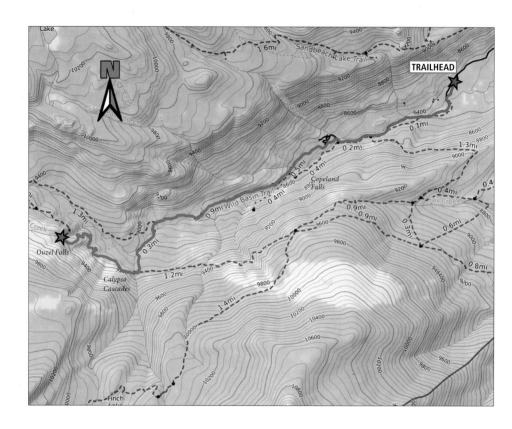

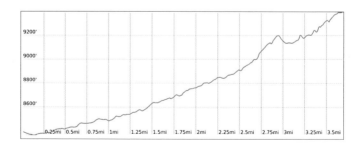

16. Allenspark Trail & Finch Lake

OPTION 1		
	ROUND TRIP	From Allenspark, 3.2 miles to overlook; 7 miles to Finch Lake
	DIFFICULTY	Moderate to challenging
	SKILL LEVEL	Intermediate
	HIGH POINT	9,760 feet at overlook; 9,912 feet at Finch Lake
	ELEVATION GAIN	800 feet to overlook; 952 feet to Finch Lake

OPTION 2		
	ROUND TRIP	From Wild Basin road closure, 7.6 miles to overlook; 11.4 miles to Finch Lake
	DIFFICULTY	Moderate to challenging depending on distance
	SKILL LEVEL	Novice to falls; intermediate to expert to Finch Lake
	HIGH POINT	9,760 feet at overlook; 9,912 feet at Finch Lake
	ELEVATION GAIN	1,440 feet to overlook; 1,592 feet to Finch Lake

AVALANCHE DANGER	None to low
MAP	Trails Illustrated #200, Rocky Mountain National Park
CONTACT	Rocky Mountain National Park, nps.gov/romo

COMMENT: This trek offers two starting points that take you high above Wild Basin. You can begin at either the Wild Basin road closure at Copeland Lake, climbing up from the Wild Basin Valley, or the Allenspark trailhead higher up. The Allenspark trailhead is about 640 feet higher and 2 miles shorter than the trailhead on the Wild Basin road. From either, you ski to an overlook where the two trails intersect, continuing up to Finch Lake if desired. You don't have to ski all the way to the lake to enjoy a great view of Wild Basin. It is an interesting short side trip (out and back) to climb to the ridge above Wild Basin. At the overlook you are rewarded with spectacular views of this glacier-carved valley and the peaks that surround it. Mount Meeker and Chiefs Head Peak are just a couple of the many visible gems.

You can ski this trail on skinny skis, but mid-width would be more comfortable on the descent. You can ski to Finch Lake with good snow.

GETTING THERE: Copeland Lake Trailhead: From Lyons, travel west and north on Highway 7 to Allenspark. Wild Basin is between the small towns of Allenspark on the south and Meeker Park on the north. From Highway 7, drive west on the Wild

North Saint Vrain Creek on Finch Lake trail from Wild Basin.

Basin road; proceed past the lodge to Copeland Lake and around the lake to the left. The road narrows to almost single-car width. The road is closed near Copeland Lake (8,320 feet).

Allenspark trailhead: From Highway 7, follow signs for the Allenspark/Ferncliff business route. When you reach the center of this small town, near the post office and church, turn west on CR 90. Stay on this road as it meanders for several miles. When you see Meadow Mountain Drive, turn right and reach the trailhead and parking lot in approximately 200 feet. The road from this point might not be passable in winter unless you have 4WD.

THE ROUTE: From Copeland Lake Trailhead: From the parking area, take either the flat road or the adjacent horse trail on the left side of the road for about 1.4 miles to the Finch Lake–Pear Lake trailhead on the left, before you reach the ranger station. It is about a 1.5-mile trek from this trailhead and about 3.8 miles one way from the road closure to the overlook near the top of the ridge, with an approximately 1,440-foot climb on switchbacks to reach the ridge. Upon arriving you have great views of Meeker, Longs, Chiefs Head, Pagoda, and the entire Wild Basin stretched before your feet. At this point you could turn around and have a satisfying round-trip. To continue to Finch Lake, see below.

The Allenspark Trail is more scenic than the trail from the Wild Basin valley floor; it is a steady climb with some variation all the way to the overlook. At about 0.8 mile, there is a trail on the right—a short connector to the Wild Basin Trail. Continue straight/left. After approximately the first mile there are breaks in the trees and you start getting nice views of Chiefs Head, Pagoda Mountain, Meeker, and a bit of Longs Peak. The last 0.5 mile to the overlook provides even more nice views, with the grand finale, the overlook itself, at 1.6 miles, where you get a 180-degree view of the peaks and the valley.

Overlook to Finch Lake: This is a challenging addition to either of the routes. From the trail junction at the overlook, the Allenspark Trail continues straight ahead, and the trail down to the right goes to Wild Basin Road; take the Finch Lake–Pear Lake Trail to the left (southwest). You reenter the trees and climb steadily toward the lake, passing through a small section of trail that was burned in the 1978 fire. In about 1 mile you cross a stream. After the first stream crossing, you dip into and out of the drainage and reach another stream crossing in about 0.5 mile. The trail then follows a small ridge 0.4 mile down to the lake in 1.9 miles from the overlook.

Photo by John Pennell, iStock

SPOT A PTARMIGAN IF YOU CAN

These snow-white birds undergo seasonal changes in plumage, from white in winter to gray or mottled brown in the spring and summer, and they blend into their surroundings so well you'll be a lucky skier to spot one. Ptarmigans (the "p" is silent) move slowly as they browse on shrubs and scratch up lichens and leaves with toes that are covered with stiff feathers above and below. They burrow into the snow to sleep, becoming almost totally invisible. For such a serene looking bird, ptarmigan males have a harsh cackling call.

ALLENSPARK TRAIL & FINCH LAKE

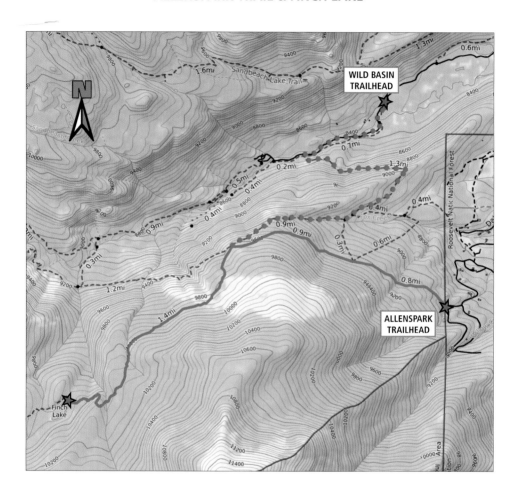

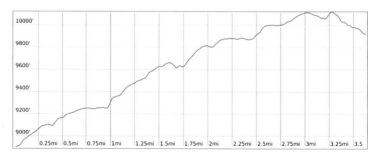

Indian Peaks Area

Chapter 3

PEACEFUL VALLEY AREA

*"I am glad I shall never be young without wild country to be young in.
Of what avail are forty freedoms without a blank spot on the map?"*

—Aldo Leopold, *A Sand County Almanac*

True to its name, Peaceful Valley is a tranquil riparian area northwest of Boulder just outside the Indian Peaks Wilderness. Enjoy spectacular views of jagged Sawtooth Mountain and its soaring 12,000-foot unnamed neighbor, which guard Buchanan Pass on the south and north, respectively. Meander the Middle Saint Vrain Creek drainage and experience a mixture of high-mountain meadows, rock outcrops, and a variety of evergreen and aspen trees. At 8,500 feet, this heavily forested area below treeline offers some of the lowest and easiest trails with consistent snow.

The area absorbs a lot of weekenders because it offers many skiing routes to choose from. Begin just before the Peaceful Valley Campground at a trailhead known by several monikers: Middle Saint Vrain, Buchanan Pass, and Peaceful Valley. This gives you the option of using either Middle Saint Vrain Road or the Buchanan Pass Trail for an out-and-back or loop. Other options would be to start at trailheads near Beaver Reservoir off CR 96 to explore Coney Flats Trail or the Sourdough Trails.

Skiing has a long history in Allenspark. Skiers slid down courses and flew into the air off jumps in the early 1900s. In the 1920s and 1930s, huge crowds came to watch jumping competitions, and when skiers learned how to turn their skis in the early 1930s, the Allenspark area was one of the first to jump on board. Often as many as 1,500 spectators came to watch slalom competitions. For a short few years in the late 1940s and early 1950s the Rock Creek Ski Area catered to participants in the new sport, and today's backcountry skiers can enjoy the same terrain and abundant snow conditions.

The Peaceful Valley area and Allenspark can be reached from Nederland, Lyons, or Estes Park.

Taking a few turns above the Caribou townsite.

17. Rock Creek Ski Area

ROUND TRIP	2.3 miles to base of ski area; 8 miles to summit of ski area
DIFFICULTY	Easy to moderate
SKILL LEVEL	Novice to advanced
HIGH POINT	9,130 feet at base of ski area; 10,810 feet at summit of ski area
ELEVATION GAIN	465 feet to base of ski area; 2,110 feet to summit of ski area
AVALANCHE DANGER	None to low
MAP	Trails Illustrated #102, Indian Peaks, Gold Hill
CONTACT	Boulder Ranger District, Roosevelt National Forest, 303-541-2500

COMMENT: The Rock Creek route follows an old road and the creek to the base area of the Rock Creek Ski Area, which operated from 1946 to 1952. Although overgrown, some of the ski area trails are visible, and it's possible to continue your trip to the top of the old area and make turns on your way back down. Experienced skiers can use any kind of ski, but if the snow is deep, wider skis will be necessary for making turns.

GETTING THERE: Turn into the town of Allenspark at the west entrance from CO 7 and go several hundred feet south past Allenspark Community Church. Take a left on 2nd Street and then a right onto the narrow, curving, and sometimes one-way Ski Road (County Road 107). Continue south for about 1.5 miles to the junction of Forest Service Roads 116.1 and 116.2. The road is not plowed beyond here. There is limited parking along the wider sections of the road, but don't continue beyond the junction as there may not be a place to turn around beyond the plowed road, and you don't want to get stuck. The road to the right continues uphill to the Saint Vrain Mountain Trailhead. The road to Rock Creek Ski Area is the left fork.

THE ROUTE: The snow can be a little thin at the beginning of the route as it descends to a creek crossing, but don't be discouraged; the reason a ski area was built here is because the Rock Creek valley holds snow, as you will soon discover. When the trail turns southwest again, it will follow the creek up the valley to the base of the old ski area in a broad open area at 1.1 miles. Rock Creek had three runs, a 30-meter jump, and a number of open snowfields serviced by rope tows that were powered by truck engines, along with a warming lodge and snack bar. It operated from 1946 to 1952. You can still see some of the overgrown runs and ski jumps.

Deep snow on the road to the old Rock Creek Ski Area.

If you want to continue your adventure from here, the trail narrows and climbs through some switchbacks to a junction with FS trail 116-2C. Take a hard left and stay on the trail that is marked simply 116. The trail will make another couple of switchbacks. Leave the trail at mile 3.1 and head through the trees south-southeast for about 0.1 mile to the crest of Ironclad Ridge. From here, turn east and in about 0.75 mile you will arrive at the summit of the old Rock Creek Ski Area. Reversing your route to go back, you can carve turns all the way back down to the old base area.

ROCK CREEK SKI AREA

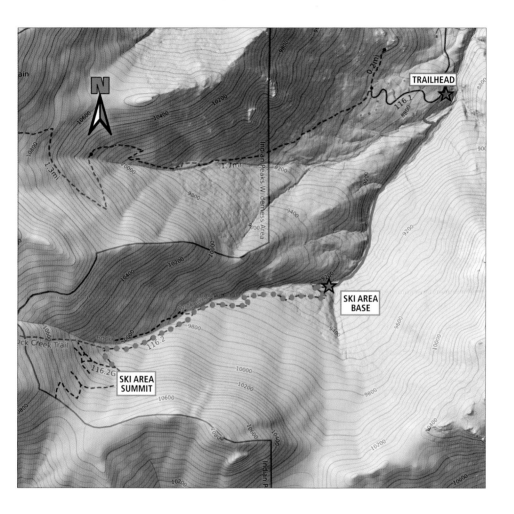

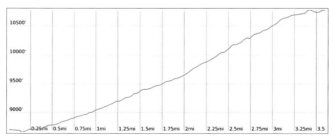

18. Buchanan Pass Trail & Middle Saint Vrain Creek

ROUND TRIP	10.8 miles to treeline
DIFFICULTY	Easy to moderate
SKILL LEVEL	Intermediate
HIGH POINT	9,880 feet at treeline
ELEVATION GAIN	1,360 feet to treeline
AVALANCHE DANGER	None to low
MAP	Trails Illustrated #102, Indian Peaks, Gold Hill
CONTACT	Boulder Ranger District, Roosevelt National Forest, 303-541-2500

COMMENT: This is an easy trek on a heavily used trail that starts on a road and then parallels it while passing through rolling, forested terrain. It is wise to arrive early to avoid the large, midday weekend crowds. This trail is a good place to go on windy days because of the heavy tree cover that shields you from the wintry blasts once you get beyond Camp Dick Campground.

The first mile is sun and wind exposed and usually has crusty snow, but after that the tree cover usually provides good snow protection, making the skiing better in the trees. This route can be skied with skinny or mid-width skis if you have good ski skills. You can ski out on the trail and back on the road if you want a quicker descent. The road is sometimes hard-packed and icy, so you will want metal edges on your skis.

GETTING THERE: From Denver, take I-25 to Highway 66; go west 16 miles to Lyons.

From Fort Collins, drive US 287 south to Highway 66 and go west to Lyons. From Boulder, take Highway 36 north to Highway 66, and then turn west on 66 to Lyons.

From Lyons, turn south on Highway 7 and drive 14 miles to Highway 72, the Peak to Peak Highway, then turn south on Highway 72 toward Nederland. The Peaceful Valley area is west of Highway 72 a couple of miles south of Raymond. From Nederland, drive north on Highway 72 about 5 miles past Ward.

On Highway 72 heading south, when you see the turnoff for Peaceful Valley about 3.5 miles south of Raymond, you are close, but don't take the Peaceful Valley turnoff. Take the second turnoff on the right (west) after Peaceful Valley. Look for signs for Peaceful Valley Campground, Forest Access, or Camp Dick. The highway marker is a small brown sign with a tent symbol on it. Turn onto FR 114. The turnoff is approximately 6 miles north of Ward.

Mountain view from Buchanan Pass Trail.

THE ROUTE: At the beginning of this route the snow can be a bit thin. Some of the best views for photography are at the beginning of the trail and in the Peaceful Valley Campground. If it is pictures of peaks you want, snap away at Mount Audubon and Sawtooth Mountain here, because in about a mile you will reach heavy forest. For the first 1 mile the route follows the road between Peaceful Valley Campground and Camp Dick Campground, crossing Middle Saint Vrain Creek twice. Past the gate at the far end of the road, the unpaved road continues along the south side of the creek; take the trail, which crosses to the creek's north side on a small footbridge. The snow improves dramatically once you enter the trees. The streamside and short hill are a pretty setting here, and after 1 mile of skiing it is a good place for a water break and/ or photos.

At around 2 miles, you will pass through some open meadows. Enjoy the warm sunshine before entering the cool forest. Some nice rock outcrops are good for loung- ing in the sun while you have a snack. It is a very wide valley. The road and trail climb very gently, offering a variety of mountain scenery. There is a side trail for horses that, because it is less traveled, offers powder rather than the hard-packed snow on the main trail. Though the horse trail is not shown on maps, it is within view of the main trail. It offers more rolling terrain and rock outcrops to climb for variety.

On the main trail at 2.5 miles, cross a side stream; at 3 miles is another open meadow. The challenging spots on the horse trail are at about the 3-mile mark where the trail narrows around a rock and above a drop into the creek, where there is a bypass with extra climbing. The main trail crosses another side stream at 3.5 miles. At 4.5 miles the end of the road crosses the creek and joins the trail. It is about 0.4 mile farther to the Indian Peaks Wilderness boundary and a trail junction. A treeline of sorts is another 0.5 mile beyond the wilderness boundary and is a good spot to begin your return trek.

BUCHANAN PASS TRAIL & MIDDLE SAINT VRAIN CREEK

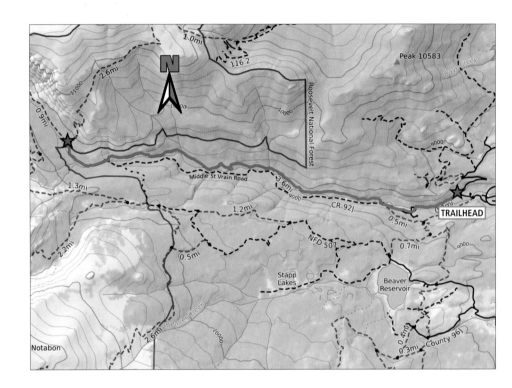

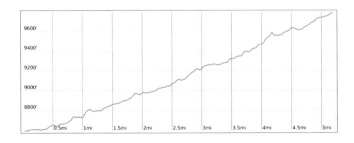

19. Beaver Reservoir–Coney Flats Trail

ROUND TRIP	7 miles to treeline
DIFFICULTY	Easy to moderate
SKILL LEVEL	Intermediate
HIGH POINT	9,800 feet
ELEVATION GAIN	600 feet
AVALANCHE DANGER	None to low
MAP	Trails Illustrated #102, Indian Peaks, Gold Hill
CONTACT	Boulder Ranger District, Roosevelt National Forest, 303-541-2500

COMMENT: This relatively easy, out-of-the-way trail is primarily in the trees but does offer some nice views along the way of St. Vrain and Meadow mountains. There are some great views of the Indian Peaks from Beaver Reservoir including Sawtooth Mountain. If the weather is iffy and you want peak pictures, take them before using the trail in case the weather socks in. Go as far as you like before turning around. This is a rolling and climbing skinny or mid-width ski trail.

GETTING THERE: From Denver, take I-25 to Highway 66; go west 16 miles to Lyons.

From Fort Collins, drive US 287 south to Highway 66, and go west to Lyons. From Boulder, take Highway 36 north and then Highway 66 west to Lyons, or from Boulder take Canyon Boulevard/Highway 119 west to Nederland.

From Lyons, turn south on Highway 7 and drive 14 miles to Highway 72, the Peak to Peak Highway, then turn south on Highway 72 toward Nederland. The Peaceful Valley area is west of Highway 72 a couple of miles south of Raymond. From Nederland, drive north on Highway 72 about 5 miles past Ward. In 3 miles (past the Peaceful Valley turnoff and past the Middle Saint Vrain/Camp Dick Campground turnoff) look on the west side of the highway for the one sign for CR 96 and the Tahosa Boy Scout Camp. The CR 96 turnoff is approximately 2.5 miles north of Ward and the Brainard Lake Recreation Area. Drive west on CR 96, passing the entrance to the Boy Scout camp, the Sourdough Trailhead on the south side of the road in 2 miles, and the spillway of Beaver Reservoir at 2.75 miles. Look for the trail on the right/north side of the road. You can turn around at a wide spot about 0.25 mile west and then park as close as you can get to the trailhead gate.

THE ROUTE: A trailhead sign gives the distance to Coney Flats as 4 miles, one way. You can have an excellent ski in less than that distance. The main 507 Trail

View from Beaver Reservoir.

passes the Cutoff Trail to Camp Dick, which is on the right in less than 100 yards, bear straight/left. (If you want to take the Cutoff Trail down to Camp Dick, be ready for a steep, windy, challenging descent.) The main trail climbs after the Cutoff Trail and then descends and climbs again repeatedly. You will see several false trails coming in from the left and right; ignore them. The main trail shows signs of heavier usage and has some 507 signs.

After 0.5 mile, the 507B Trail option will be on your left. It is less heavily trafficked and generally more powdery than the main trail. It also winds and climbs a bit more steeply, rejoining the main trail in about 1 mile. Less-experienced skiers should stay on the main trail. If you want a short loop, go up the main trail and back on the 507B Trail. The trail rolls as it climbs, so you will climb at least 300 to 400 feet in the first 1.4 miles. You will reach a large sign that says skiers and hikers go right/straight, bikers and cars left.

If you want a view, venture into the trees to the right of the trail and you can see Saint Vrain and Meadow mountains on a clear day. Some turn around here for a nice, short family outing. The main trail descends a bit more steeply for 0.25 mile before leveling and then continuing to roll up and down. If you want a longer, steeper climb-and-descent adventure, go left on the Coney Flats Road at the large sign, rather than straight on the main trail. You will wind up hill and down dale and rejoin the main trail in 1.8 miles versus 1.2 miles. Don't attempt it unless you have excellent routefinding skills, since it isn't as heavily used or well-marked. When the Coney Flats Road rejoins the trail you will be 0.6 mile from the Coney Flats/Creek Trailhead. Go straight for Buchanan Pass, or left for the Coney Creek Trail. Coney Creek goes toward Coney Lake below avalanche terrain; the pass climbs much more steeply, though safely. A hard right will take you down to the Middle Saint Vrain Road/Trail where you might see snowmobilers. You will have a 6.4-mile round-trip from this intersection if you turn around. On a clear day, you will earn some nice views to savor for your efforts, but probably some wind, too.

BEAVER RESERVOIR–CONEY FLATS TRAIL

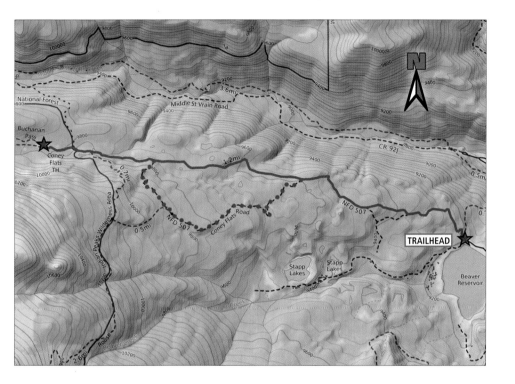

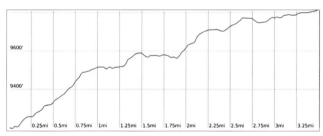

WHAT'S THAT SQUEAKING?

The coney, or cony, is also known as a pika. The name pika comes from the Mongols of the Ural Mountains. Pikas live in rockpiles, usually above timberline, but they don't hibernate, so there's a chance you'll see one when skiing in the high country. Actually, it's much more likely that you'll hear its high-pitched squeak before you'll catch sight of the small, rock-colored, fast-moving animal.

20. North Sourdough Trail

OPTION 1		
	NORTH ONE WAY	1.25 miles to Middle Saint Vrain Creek
	DIFFICULTY	Easy to moderate
	SKILL LEVEL	Intermediate
	HIGH POINT	9,140 feet at trailhead
	ELEVATION GAIN	540 feet
OPTION 2		
	NORTH ONE WAY	1.5 miles via Beaver Reservoir Cutoff Trail
	DIFFICULTY	Easy
	SKILL LEVEL	Intermediate
	HIGH POINT	9,200 feet
	ELEVATION GAIN	60 feet
OPTION 3		
	SOUTH ONE WAY	5 miles to Red Rock Trailhead
	DIFFICULTY	Moderate to challenging
	SKILL LEVEL	Intermediate
	HIGH POINT	10,000 feet
	ELEVATION GAIN	860 feet

AVALANCHE DANGER	Low
MAP	Trails Illustrated #102, Indian Peaks, Gold Hill
CONTACT	Boulder Ranger District, Roosevelt National Forest, 303-541-2500

COMMENT: From Beaver Reservoir you can take the North Sourdough Trail either north or south. The snow is generally better to the north. The route to the south, between Beaver Reservoir and Red Rock Trailhead, is often plagued by spotty snow and is quite rocky in the early or late season. If there has been a major spring snowfall in the area, it will be okay. The route south from Beaver Reservoir to Red Rock Lake is best done one-way with a vehicle shuttle. More accessible, popular access points for the South Sourdough Trail are in the Brainard Lake Recreation Area at Red Rock Trailhead, or farther south at Rainbow Lakes Trailhead. The South Sourdough Trail from Red Rock Trailhead to Rainbow Lakes usually has more reliable snow and is better for skiing because it is less wind and sun exposed. Skinny skis are adequate.

GETTING THERE: From Denver, take I-25 to Highway 66; go west 16 miles to Lyons.

From Fort Collins, drive US 287 south to Highway 66, and go west to Lyons.

From Boulder, take Highway 36 North and then Highway 66 west to Lyons, or from Boulder take Canyon Boulevard/Highway 119 west to Nederland.

From Lyons, turn south on Highway 7 and drive 14 miles to Highway 72, the Peak to Peak Highway, then turn south on Highway 72 toward Nederland. The Peaceful Valley area is west of Highway 72 a couple of miles south of Raymond.

From Nederland, drive north on Highway 72 about 5 miles past Ward. In 3 miles past the turnoff for Peaceful Valley and past the Middle Saint Vrain/Camp Dick Campground turnoff, look on the west side of the highway for the one sign for CR 96 and the Tahosa Boy Scout Camp. The CR 96 turnoff is approximately 2.5 miles north of Ward and the Brainard Lake Recreation Area.

New snow on the trail.

Drive west on CR 96, passing the entrance to the Boy Scout camp. The Sourdough Trailhead is 2 miles west of Highway 72, about 0.25 mile before Beaver Reservoir, on the south side of the road. Another access point is at the Coney Flats trailhead, on the right/east side of the road a little more than 0.75 mile farther. It is called the Beaver Reservoir Cutoff Trail on some maps.

THE ROUTE: North: From the Sourdough Trailhead, the trail to the north is a short route to Middle Saint Vrain Creek. In 0.25 mile it crosses Beaver Creek, and at about 0.75 mile the Beaver Reservoir Cutoff Trail comes in on the left. Continue straight to reach Middle Saint Vrain Creek. If you turn left onto the hilly, heavily forested Beaver Reservoir Cutoff Trail, it takes you uphill to the Coney Flats Trail and the Beaver Reservoir Trailhead in another 0.75 mile. It can be a fun, short trip with a car shuttle, or you can take your skis off and walk 0.75 mile on the road back to your car to close the loop at 2.25 miles.

South: From the Sourdough Trailhead, the trail to the south climbs between two hills, crosses a gated road at about 0.75 mile, and intersects with the Baptiste Ski Trail at about 1.4 miles, and with the Wapiti Ski Trail at about 2.4 miles. It travels down and then up to a trail junction at about 3.1 miles where the South Saint Vrain Trail goes straight/right up to Brainard Lake. Go left on the South Saint Vrain Trail toward the Red Rock Trailhead.

In about a mile is another trail junction. The South Saint Vrain Trail continues straight/left; go right on the Sourdough Trail and cross South Saint Vrain Creek. You will reach the Red Rock Lake Trailhead at a little over 5 miles. It is a long, hilly trek.

NORTH SOURDOUGH TRAIL

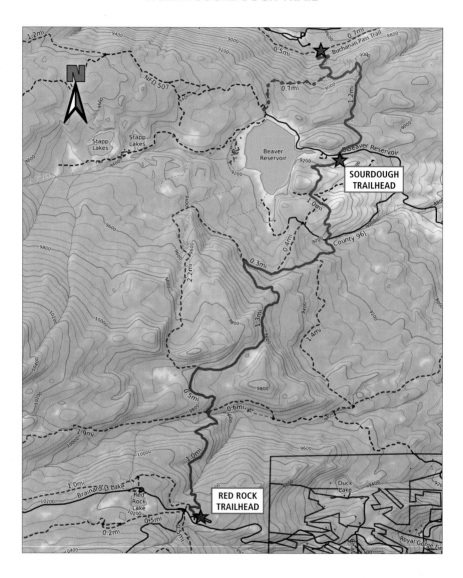

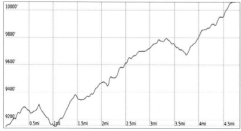

Sourdough Trailhead to Red Rock Trailhead

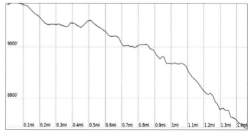

Sourdough Trailhead to Middle Saint Vrain Creek

Chapter 4
BRAINARD LAKE RECREATION AREA

"Twenty years from now you will be more disappointed by the things that you didn't do, than by the ones you did do. So throw off the bowlines. Sail away from the safe harbor...Explore. Dream. Discover."

—Mark Twain

Brainard Lake Recreation Area borders the Indian Peaks Wilderness Area and is one of the most popular places in the state for cross-country skiing. When you see the stunning setting, you will know why. The Indian Peaks are a formidable and thoroughly enticing backdrop that makes it worthwhile to endure the popularity of this place. This glacier-carved Continental Divide mountain "wall" was once proposed to become part of Rocky Mountain National Park to protect the area, but it was feared the designation would cause it to be overrun with people. It is hard to imagine that it could be used more heavily than it is; however, it absorbs a large number of people very well because of the number of trail options. Weekday visits are highly recommended. If that isn't possible, then early arrival for a parking space is suggested, though new parking lots help ease the situation.

The U.S. Forest Service (USFS) strives to spread out the users and maintain the wilderness appeal of the area. First, the USFS asks that, if at all possible, you leave your pets at home. The heavy usage in the relatively small area is much more palatable with fewer dogs. Three trails are designated dog-free: Little Raven, Waldrop, and the Colorado Mountain Club (CMC) Trail. The USFS also has some separate trails for skiers and snowshoers so that snowshoers don't have to walk in skiers' tracks and skiers don't have to zoom around the slower snowshoers.

To get there from Boulder, take Canyon Boulevard/Highway 119 west for 17 miles to Nederland. At Nederland, turn right/north on Highway 72, the Peak to Peak Highway, and go approximately 9 miles. The town of Ward is on the right/east side of the road. Watch for the Brainard Lake Recreation Area turnoff immediately on the left/west side of the road after the Ward turnoff.

The author's ski tracks on Niwot Mountain Trail.

21. South Sourdough Trail

ROUND TRIP	12 miles
DIFFICULTY	Moderate (one-way or out-and-back) to challenging (round-trip)
SKILL LEVEL	Intermediate
HIGH POINT	10,200 feet
ELEVATION GAIN	From Red Rock Trailhead to Rainbow Lake, gain of 500 feet, loss of 900 feet; From Rainbow Lakes Trailhead, gain of 1,000 feet, loss of 400 feet
AVALANCHE DANGER	Low
MAP	Latitude 40° Boulder Nederland; USGS Ward
CONTACT	Boulder Ranger District, Roosevelt National Forest, 303-541-2500

COMMENT: The South Sourdough Trail, though popular, has much less traffic than other trails in and around the Brainard Lake Recreation Area. You won't get quite the stunning views of the Indian Peaks Wilderness, but you will get beautiful views of the foothills and plains.

From the Red Rock Trailhead you can go either north or south. Both routes offer a rolling, hilly, sheltered trail. The route to the south is a bit easier than going north toward Beaver Reservoir. You can go south for as far as you like and then turn around. You can easily have an enjoyable hour or two with an out-and-back route. Going all the way to the Rainbow Lakes Trail is a half-day or full-day adventure with a descent to the Rainbow Lakes parking area at the end. The Brainard Lake–Red Rock end is higher, so starting at the Rainbow Lakes end is a climb of 1,000 feet. This trail is well-marked with blue diamonds and arrows and is equally popular with skiers and snowshoers. It is an advanced ski trail because of some steep sections and tight turns. Experienced skiers can use any style of ski on this route, although skinny skies are adequate.

GETTING THERE: From Nederland, turn right/north on Highway 72, the Peak to Peak Highway, and go approximately 9 miles. The town of Ward is on the right/east side of the road. Watch for the Brainard Lake Recreation Area turnoff immediately on the left/west side of the road after the Ward turnoff. From Highway 72, drive west on the Brainard Lake Road to the gate closure in about 3 miles. The Sourdough Trail is just east of the gate closure, crossing the road at the Red Rock Trailhead parking area.

From Boulder, take Canyon Boulevard/Highway 119 west 14 miles to Nederland. At Nederland, turn right/north on Highway 72, the Peak to Peak Highway, for approximately 6 miles. Turn west on the Rainbow Lakes campground road, also marked for the University of Colorado Mountain Research Station. The parking lot is approximately 1 mile on the south/left side of the road.

THE ROUTE: From the Red Rock Trailhead parking area on Brainard Lake Road: Go toward the summer entrance and turn left. Take the Sourdough Trail south and go downhill to cross Left Hand Creek. The trail then climbs as it rolls to introduce you to the Sourdough routine. The trail gradually ascends and in about 0.4 mile the Little Raven Trail goes off to the right; continue straight/left in thick trees. The trail rolls up and down and twists while gradually climbing for another 0.8 mile, where it reaches its high point at 10,200 feet. Enjoy the trees, the intermittent views, and the roller coaster as the trail rolls along at around 10,000 feet. It then climbs to another stream crossing at about 1.75 miles. The trail levels and continues due south for 0.75

SOURDOUGH IN HARDSCRABBLE TIMES

The hills and mountains around Ward and Nederland were the site of many gold and silver mines during the Colorado Gold Rush, which began around 1849 and lasted through the 1800s. Most of the miners searched the hills unsuccessfully for gold and survived on sourdough bread, sourdough flapjack pancakes, and beans. Sourdough bread is made by using fermenting dough left over from the previous batch of bread, and experienced prospectors and old-timers were also referred to as sourdoughs. The Sourdough Trail is named to honor the miners and the sourdough staples that kept them alive through their hardscrabble times.

mile, affording nice views. Then it turns sharply west/right at about 2.6 miles. In another mile it drops to Four Mile Creek, and then to the Peace Memorial Bridge at around 3.5 miles. This is a good turnaround point for an out-and-back, or you can turn around before descending 100 feet into the drainage to save the climb back out. The trail switchbacks into the drainage to cross Four Mile Creek, then climbs back up and continues due south another 0.75 mile or so. At about 4 miles the trail winds to the east and then south for 1 mile, descending the ridgeline to the Rainbow Lakes Road at 6 miles.

From the Rainbow Lakes parking area: This starting point will provide you with an 800-foot climb, from around 9,200 feet to around 10,000 feet, over the first 2.5 miles. The high point of the trail, 10,200 feet, is at the north end. You will then gain and lose at least another 200 feet along the way on the roller coaster, dropping into and out of a couple of creek drainages. The trail is north of the parking area. It travels gradually uphill west, levels, and resumes with a steeper climb. Bear right at the first arrow, and then left at the next one as the trail turns west and opens up to a view of Niwot Ridge and Niwot Mountain at around 9,400 feet. The trail turns sharply left/ south, and begins a series of steeper switchbacks, paralleling the University of Colorado Mountain Research Station road.

At 1 mile, it levels at the top of the switchbacks at 9,600 feet and tracks north, crosses a power line with views of the Peak to Peak Highway, and then travels west along the ridge with views of Niwot Mountain as you climb to around 9,700 feet. In an open aspen area, the trail turns sharply north/right and climbs up to 9,800 feet, then descends briefly before climbing up to a Sourdough Trail sign that says it is still 5 miles to the other end at the Red Rock Trailhead (sigh). There is a flat stretch for 0.3 mile to the north, and then a steep uphill to the northwest that ends at almost 9,900 feet, with a short descent to the Peace Memorial Bridge at Four Mile Creek.

This is a good place to turn around, giving you almost a 5-mile round-trip, unless you want to climb higher and see a few views of Golden Gate Canyon State Park in the distance as the trail tracks north. The trail climbs again, turning sharply left/south to begin switchbacks up to 10,000 feet. Once you reach 10,000 feet you will enjoy another roller coaster ride with intermittent views.

LITTLE RAVEN TRAIL: This short connector trail between the South Sourdough Trail and Left Hand Reservoir Road is a fun, challenging endeavor for experienced skiers with excellent ski skills. You will want wider AT or telemark skis for the descent, though it can be done on skinny skis. You can access the trail from Left Hand Reservoir Road, about 1 mile from the winter trailhead. Trek left at the first intersection and be ready for a steep, twisty descent down to the South Sourdough Trail. You can also access it by going south on the Sourdough Trail from the Red Rock Trailhead in the Brainard winter parking lot.

SOUTH SOURDOUGH TRAIL

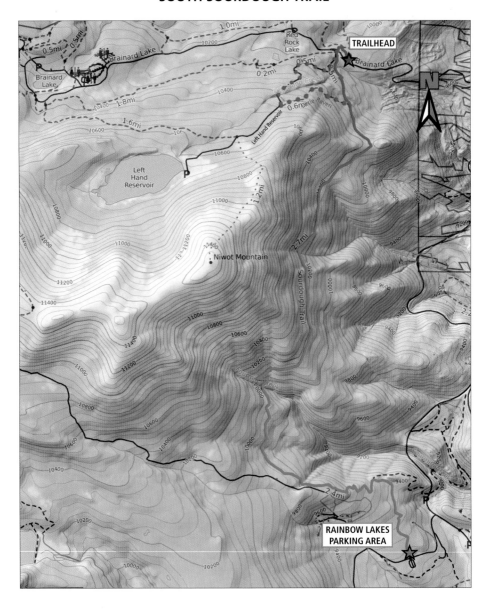

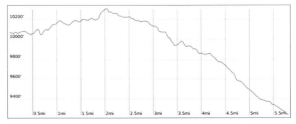

22. Niwot Mountain & Niwot Ridge

ROUND TRIP	6 miles
DIFFICULTY	Challenging
SKILL LEVEL	Intermediate to expert
HIGH POINT	11,557 feet
ELEVATION GAIN	1,557 feet
AVALANCHE DANGER	Low to moderate
MAP	Latitude 40° Boulder Nederland
CONTACT	Boulder Ranger District, Roosevelt National Forest, 303-541-2500

COMMENT: This high ridge towering to the south of the Brainard Lake area can offer an interesting winter adventure. It has a grand view of the majestic Indian Peaks and Longs Peak without requiring you to travel the length of Brainard Lake Road. There are two approaches to Niwot Ridge, but one of them—the western approach from Long Lake—is not recommended because of distance and the lack of trail markers. You can reach the eastern approach from either the Left Hand Park Reservoir Road or the Sourdough and Little Raven trails. There is no marked trail on this approach to the ridge top, so good routefinding and bushwhacking skills are required, plus a topographic map and compass. This climb is best attempted on a calm day.

Niwot Mountain and Niwot Ridge are often windswept, so be prepared for a little hiking. Most of the slopes are low-angle, and avalanche-hazard areas can be avoided. You will want AT or telemark skis for this rare adventure. You need a major snow-storm and no wind, a rare combination for this route. It is usually wind-scoured and crusty, but occasionally you can get lucky and experience lots of nice turns.

GETTING THERE: From Nederland, turn right/north on Highway 72, the Peak to Peak Highway, and go approximately 9 miles. The town of Ward is on the right/east side of the road. Watch for the Brainard Lake Recreation Area turnoff immediately on the left/west side of the road after the Ward turnoff. From Highway 72, drive west on the Brainard Lake Road to the gate closure in about 3 miles. The Red Rock Trailhead parking lot is just east of the gate closure. Left Hand Reservoir Road is at the entrance station west of the Red Rock Trailhead parking lot. The Sourdough Trail is across the road from the parking area. The route described here takes the trails on the way up and then the road, which is about 0.3 mile shorter, on the way down.

THE ROUTE: Take the Sourdough Trail south and cross Left Hand Creek. The trail rolls gently approximately 0.5 mile to reach the intersection with the Little Raven

Clouds over Niwot Mountain.

Trail. There should be a sign marking the Little Raven Trail. Turn right/west onto the Little Raven Trail (the South Sourdough Trail continues straight/left). The Little Raven Trail alternates between steep and moderate climbing. As it nears Left Hand Park Reservoir Road it levels out a bit and climbs more slowly. In approximately 0.6 mile you will reach the intersection with Left Hand Park Reservoir Road at 1.1 miles. Turn left/southwest onto the road (to the right is your return path). There is a sign on the right for the Little Raven Trail, which goes on to Brainard Lake; stay on the road. Climb approximately 150 yards up the Left Hand Park Reservoir Road to an old gravel pit or mine on the south side of the road, where you leave the road for the ridge at about 1.2 miles.

Climb up the hill to the left/east side of the mine, then bear southeast/left when you enter the trees. You climb steeply and gain about 200 feet in the first 0.25 mile through thick trees. After 0.15 mile, you are on a more gradual ascent path at around 10,600 feet and about 1.5 miles from the trailhead; pick the best route and angle to the southwest. After climbing another 0.25 mile and another 200 feet to 10,800 feet, you will encounter stunted pine trees at 1.7 miles. At this point you already have great views of Longs Peak to the north and Mount Toll, Pawnee Peak, and Mount Audubon to the west. If the wind is howling, turn around.

If it is one of those rare calm days, note carefully where you have emerged from the trees and pick your way southwest up the ridge for 0.5 mile. Look back frequently so you'll know where to reenter the trees on your return. At about 2.3 miles, angle south toward the rock shelter visible on the top of the ridge. It offers a nice windbreak for a snack or photos. The Niwot Mountain summit is the high point at the east end of the ridge at 11,471 feet. Continue about a mile southwest along the ridge to the second highpoint at 11,557 and 3.25 miles. If you are in a highpoint–bagging mood, you can continue slightly northwest another mile to 11,679 feet. You must turn around before the Boulder watershed boundary.

On the return when you reach Left Hand Park Reservoir Road, stay on it. About 0.1 mile after the intersection to the right with the Little Raven Trail, cross Left Hand Creek. The road continues with some nice views to the north and then descends for 1 mile back to Brainard Lake Road.

NIWOT MOUNTAIN & RIDGE

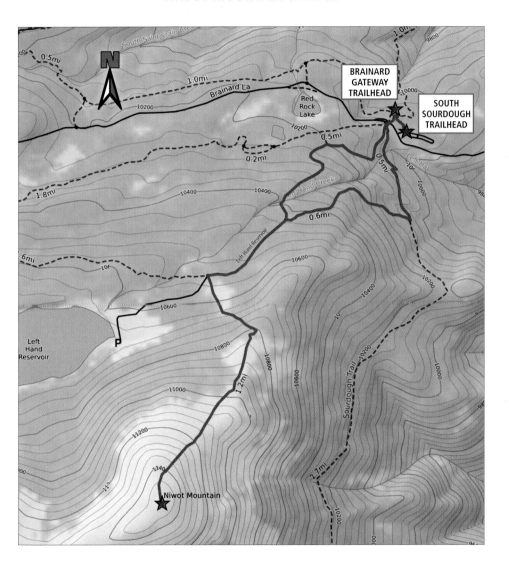

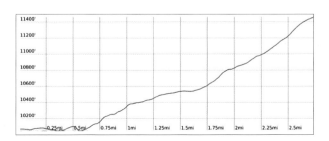

23. Brainard Lake Road

OPTION 1		
ONE WAY	2.2 miles to Brainard Lake
DIFFICULTY	Easy
SKILL LEVEL	Novice
HIGH POINT	10,300 feet
ELEVATION GAIN	300 feet

OPTION 2		
LOOP	1.2 miles around Brainard Lake
DIFFICULTY	Easy
SKILL LEVEL	Novice
HIGH POINT	10,370 feet
ELEVATION GAIN	70 feet

AVALANCHE DANGER	None
MAPS	Latitude 40° Boulder Nederland; USGS Ward
CONTACT	Boulder Ranger District, Roosevelt National Forest, 303-541-2500

COMMENT: One of the reasons the Brainard Lake Recreation Area is popular is its proximity to Denver and Boulder; another is its ease of use for family or novice outings. It is almost impossible to get lost, and the views of the surrounding Indian Peaks are spectacular. Brainard Lake Road can be skied as an out-and-back to Brainard Lake, or any distance short of the lake. The road rolls gently and the snow is usually packed down firmly by midmorning. You pay for the convenience, however, by encountering large numbers of dogs and people on the road. You can extend your trip with a nice kick-and-glide ski tour around Brainard Lake on skinny Nordic skis.

GETTING THERE: From Nederland, turn right/north on Highway 72, the Peak to Peak Highway, and go approximately 9 miles. The town of Ward is on the right/east side of the road. Watch for the Brainard Lake Recreation Area turnoff immediately on the left/west side of the road after the Ward turnoff. From Highway 72, drive west on the Brainard Lake Road to the gate closure in about 3 miles. Do not confuse this with the Red Rock Trailhead just east of the gate—that is the entry point for the superb but challenging Waldrop, Saint Vrain Creek, and Sourdough Trails. Turn right into the Brainard Gateway parking area where you will find a waxing room and restrooms.

A family ski outing on Brainard Lake Road.

THE ROUTE: Walk from the parking area west to the Brainard Lake Road closure and go around the gate. You can ski west on the Brainard Lake Road all the way to the lake, or only as far you'd like for a nice out-and-back trip. When you reach the lake, you can opt to ski around it before returning to the parking area. Various trails will intersect the road, but you can't get lost if you stay on the wide road.

BRAINARD LAKE ROAD: From the gate closure the road climbs gradually northwest; in 0.5 mile you cross Red Rock Lake's outlet stream. The Brainard Lake Road climbs slightly, curving southwest and then leveling off, reaching the midpoint intersections with the snowshoers-only trail at 1.25 miles. The road resumes climbing southwest, and in 0.5 mile reaches the side loops for Pawnee Campground. In another 0.25 mile, at approximately 2 miles, you will reach a stunning high-mountain panorama. This is a good spot to turn around unless you decide to continue to loop around the lake.

BRAINARD LAKE LOOP: Where the road splits you can continue around the lake to enjoy views of the Indian Peaks or to reach the roads to the trailheads for Mitchell and Blue Lakes, Long Lake, and Lake Isabelle. From where Brainard Lake Road first reaches the lake, go right (counterclockwise). In 50 yards, the north leg of the snowshoers-only trail comes in from the right; in another 25 yards you cross the lake's outlet stream. You will see the Arickaree Picnic Area, and in another 25 yards a trail goes off to the right. At a little over 0.3 mile you cross Mitchell Creek, and less than 100 yards later is the Mitchell Creek Picnic Area, which is at the intersection with the road to Mitchell, Blue, and Long Lakes and Lake Isabelle on the right at 0.4 mile.

At the west end of the lake, where the other trailheads split off, you are in the trees. From there you can turn right to proceed to another trailhead; stay straight/left on the road to continue around the lake. At 0.7 mile the Niwot Cutoff Trail comes in from the right. You soon have nice views to the north and west across Brainard Lake. Now the road climbs a small hill in 0.4 mile and you are back to the start of the loop.

BRAINARD LAKE ROAD

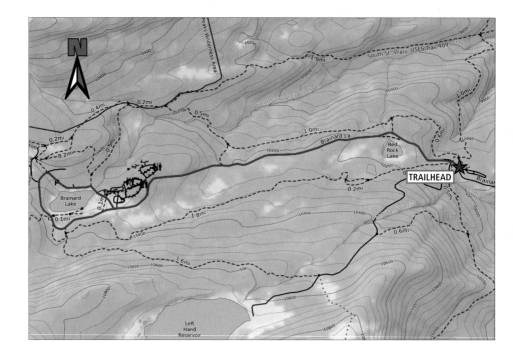

24. Left Hand Park Reservoir Road

ROUND TRIP	3.5 miles
DIFFICULTY	Moderate
SKILL LEVEL	Novice
HIGH POINT	10,650 feet
ELEVATION GAIN	600 feet
AVALANCHE DANGER	None
MAPS	Latitude 40° Boulder Nederland; USGS Ward
CONTACT	Boulder Ranger District, Roosevelt National Forest, 303-541-2500

COMMENT: Although there are a couple of spots that can blow free of snow, this is an easy out-and-back route that will give you sweeping views from the reservoir as a reward. It also can feature a quick descent on the road depending on snow conditions. This road can be skied on any ski, but wider skis are more fun for the descent.

GETTING THERE: From Nederland, turn right/north on Highway 72, the Peak to Peak Highway, and go approximately 9 miles. The town of Ward is on the right/east side of the road. Watch for the Brainard Lake Recreation Area turnoff immediately on

The view from Left Hand Park Reservoir Road.

Skiing the Left Hand Park Reservoir Road.

the left/west side of the road after the Ward turnoff. From Highway 72, drive west on the Brainard Lake Road to the gate closure in about 3 miles and park in the Brainard Gateway parking lot. Do not confuse this with the Red Rock Trailhead just east of the gate—that is the entry point for the superb but challenging Waldrop, Saint Vrain Creek, and Sourdough Trails.

THE ROUTE: From the winter trailhead go toward the entrance station and around the closed gate. Look immediately to your left for Left Hand Park Reservoir Road. You will pass three other trailheads for Sourdough South and CMC. Continue up the road past the Little Raven Trail at 1 mile, and then past the continuation of Little Raven in another 0.75 mile on the right, go straight toward the reservoir. The best views are on the edge of the reservoir, so enjoy the view and turn around to go back. If you want a twisty, turny, narrow route back, take the Little Raven Trail to the CMC trail, which would extend your ski by 1.75 miles.

LEFT HAND PARK RESERVOIR ROAD

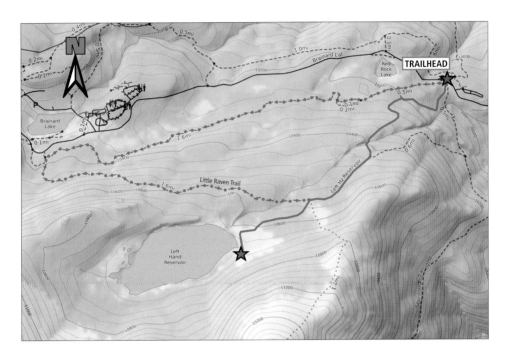

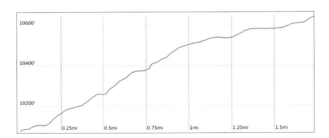

25. Little Raven–Left Hand Park Reservoir Road–CMC South Trail Loop

ROUND TRIP	5.5 miles
DIFFICULTY	Moderate
SKILL LEVEL	Intermediate to advanced
HIGH POINT	10,900 feet
ELEVATION GAIN	700 feet
AVALANCHE DANGER	None
MAP	Latitude 40° Boulder Nederland
CONTACT	Boulder Ranger District, Roosevelt National Forest, 303-541-2500

COMMENT: This is one of the most enjoyable loop of trails in the Brainard Lake area. It offers nice scenery and a variety of intermediate and advanced skiing options with easy sections and more challenging descents. The bottom section of the Little Raven Trail between the reservoir road and the Sourdough Trail is the most challenging descent and can be avoided or embraced. It is great fun on a powder day if you're a solid intermediate skier. It is steep and narrow with some sharp turns; not as much fun on old, hard-packed snow. If you want to avoid it, you can start the clockwise approach by climbing it. Midwidth skis are the best choice, but you can survive on skinny skis with good skills.

GETTING THERE: From Boulder, take Canyon Boulevard/Highway 119 west for 17 miles to Nederland. At Nederland, turn right/north on Highway 72, the Peak to Peak Highway, and go approximately 9 miles. The town of Ward is on the right/east side of the road. Watch for the Brainard Lake Recreation Area turnoff immediately on the left/west side of the road after the Ward turnoff. Go west on Brainard Lake Road 3 miles to the winter road closure. The Brainard Gateway parking area, restrooms, and warming hut are on your right.

THE ROUTE: Clockwise Approach: From the Brainard Gateway parking lot, go south on the road to the gate closure. Go around the gate and look to the left for Left Hand Park Reservoir Road. The entrance to the South Sourdough Trail is next to the road on the left/east side. The trail initially descends and then climbs gradually 0.4 miles to the intersection of the Little Raven Trail (USFS Trail 802). Go uphill to the right/west to ascend as the trail winds its way steeply through the thick tree cover; it's nice on a windy day. It is around 0.6 mile to the top where the trail levels and goes north to intersect the reservoir road. Turn left/west on the road and ascend less steeply 0.4 mile to the continuation of the Little Raven Trail and the intersection on the right/north side of the road, across from a former mine. If you want a great view, trek south to the mine and uphill for an Indian Peaks panorama before getting on Little Raven Trail.

Taking advantage of a sunny day on the Brainard Lake trails.

Once on Little Raven Trail, it is level for around 0.25 mile then descends more steeply to the intersection with the Colorado Mountain Club (CMC) South Trail (USFS Trail 814.2) in about 1 mile. Hang on to your hat as the trail turns 90 degrees to the east around a sharp descending curve. The trail plunges again to reach more level terrain, where you can take a side trail on the left down to the Brainard Lake Road if you or someone with you isn't enjoying the twists and turns of the trail. Turn right/east on the road to return to the trailhead on the much less challenging road that features gently rolling hills. If you opt to return on the trail, you will have another lovely 2.8 miles from the intersection through the trees back to the parking lot. The CMC trail mellows as it gradually descends to the east with a few interesting twists and turns through the forest.

Counterclockwise: Going counterclockwise means you will be climbing through the steep hairpin turns on the Little Raven and CMC trails. Start the route by going around the closed gate and looking on the left for the reservoir road. Just above the intersection on the right you will see the Snowshoers Only trail and the skiers only CMC ski trail trailheads. On the CMC Trail you will enjoy the gradual climb for around 1.5 miles before it gets steeper. You will reach the intersection with the Little Raven Trail after 2.8 miles and the Left Hand Park Reservoir road after a total of 4.5 miles of climbing. When you reach the road you get to enjoy the benefits of all of the climbing and cruise down the wide road to the intersection with the lower section of the Little Raven on the right/south side. You can stay on the road for the rest of the descent or choose the more challenging twists and turns of the Little Raven Trail. "The Raven" is best enjoyed after a dump of fresh snow. The road is generally easier though there is often a blow-off section just below the Raven intersection.

LITTLE RAVEN–
LEFT HAND PARK RESERVOIR ROAD–
CMC SOUTH TRAIL LOOP

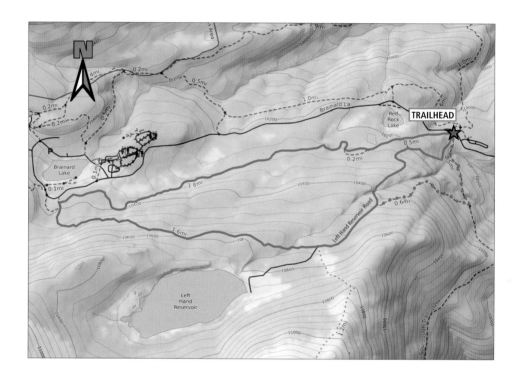

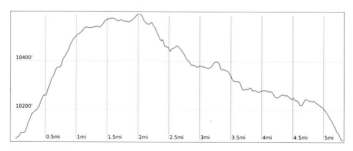

Clockwise loop

26. Waldrop Trail

ROUND TRIP	Up to 8.75 miles
DIFFICULTY	Moderate
SKILL LEVEL	Intermediate
HIGH POINT	10,200 feet
ELEVATION GAIN	1,000 feet
AVALANCHE DANGER	None
MAP	Latitude 40° Boulder Nederland
CONTACT	Boulder Ranger District, Roosevelt National Forest, 303-541-2500

COMMENT: The Waldrop Trail is a scenic connector trail that can be used for either a long loop or a shorter out-and-back. Skinny or mid-width skis would work. It is a roller coaster with lots of short climbs and descents requiring intermediate ski skills, especially when hard-packed, due to a few sharp turns and steep descents. You will see some nice views of Mount Audubon after the first mile.

It can be used for one of the most direct routes to the Colorado Mountain Club (CMC) Arestua Cabin or for longer loops. You can create loops with the Brainard Lake Road, CMC South Trail, or South Saint Vrain and North Sourdough Trails.

Tracks on the Waldrop Trail.

GETTING THERE: From Boulder, take Canyon Boulevard/Highway 119 west for 17 miles to Nederland. At Nederland, turn right/north on Highway 72, the Peak to Peak Highway, and go approximately 9 miles. The town of Ward is on the right/east side of the road. Watch for the Brainard Lake Recreation Area turnoff immediately on the left/west side of the road after the Ward turnoff. Go west on Brainard Lake Road 3 miles to the winter road closure and the Brainard Gateway parking lot.

THE ROUTE: Starting from the Brainard Gateway parking lot go south next to the warming hut, then west around the end of the hut, and then northwest. In 100 feet you will reach an intersection with the Sourdough Trail; go straight. You will go gently downhill and then climb for 0.6 mile to the Red Rock Lake intersection; continue straight west. The trail goes down and then begins its roller coaster ride up and down hills with a couple of steep climbs and descents. You will see views of Mount Audubon after the first mile. The trail then gradually descends into the South Saint Vrain Creek drainage and continues to rollercoaster. It intersects the Snowshoe Trail and crosses the creek climbing toward the South Saint Vrain Trail.

You can turn around and go back the way you came, or go west to create a loop with either Brainard Lake Road or the CMC South Trail; go east/right to create a loop with the South Saint Vrain and North Sourdough Trails. The latter option is more challenging because it ends with a steeper climb up the often rocky North Sourdough Trail. Excellent snow conditions are advised for the rocky North Sourdough.

WALDROP TRAIL

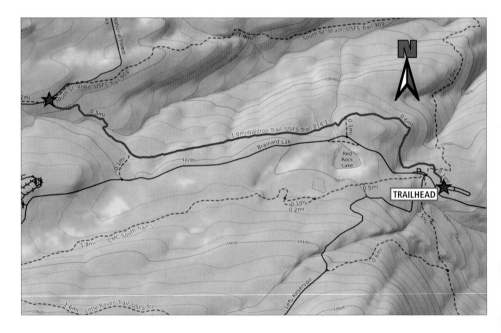

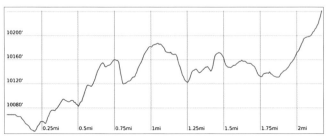

27. Mitchell and Blue Lakes & Mount Toll

ROUND TRIP	7.2 miles to Mitchell Lake; 10 miles to Blue Lake
DIFFICULTY	Moderate to challenging
SKILL LEVEL	Novice to Mitchell Lake, intermediate to expert to Blue Lake
HIGH POINT	10,700 feet at Mitchell Lake; 11,300 feet at Blue Lake; 12,979 feet at Mount Toll
ELEVATION GAIN	700 feet to Mitchell Lake; 1,300 feet to Blue Lake; 2,900 feet to Mount Toll
AVALANCHE DANGER	Low to considerable on Mount Toll
MAP	Latitude 40° Boulder Nederland
CONTACT	Boulder Ranger District, Roosevelt National Forest, 303-541-2500

COMMENT: You need good weather and snow conditions and/or to get an early start to make the round-trip to Mitchell Lake from the Brainard Lake Road gate closure. It is worth the trip to see the setting of this large, high-mountain lake and the backdrop of the Indian Peaks. If conditions permit, you can continue on the Mitchell Lake Trail 1.4 miles to Blue Lake. This is a tougher trek than the trek from Long Lake to Lake Isabelle, but it is spectacular. Fortunately, the return is mostly downhill except for one small hill. Toll Mountain is best skied in the spring after the snow has stabilized, since it is definitely steep enough to avalanche at any time. You need expert ski skills and AT or telemark skis to ski it. Most people who ski it don't climb all the way to the summit. You can make it to either Mitchell or Blue Lake on skinny skis but the descent is more fun on wider skis.

GETTING THERE: From Nederland, turn right/north on Highway 72, the Peak to Peak Highway, and go approximately 9 miles. The town of Ward is on the right/east side of the road. Watch for the Brainard Lake Recreation Area turnoff immediately on the left/west side of the road after the Ward turnoff. From Highway 72, drive west on the Brainard Lake Road to the gate closure in about 3 miles. The Red Rock Trailhead parking lot is just east of the gate closure.

THE ROUTE: From the Brainard Lake gate closure, follow Brainard Lake Road 2 miles one way (or 2.8 miles on the CMC South Trail) to reach the lake, then follow the loop

Tracks on the Mitchell and Blue Lake trail beneath the towering Indian Peaks.

0.4 mile around the lake to the turnoff for summer trailheads at 2.4 miles. At the well-marked turnoff for Mitchell and Long lakes on the right/north side (or the left/north side if you approach from the CMC South Trail) of Brainard Lake Road, the trailhead road turns to the north and in 0.1 mile, forks; take the right-hand branch (the left branch goes to Long Lake and Lake Isabelle). In about 100 yards the road crosses Mitchell Creek, and Waldrop North Trail comes in from the right here. At 0.25 mile from the turnoff the South Saint Vrain Trail comes in from the right, and the road curves left (west). Meander through the thick tree cover gradually uphill to the summer trailhead parking lot (10,500 feet) at 0.4 mile (a 200-foot elevation gain) from the turnoff from Brainard Lake Road, 2.9 miles from the gate closure.

From the summer trailhead, the trail levels before climbing steadily next to Mitchell Creek. You will continue in trees most of the way. In about 0.3 mile, at the boundary for the Indian Peaks Wilderness, a path comes in from the left at 3.2 miles. Shortly after, the trail opens up and you will see several nice views of the pointed summit of Mount Toll. In a little more than 0.3 mile you cross the southern shore of a little lake at 3.5 miles, and about 0.1 mile after, at 3.6 miles, you reach the shoreline of Mitchell Lake. After the first shoreline access to Mitchell Lake you will cross its outlet and continue to climb around its southern shore. There are several more opportunities to descend to the lakeshore and enjoy the views of Mount Toll, Pawnee Peak, and Shoshoni Peak. You will reach the inlet stream from Blue Lake at 3.9 miles. If you don't want to go all the way to Blue Lake but would like a nice view above the trees, continue on the trail and climb the steep hill just west beyond Mitchell Lake. It is worth the price of admission to see the view back to the east.

As you continue to Blue Lake, the trail is steeper throughout, although there are a few flat stretches. It is not a good early season trail. At 4.1 miles you will cross the stream, and then will do so again at 4.2 miles. After the first steep hill beyond Mitchell Lake, you are well out of the trees. On a clear day you have a steady diet of nice views all the way of Niwot Ridge. Numerous waves of ridges roll away under your feet as you climb one false summit ridge after another. The several little lakes to your left are not yet Blue Lake.

Finally, at 5 miles from the gate closure, you reach the southeastern shore of Blue Lake at its outlet; the lake is above tree line in a glacial cirque beneath Mount Toll and Pawnee Peak. If you want to ski Mount Toll you will have to circumnavigate Blue Lake. Crossing the lake for a direct approach can be risky in the spring when ice is melting. As with many of the trails in this book, even if you turn around short of Blue Lake, you will have had a very enjoyable adventure. Just remember that the return trip will seem longer. Be conservative in your turnaround time.

MITCHELL AND BLUE LAKES

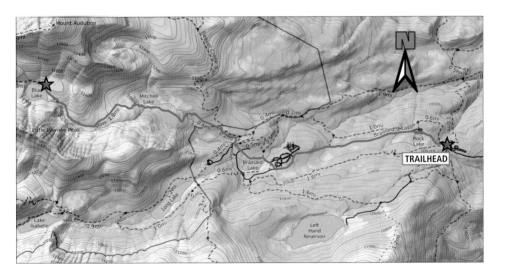

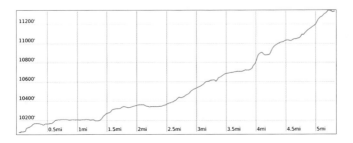

28. Mount Audubon

ROUND TRIP	14.8 miles for the summit
DIFFICULTY	Challenging
SKILL LEVEL	Expert, with winter mountaineering skills
HIGH POINT	13,223 feet
ELEVATION GAIN	2,700 feet
AVALANCHE DANGER	Low to moderate
MAP	Latitude 40° Boulder Nederland
CONTACT	Boulder Ranger District, Roosevelt National Forest, 303-541-2500

COMMENT: You have to have good weather and snow conditions and/or get a very early start to make the round-trip to the top of Mount Audubon from the Brainard Lake Road gate closure. The easiest way to reach the summit is to climb it before the road closes for the season, or as soon as it opens, saving around 6 miles round-trip. The late spring approach guarantees more complete snow coverage. Skiing all of the way on the road is another very viable alternative. The higher reaches of Mount Audubon are often blown free of snow, so expect to alternate between skiing and hiking.

The summit is 7.4 miles one way from the gate closure. Excellent routefinding skills and fitness are required to see the stunning view of the Indian Peaks from the top. You will want AT or telemark skis for this route, as it features lots of steep descents on the return. There is a good, relatively safe, slope for taking turns on the south side to the west of the main trail 0.5 mile after the trail steepens. There are also some skiable slopes on the east side of the trail that are steeper and more avalanche prone. The best skiing conditions are usually on the lower slopes rather than near the summit.

GETTING THERE: From Boulder, take Canyon Boulevard/Highway 119 west for 17 miles to Nederland. At Nederland, turn right/north on Highway 72, the Peak to Peak Highway, and go approximately 9 miles. The town of Ward is on the right/east side of the road. Watch for the Brainard Lake Recreation Area turnoff immediately on the left/west side of the road after the Ward turnoff. Go west on Brainard Lake Road 3 miles to the winter road closure.

THE ROUTE: From the Brainard Lake gate closure, follow Brainard Lake Road 2 miles one way to reach the lake, then follow the loop 0.4 mile around the lake to the turnoff for summer trailheads at 2.4 miles. If you don't want to ski on the road, you can take the Waldrop North Trail to the South Saint Vrain Trail for a direct but rolling route. At the well-marked turnoff for Mitchell and Long Lakes on the right/north side of Brain-

The view from the summit of Mount Audubon.

ard Lake Road, the trailhead road turns to the north and in 0.1 mile, forks; take the right-hand branch (the left goes to Long Lake and Lake Isabelle). In about 100 yards the road crosses Mitchell Creek, and Waldrop North Trail comes in from the right. At 0.25 mile from the turnoff, the South Saint Vrain Trail comes in from the right and the road curves left/west. Meander through the thick tree cover gradually uphill to the summer trailhead parking lot (10,500 feet) at 0.4 mile (200-foot elevation gain) from the turnoff from Brainard Lake Road, which is 2.9 miles from the gate closure.

The Mount Audubon Trailhead is at the north/right end of the summer parking, separate from the Mitchell/Blue Lakes Trailhead. You will be traveling west and northwest as you gradually climb to a headwall at around 10,600 feet. It is around 1 mile to reach the headwall, where you turn right/north and climb more steeply on switchbacks. The long switchbacks will take you up about 200 feet where the trail levels a bit. You will see the summit to the southwest, and most of the route ahead. The skiable south-facing slope is to the west; the east-facing slopes are to the east. The sign for the Buchanan Pass Trail is in 0.5 mile. In another 0.25 mile, switchbacks begin again around 10,900 feet, and then the trail travels more gradually as it traverses northwest for almost a mile.

Some skiers prefer to turn to the west and ski the steep south slopes rather than going for the summit. They are steep enough to avalanche. If you stay on the main trail, you will see steep cliffs that drop off to the north, and a very steep slope to the summit. There are multiple cairned routes (if they aren't completely buried under the snow) to the summit, which is to the west and then southwest from the bottom of the slope. Pick what looks like promising snow cover as you go, making your own switchbacks. Unless there has been a recent storm and no wind, it is unlikely that you will have great snow all the way to the summit for skiing. You can still get in a good round-trip regardless of your turn-around point.

MOUNT AUDUBON

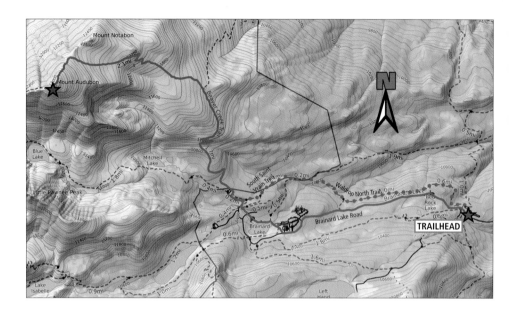

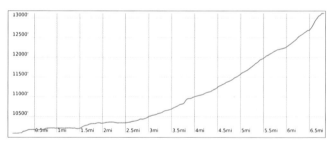

PARKING ETIQUETTE

On a number of routes in this book the parking is limited, so consider your fellow skiers and private landowners when you park. Don't block another car, or park so close that it will make it hard to access the trunk of the car in front. Do not share your music with the world by blaring your stereo while you gear up. The rest of us are not that much into Electro-Norwegian-Reggae-Punk. When you are gearing up, don't hold up traffic because you are standing in the middle of the parking lot putting on your gaiters, or loading your pack, or herding kids. Some of these routes abut private property. While you have a perfect right to park your car on unposted city, county, or state easements along the road, you do not have a right to trespass on private property. Letting dogs run free or pee on private property is bad form, and it is even worse when you do.

29. Long Lake & Lake Isabelle

ROUND TRIP	6.3 miles to Long Lake; 9.3 miles to Lake Isabelle
DIFFICULTY	Easy for Long Lake; challenging for Lake Isabelle
SKILL LEVEL	Intermediate
HIGH POINT	10,600 feet at Long Lake; 10,800 feet at Lake Isabelle
ELEVATION GAIN	600 feet to Long Lake; 800 feet to Lake Isabelle
AVALANCHE DANGER	Low
MAP	Latitude 40° Boulder Nederland
CONTACT	Boulder Ranger District, Roosevelt National Forest, 303-541-2500

COMMENT: Long Lake enjoys a stunning setting, and the trek has its own rewards. Lake Isabelle, another 1.5 miles beyond, is reached on one of the more beautiful trails in the Front Range. It is a steady climb from Long Lake but not particularly steep until you are very near Lake Isabelle. From this lake you can also safely venture another 0.5 mile up the Pawnee Pass Trail before entering an avalanche hazard area. You can circle Long Lake by using the Jean Lunning Trail on the south side as part of the loop. You can ski to Long Lake on skinny skis and to Lake Isabelle on mid-width or skinny skis.

GETTING THERE: From Boulder, take Canyon Boulevard/Highway 119 west for 17 miles to Nederland. At Nederland, turn right/north on Highway 72, the Peak to Peak Highway, and go approximately 9 miles. The town of Ward is on the right/east side of the road. Watch for the Brainard Lake Recreation Area turnoff immediately on the left/west side of the road after the Ward turnoff. Go west on Brainard Lake Road 3 miles to the winter road closure.

THE ROUTE: From the Brainard Lake gate closure, follow Brainard Lake Road 2 miles one way to reach the lake, then follow the loop 0.4 mile around the lake to the turnoff for summer trailheads at 2.4 miles. At the well-marked turnoff for Long and Mitchell lakes on the right/north side of Brainard Lake Road, the trailhead road turns to the north and in 0.1 mile, forks; take the lefthand branch (the right goes to Mitchell and Blue lakes). The road gradually climbs southwest 0.4 mile to the summer trailhead parking lot (10,500 feet) at 2.9 miles from the gate closure.

From the trailhead, you have nice views of Niwot Ridge along the way to Long Lake. On the left is a short connector to the Jean Lunning Trail, which is mostly in the trees and doesn't offer the great views of the Pawnee Pass Trail; stay straight/

Tracks on the ski trail that skirts Long Lake.

right. When you reach the lake at about 3.2 miles, there is a spectacular and unique view of the Indian Peaks. If it is a windy day, hang on to your hat to enjoy the view for any length of time. If it isn't windy, the lakeshore is a delightful place for a lunch or snack break.

As you continue west and then southwest along the shore of Long Lake for 0.5 mile, you are rewarded with superb views almost all the way, since most of the trail has openings through the trees to Niwot Ridge. There is a trail junction at 4 miles with the other end of the Jean Lunning Trail to the left; for Lake Isabelle, stay straight/right. In about 0.4 mile beyond the intersection you come to a very nice, open meadow area at 4.4 miles that affords a terrific view of the ridge and some of the peaks beyond. It is a good place for a rest break because it has southern exposure and is still relatively sheltered from the wind. After this, the trail steepens considerably and switchbacks up through trees 0.25 mile to Lake Isabelle at 4.6 miles. The view from here of the Indian Peaks is nothing less than stunning.

OTHER TRAILS TO EXPLORE: From Lake Isabelle you can continue higher up the Pawnee Pass Trail, but stop when the trail starts to near the ridgeline with cliffs above. This area is very avalanche-prone. The route is safe up to that point. You need an early start to make this a fun trip on short winter days.

Along the way, notice what may be a glacial terminal moraine with a meadow on the uphill side. The meadow may once have been a lake.

LONG LAKE & LAKE ISABELLE

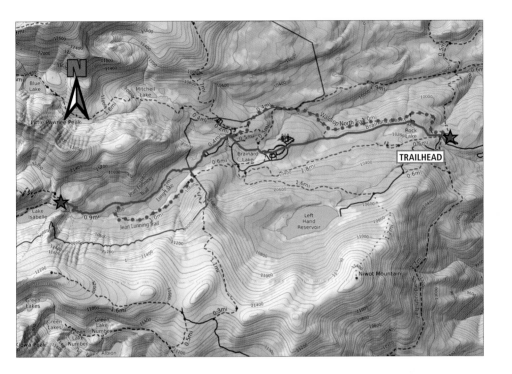

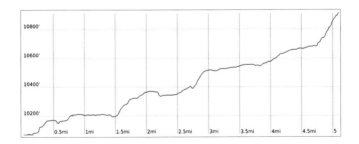

30. Rainbow Lakes & Arapaho Glacier Overlook Trail

ROUND TRIP	8 miles to the lakes
DIFFICULTY	Easy to moderate
SKILL LEVEL	Novice to lakes; intermediate to overlook
HIGH POINT	10,100 feet
ELEVATION GAIN	800 feet
AVALANCHE DANGER	Low
MAP	Latitude 40° Boulder Nederland
CONTACT	Boulder Ranger District, Roosevelt National Forest, 303-541-2500

COMMENT: The majestic high-alpine terrain of the Arapaho Glacier Overlook and Rainbow Lakes is heavily trod in the summer but not as heavily used in the winter, making it a treat for skiers. Access Rainbow Lakes and encounter the massive spectacles of Niwot and Caribou Ridges, brooding Bald and Pomeroy Mountains, and the high and distant summit ridge of the Arapaho Peaks. The area is south of the busy Brainard Lake area and west of a bustling parking lot that is at the south end of the Sourdough Trail. The Rainbow Lakes road beyond the Sourdough parking lot is impassable in the winter, but a trek on the road to the Rainbow Lakes Trailhead will reward you with views of the area's rugged peaks.

The Rainbow Lakes are in a spectacular high-mountain setting, nestled next to the soaring tundra of the glacier-carved Caribou ridgeline. The road is closed to winter travel, so it can be used for a nice ski toward the trailhead. You will have good views of both the Caribou and Niwot Ridges and some of the towering Indian Peaks on the way, though making it all the way to the lakes and back is a long day unless you are very fast on skis. Skiing just part of the road is a worthwhile adventure since it climbs very gradually and offers mountain views. Sections of the road might be snow-free because of wind and sun, so be prepared to carry your skis for short parts of the road. You can use skinny Nordic skis for this outing, and if someone breaks trail for you it can be a round-trip ski and glide. If you want to add to the adventure, have lots of stamina, and are on wider skis, start early and take the side trail on the north toward the Arapaho Glacier Overlook.

The road is a beginners ski route, but the Glacier Trail requires expert ski skills.

GETTING THERE: From Boulder, take Canyon Boulevard/Highway 119 west for 17 miles to Nederland. At Nederland, turn right/north on Highway 72, the Peak to Peak

A ski adventure on the Rainbow Lakes road.

Highway, and go approximately 6 miles. Turn west on the Rainbow Lakes Campground road, also marked for the University of Colorado Mountain Research Station. The parking lot is approximately 1 mile on the south/left side of the road.

THE ROUTE: It is 3 miles one way to the Rainbow Lakes Trailhead, and another mile to the first of the lakes. You will have to park in the Sourdough Trail parking lot and walk 0.5 mile to the Rainbow Lakes road closure. The road to the University of Colorado Mountain Research Station is on the right at 0.6 mile. Rainbow Lakes road is on the left/south side of the research road. The route starts at the closure gate and turns sharply south for a mile, then climbs gradually to 9,600 feet. At about 1.25 miles the road turns west. You will see views through the aspen on the left. At 1.5 miles, towering Pomeroy and Klondike Mountains come into view as the road descends toward North Boulder Creek. At about 2.25 miles it crosses North Boulder Creek. The road then climbs back up to 9,700 feet, then to 9,900 feet as it nears Rainbow Lakes Campground.

The trailhead for the lakes is at the very end of the campground road loop, next to the trailhead map. If you make it to the trailhead, the lakes trail rolls gently for another mile to the lakes to the northwest alongside a creek. You'll have some nice views along the way. In a mile you reach the lakes, which are surrounded by Caribou and Arapaho Ridges at around 10,000 feet. The real treat is the view from the lakes if you make it that far. Don't dawdle too long, as you have a long trek back.

As mentioned, you can skip the lakes and go for the Arapaho Glacier Overlook Trail. It is 12 miles round-trip to the overlook but only 4 miles round-trip to the spectacular overlook of the Boulder watershed and a view of Mount Albion. You will want AT or telemark skis for this route, and the longer days of spring.

RAINBOW LAKES & ARAPAHO GLACIER OVERLOOK TRAIL

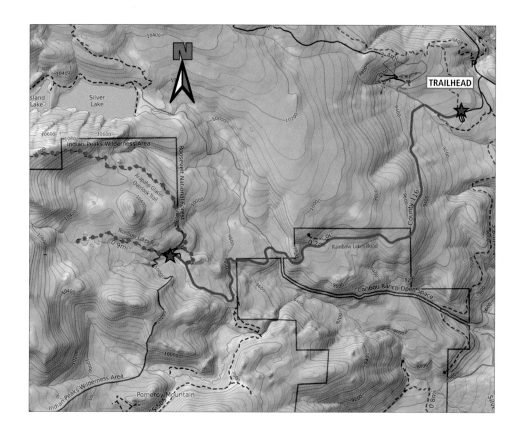

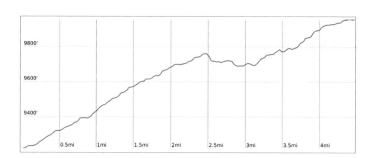

Nederland Area

Chapter 5

NEDERLAND

"If we had the courage to follow those unknown canyons...we might walk right into Eden."
—James C. Work, *Windmills, The River & Dust: One Man's West*

The Nederland area, 17 miles from Boulder, offers a variety of trails at the foot of the Indian Peaks. The magnificent backdrop of the Continental Divide invites the uninitiated into the high foothills and mountains of the Front Range. Enjoy the windswept meadows, frozen sparkling lakes and streams, and the aspen and conifer forests. Nederland is surrounded by Roosevelt National Forest, and Boulder County's Mud Lake Open Space borders town on the north. Mud Lake Open Space connects to the county's Caribou Ranch Open Space. The rolling Magnolia Trails network is minutes from town.

The town of Nederland features more than the famous Frozen Dead Guy and the annual winter festival celebrating him; there are a dozen excellent restaurants, bakeries, coffee shops, and brewpubs. If you don't want to make the drive from Boulder by car, you can hop on an RTD bus to Nederland, and if you want to spend the night, there are affordable and unique lodging options.

The best way to get to Nederland is to drive west up Boulder Canyon/Highway 119 from Boulder.

THE SWITZERLAND TRAIL

The Switzerland Trail was a narrow-gauge railroad line that operated around the turn of the twentieth century between Nederland and Ward. It carried supplies and ore to and from mining camps and the mills, and then, as mining declined, the railroad began bringing tourists from towns in the Front Range to the spectacular mountain vistas and playgrounds. The railbed is now popular for hiking and biking.

Looking across the valley at Eldora Mountain Resort.

CARIBOU RANCH RECORDING STUDIO

There was a barn on private property near the open space also called Caribou Ranch that was famous as a music recording studio in the 1970s and used by Elton John, U2, John Lennon, Joe Walsh, some of the Eagles, Stephen Stills, and other well-known musicians. It burned down in 1985 and the property was then used for a gated, high-end real estate development. The rest of the ranch was purchased by Boulder County and became the Caribou Ranch Open Space.

31. Caribou Ranch Open Space

ROUND TRIP	3.1 miles total: DeLonde Homestead 1.2 miles; Blue Bird Loop 1.9 miles
DIFFICULTY	Easy
SKILL LEVEL	Novice
HIGH POINT	8,300 feet
ELEVATION GAIN	200 feet
AVALANCHE DANGER	None
MAP	Trails Illustrated #102, Indian Peaks, Gold Hill
CONTACT	Boulder County Open Space, bouldercounty.org/open-space/parks-and-trails/caribou-ranch/
RESTRICTIONS	Dogs and bicycles prohibited The open space is closed from April 1 through June 30 to protect calving elk and migratory birds

COMMENT: The Boulder County Open Space area called Caribou Ranch includes the historic DeLonde Homestead, with a striking aspen- and pine-ringed high-mountain meadow, as well as the nineteenth-century Blue Bird Mine complex. The ranch was used as a site to film movies between 1936 and 1971, including the 1966 remake of Stagecoach starring Bing Crosby and Stephanie Powers. Most of the historic buildings have been preserved. You can see into the close quarters the miners used. Enjoy a stream, a waterfall, diverse trees, and animals. This trail has enough snow only after a major easterly upslope storm or the snows of mid-winter. Wait until after January unless you hear Nederland has good snow cover. This can be an easy Nordic skinny ski tour after a major Front Range storm, but not before.

GETTING THERE: From the Nederland roundabout, turn north onto Peak to Peak Highway 72. Travel 2.0 miles to CR 126; turn left/west on CR 126 and go 1 mile to the Caribou Ranch parking lot.

THE ROUTE: You will travel northwest from the parking area and go gradually uphill in thick trees. In 0.5 mile, you crest the ridge and have a sweeping view of part of the ranch and the hilly, forested terrain. This section of the trail is often blown free of snow. Descend a short hill and reenter the trees, coming to a comely small meadow and another section of sun-exposed trail. You might have to carry your skis. The trail turns sharply north and goes downhill with a historical marker about the Switzerland

The trail to DeLonde Homestead on Caribou Ranch Open Space.

Trail excursion train. You will reach an intersection in 0.25 mile. If you are not sure you want to ski the entire loop, turn right and go down a short hill to the historic DeLonde Homestead and beaver pond.

From the homestead you can make a slight detour to a picnic area to the southeast where you can see the beaver pond and a wildlife description. If you don't want to ski the entire loop, this can make a good turnaround spot.

If you decide to continue to the mine, continue north from the homestead. The next section is uphill through rocky terrain for over 0.5 mile. You might have to carry your skis through part of it. You will see signage for Boulder Creek, and then the Blue Bird Mine. If you visit the mine, continue past the structures for 0.25 mile to reach the streamside picnic area and a small, possibly frozen waterfall. When you go back downhill, look to your left for the trail—it is easy to miss the trail and end up on the service road.

When you return to the trail from the mine, continue for another 1.5 miles back to the trailhead by traveling west/right; or make your trek a shorter route by retracing your steps. It is worth completing the entire circuit so you can enjoy the meadow and the stately stands of aspen. If you continue west, the trail crests a small hill and then goes downhill before leveling. There is a viewpoint less than 0.5 mile on the left that is good for photos. When you round the bend in the trail, it travels southeast and begins a gentle climb back to where you started.

CARIBOU RANCH OPEN SPACE

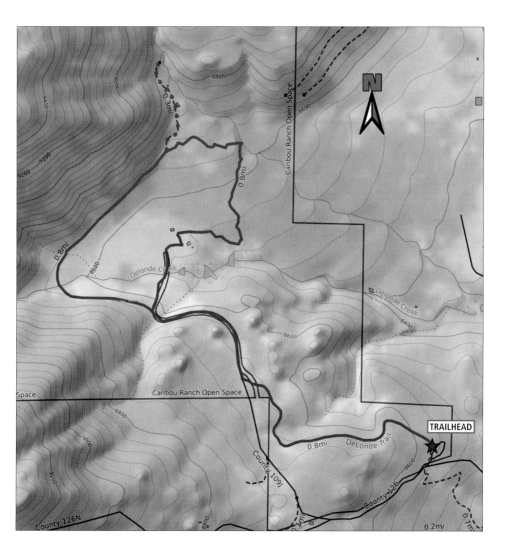

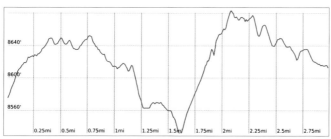

32. Mud Lake Open Space

ROUND TRIP	2.4 miles via: Kinnickinnick Loop, 1.1 miles; Tungsten Loop, 0.8 mile; and Caribou Ranch connector trail, 0.5 mile
DIFFICULTY	Easy
SKILL LEVEL	Intermediate
HIGH POINT	8,300 feet
ELEVATION GAIN	200 feet
AVALANCHE DANGER	None
MAP	Trails Illustrated #102, Indian Peaks, Gold Hill
CONTACT	Boulder County Open Space, bouldercounty.org/open-space/parks-and-trails/mud-lake/
RESTRICTIONS	Dogs are allowed on leash at Mud Lake, but not at Caribou Ranch Open Space

COMMENT: This is a beautiful Boulder County Open Space area featuring stately aspen, a frozen lake, and views of the nearby peaks. It is an easy figure-eight loop in gently rolling terrain that also features a pine, fir, and spruce forest with views of Bald and Pomeroy Mountains. This trail has enough snow only after a major easterly upslope storm or after the snows of mid-winter because of its relatively low 8,200-foot elevation. Wait until after January, unless you hear Nederland has good snow cover from a major early-season storm. This can be an easy Nordic ski after a major Front Range storm. Don't venture onto the lake surface unless you are absolutely sure it is frozen solid.

GETTING THERE: From Boulder, take Canyon Boulevard/Highway 119 west for 17 miles to Nederland. Go straight through the roundabout and bear right onto Peak to Peak Highway 72 north for 2.0 miles to CR 126; turn left/west on CR 126 for 0.5 mile. Turn left into the Mud Lake parking lot.

THE ROUTE: The trailhead is on the northwest edge of the parking lot. There is a map at the trailhead. You will travel uphill 50 yards to an intersection with the Tungsten Trail. Go left immediately to reach lovely, usually frozen Mud Lake. Waterfowl will be there early in the season or until it freezes solid. You can circumnavigate the lake for a very short, easy ski, or follow the entire, slightly hilly Tungsten loop for an almost 1-mile jaunt and enjoy the views from both sides of the lake. Be sure to trek over to the east side of the lake for the best photography. You will see a sweeping view of the lake with Pomeroy Mountain (a sub-peak of South Arapaho Peak) in the background.

The picnic pavilion at Mud Lake.

If you want a more extended adventure with a bit more uphill and nice views, add the 1.1 miles of the Kinnickinnick Loop. You will climb around 200 feet to include it, but the trail is not very steep and well worth it. Traveling counter-clockwise on Kinnickinnick from Tungsten will mean you will climb the steepest (northwest) section first and then have a mellow downhill. As you wind your way uphill on gentle switchbacks, you will see a bench at the top of the hill. This is also an excellent spot for pictures of Pomeroy and Bald mountains, and you might even see Mount Audubon peeking over the top in the distance if it is a clear day. If you prefer a mellower climb first, go clockwise (southeast), and enjoy a beautiful stand of aspen on the way up.

If you want to lengthen the enjoyment, include the Caribou Ranch connector trail to add another 1 mile round-trip. It is a beautiful, gradual hill route, with pretty meadows and ponderosa pine and is frequented by deer, elk, and even moose. You might have to shed your skis to cross Sherwood Creek on the wooden bridge. This trail section is more sun-exposed, so snow cover might be thin until the middle of the winter. The trail intersections are well-marked but the trails themselves are not continuously marked. For most of the winter these well-used trails will be obvious, but if you are the first to arrive after heavy snow you might have to routefind. It is difficult to get lost because the open space is relatively small. Just remember which direction the parking lot is, and that it is generally uphill from the lot and downhill to get back to it.

MUD LAKE

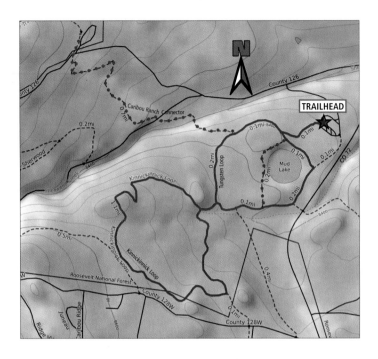

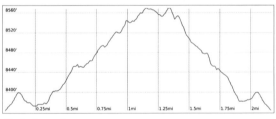

Clockwise route

KINNICKINNICK

Also called bearberry, Kinnickinnick, pronounced KINNY-kin-ICK or Kinn-ICK-innick, is frequently found on the edge of forest clearings. It grows as a ground-hugging mat of glossy evergreen leaves with red stems and white bell-shaped flowers tinged with pink that turn into red berries in the ski season. Most scholars credit the Algonquin for naming the plant Kinnickinnick, which means "smoking mixture."

33. **West Magnolia Trails**

ROUND TRIP	2 miles on trails 925A and 342; 1 mile on trails 925A and 925B; 1 mile on trail 355A
DIFFICULTY	Easy
SKILL LEVEL	Novice
HIGH POINT	8,900 feet
ELEVATION GAIN	400 feet
AVALANCHE DANGER	None
MAP	Trails Illustrated #102, Indian Peaks, Gold Hill
CONTACT	Boulder Ranger District, Roosevelt National Forest, 303-541-2500

COMMENT: This is a large network of easy trails in gently rolling terrain in an aspen, pine, fir, and spruce forest with views of South Arapaho Peak, Bald and Pomeroy mountains, as well as the Eldora Mountain Resort. The loops can be confusing, but it is difficult to get lost. These trails have enough snow only after a major upslope storm or after the snows of mid-winter. Wait until after January, unless you hear Nederland has good snow cover from an early-season storm. If you are very ambitious, you can ski from West Magnolia Campground all the way to Rollinsville. After a major storm, this area can be good for easy Nordic skiing.

GETTING THERE: From Boulder, take Canyon Boulevard/Highway 119 west for 17 miles to Nederland. Go left/south through the roundabout onto Peak to Peak Highway 72 for 2.7 miles to Magnolia Road/CR 132W; turn right/northwest, and you will see a small parking area on the right. Or, continue west for another mile, and park outside the second forest gate that is closed for the winter. Walk southwest around the gate and you will see the trailhead on the right/west side of the summer parking lot.

THE ROUTES:
TRAILS 925A/B, 342A, AND 926A
From the first parking area, you will see a sign for the 925A trail on the left/west uphill side of the trailhead. This goes gradually uphill into the trees to the north and then west. In a little over 0.25 mile you will come to the intersection with the 925B and 925F trails. If you continue straight you will end up on the 925F trail, which will take you over a hill and through the trees to Magnolia Road in about 1 mile. If you go right/north on the 925B trail, you will go downhill and circle around back to the

Skiing at West Magnolia after a spring snowstorm.

parking area in only 0.75 mile. If you go downhill on 925B and then left on 342A, you will enjoy a longer additional 0.75-mile loop through a beautiful aspen grove called Aspen Alley. You can loop the grove on 342A and 926A, and then return uphill to the parking area.

TRAIL 355A

These trails/roads are from the summer trailhead that is 1 mile west of Highway 119: 355A, 355, 926E and F, and Hobbit.

This is an easy, rolling out-and-back that travels west from the trailhead. You will probably want to continue onto the 926E and F trail to extend your trip through the forested rolling, rocky hills. There will be nice views to the north of Eldora Mountain Resort and South Arapaho Peak. When 355A dead-ends into campground loop 355, turn right to pick up 926 E and F. They will take you to a small ridge and then back around to 355, which is primarily the summer campground road. Trail 355 can also be used to extend your trek through the thick, lodgepole pine forest. If you want to go farther, take 355-I past the 355 campground road, and south onto Hobbit I. Hobbit I and II are more difficult to discern in deep snow. Give it your best effort, and if you lose the Hobbit trails, you can retreat onto the portion of 355 that is nearby. Just keep a general sense of which direction you came from or, better yet, carry a compass for orienting yourself.

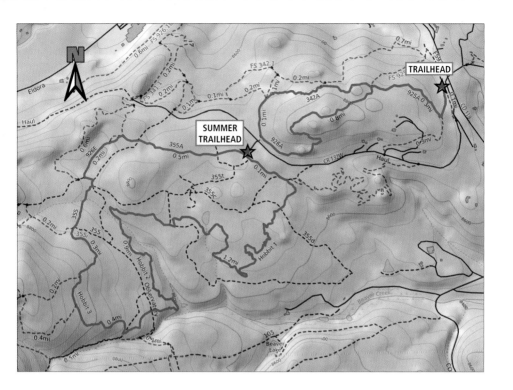

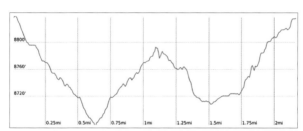

Trails 925A/B-342A-926A

South loop: trails 355A-355-925E/F-Hobbit

WEST MAGNOLIA TRAILS

Chapter 6
ELDORA MOUNTAIN RESORT & WEST

"Storms are fine speakers, and tell all they know, but their voices of lightning, torrent, and rushing wind are much less numerous than the nameless still, small voices too low for human ears; because we are poor listeners."

—John Muir, *The Mountains of California*

Nederland is a charming former mining community 19 miles west of Boulder. Eldora Mountain Resort is approximately 5 miles west of Nederland and 1,200 feet higher, with the base at 9,400 feet. Avoid driving I-70 to the larger ski areas by visiting Eldora Mountain Resort; Boulder Canyon is a short, scenic drive in comparison. There is RTD bus service from Boulder to Eldora seven days a week, so take advantage of this option if you do not want to drive on very well-maintained but snowy mountain roads.

The additional elevation and proximity to the Continental Divide mean that the resort receives much more snow than Nederland or Boulder. A warm, sunny day in Boulder can be a snowy powder day at Eldora Mountain Resort. Oddly enough, even the town of Eldora, which is just downhill from the resort and west of Nederland, is also in a different climate zone and often gets more snow and wind than its snowy, windy neighbor Nederland. This means that skiers can rely on good snow cover most of the winter.

The ski area is a bit more wind-prone than breezy Boulder, but the Nordic trails have excellent tree cover that provides good shelter from the breezes you will experience in the downhill area and parking lot.

If you want to ski, but want the predictability of a resort with warm lodges, food, and well-marked trails and are willing to pay for it, then Eldora's Nordic trails are for you. Fortunately, the trail passes for access to the Nordic Center trails are only a fraction of the cost of a downhill lift ticket, even at Eldora's less expensive prices. The Nordic Center is the starting point for the trails, and it is a good place for warming and snacks. You can ride a shuttle bus to two other lodges with more complete food and beverage service. There is a bar in the main lodge for après trail activities. There is also a wide variety of coffee shops, excellent restaurants, and pubs in Nederland, as well as lodging and entertainment. Nederland has a vibrant local music scene, with several bands that tour nationally and often appear locally for a pittance. Book a night in a local lodge and avoid the commute.

For the more adventurous, several trails start at the Caribou townsite. During its silver boom, Caribou was a thriving town of thousands. Today all that's left are a few stone foundations and some excellent skiing. The narrow dirt road to Caribou is rugged and not often plowed, necessitating four-wheel-drive and good snow tires.

Eldora and Caribou are easily reached from Nederland, which is 17 miles west of Boulder. From Boulder, take Canyon Boulevard/Highway 119.

Skiers contemplate the view of the Anchor Mine route.

34. Fourth of July Road/Trail

ROUND TRIP	7 miles
DIFFICULTY	Easy to moderate
SKILL LEVEL	Novice
HIGH POINT	9,700 feet
ELEVATION GAIN	800 feet
AVALANCHE DANGER	Low to considerable; can be avoided
MAP	Trails Illustrated #102, Indian Peaks, Gold Hill
CONTACT	Boulder County Open Space, bouldercounty.org/open-space/parks-and-trails; and Boulder Ranger District, Roosevelt National Forest, 303-541-2500

COMMENT: The Hessie Valley is a beautiful riparian area of Middle Boulder Creek just west of the town of Eldora. You will see rock formations and many peak views. It is a good route for family excursions, as even doing part of the trail is worthwhile. The Fourth of July Road will take you above the Hessie Valley for a sweeping view of the valley and the north side of Eldora Mountain Resort. You will also see the peaks of Bryan (10,810 feet), Chittenden (10,860 feet), Guinn (11,200 feet), Woodland (11,205 feet), and a more distant unnamed 12,000-foot mountain before entering the tree-lined portion of the road where you will have great views of South Arapaho Peak (13,397 feet).

The first 3.5 miles of the road are avalanche safe. As you near the steep flanks of Klondike and Bald mountains, and especially South Arapaho Peak, the avalanche danger increases. There have been fatal avalanches near the Fourth of July Trailhead, so traveling that far is not wise unless avalanche danger is low. But you can have a nice long ski and be in no avalanche danger.

This is a very popular route. Either plan to arrive early or visit during the week to avoid crowds and garner a close-in parking spot. You can ski the road with skinny Nordic or wider skis. The descent after you turn around is not steep.

GETTING THERE: From Nederland, go south through the roundabout onto Peak to Peak Highway 72 for around 1 mile, and turn right onto CR 130. In approximately 2 miles, you will see the turnoff on the left for CR 140 uphill for Eldora Mountain Resort; don't turn, go straight. The town of Eldora is another 2 miles west. The Hessie Trailhead is beyond the closed or impassable road on the west side of town. Parking is limited. Pay attention to the No Parking signs and don't block residents' access to their driveways, or you will be towed.

THE ROUTE: Your distance to the trail might vary a bit depending on where you can park. In any case, you will have at least a 0.75-mile stroll on the Fourth of July Road to reach the Hessie intersection. You will see the north side of Eldora Mountain Resort to the south as you stroll along the road. At the fork, stay on the Fourth of July Road as it goes straight uphill and the Hessie road/trail goes left downhill. The next 0.5 mile is one of the steepest sections of the road and also the most sun-exposed, so you might have to shed your skis.

It climbs more gradually after this and has some almost flat sections where the snow improves. As you climb 200 feet, enjoy the views to the south and west; this is the one of the best view sections of the

View of South Arapaho Peak from Fourth of July Road.

road. In about 0.25 mile there is an open view as the trees part at around 9,200 feet. You will see the slopes of Bryan Mountain and Guinn Mountain above Lost Lake.

As the road levels somewhat and the snow improves, enjoy the rugged flank of Chittenden Mountain while climbing to 9,300 feet. You will only gain another 200 feet over the next mellow 0.75 mile with a forest of aspen, mixed conifers, and Klondike Mountain's rocky cliffs as your view. The higher you go, the thicker the aspen get—reaching for the sky with their slender branches and defying heaven to be any nicer.

Around 9,400 feet the trail levels as you cross a tributary of the creek. This section of the road can be very icy. An S-turn climbs more steeply to 9,500 feet, where you see seasonal cabins in the Grand Island community. The road then goes downhill and mellows as the aspen trees open up with head-on views of Klondike and Bald mountains. Rounding another curve while the trail rolls, you will be startled to see a view of soaring South Arapaho Peak on the right/northwest side of the road. The road/trail climbs steeply to 9,700 feet as it sidesteps along the steep slopes of Klondike Mountain. The reward is another striking view of 13,000-foot-high South Arapaho Peak. You can also see the steep slopes of Bald and South Arapaho that create avalanche hazards for the road in about 0.5 mile. Either turn around now, or savor the additional 1-mile loop, and begin your descent.

FOURTH OF JULY ROAD

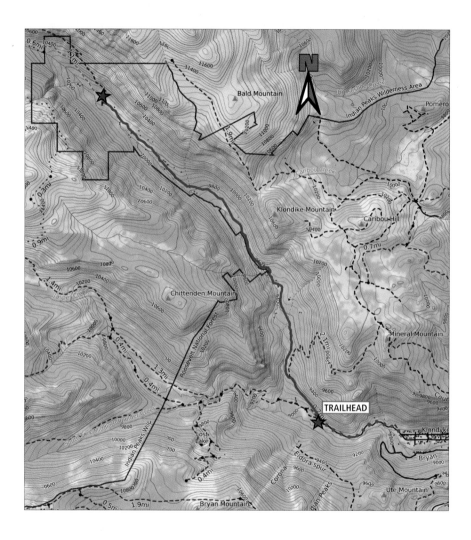

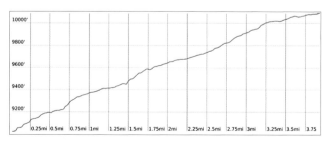

35. Lost Lake Trail

ROUND TRIP	5.5 miles
DIFFICULTY	Moderate
SKILL LEVEL	Intermediate
HIGH POINT	9,800 feet
ELEVATION GAIN	823 feet
AVALANCHE DANGER	Low to considerable; can be avoided
MAP	Trails Illustrated #102, Indian Peaks, Gold Hill
CONTACT	Boulder County Open Space, bouldercounty.org/open-space/parks-and-trails; and Boulder Ranger District, Roosevelt National Forest, 303-541-2500

COMMENT: The Hessie valley is a beautiful riparian area of Middle Boulder Creek, located just west of the town of Eldora. You will see rock formations, peak views, and moose if you are lucky. It is a good route for family excursions, since skiing just part of the trail is worthwhile. This is one of two Lost Lake trails covered in this book. The other is North Fork Trail near Estes Park. This is a much shorter and easier route that's relatively close to the Denver-Boulder area, making it very popular. Either plan to arrive early or visit during the week to avoid crowds and garner a close-in parking spot.

This trail has some narrow steep sections so mid-width skis would be better than skinny skis, though skinny skis are fine for most of the route with good snow. You will want a major Front Range storm before visiting, since much of the trail and road are sun exposed.

GETTING THERE: From Nederland, go south through the roundabout onto Peak to Peak Highway 72 for around 1 mile and turn right onto CR 130. In approximately 2 miles you will see the turnoff on the left for CR 140 uphill for Eldora Mountain Resort; don't turn, go straight. The town of Eldora is another 2 miles west, and the Hessie Trailhead is beyond the closed or impassable road on the west side of town. Parking is limited. Pay attention to the No Parking signs and don't block residents' access to their driveways, or you will be towed.

THE ROUTE: Your distance to the trail might vary a bit depending on where you can park. In any case, you will have at least a 0.75-mile stroll on the Fourth of July Road to reach the Hessie intersection. You will see the north side of the Eldora Mountain Resort to the south as you stroll. At the fork, the Fourth of July Road goes straight

Jasper Mountain massif from Lost Lake.

uphill; you will bear left downhill on the Hessie road/trail. It is another 0.7 mile to the Hessie townsite sign that notes you are at 9,000 feet. Continue straight ahead on the level trail as you enter trees. You will see some cabins on the right; bear left. In about 0.3 mile you will cross Middle Boulder Creek on either the footbridge or the frozen surface. You will then see signage for the various trailheads for numerous lakes that are all 1 mile away.

Now the real fun begins as the trail begins to climb more steeply in about 0.25 mile and switchbacks to the northeast before turning west-northwest. This part of the trail can be windswept with exposed rocks or have deep drifts to navigate. The steep slopes to the north pose a slight avalanche risk; they generally don't collect enough snow for large releases. The trail climbs 400 feet in less than 1 mile before leveling. Expansive views of the valley are your reward. You will enjoy a less steep 0.25 mile of trail in the trees and reach another stream crossing and trail intersection. You are now only 0.5 mile from Lost Lake, but you still have another 400 feet of climbing. Fortunately you are warmed up. (If some members of your party are breathless, this is a good turnaround point.)

Once you renew your determination, you will reach the lake in short order. You will see signs for the various lakes; bear left for the Lost, Woodland, and King lakes trails. The other route to the right goes to Jasper and Devil's Thumb lakes. You will climb 200 feet in 0.3 mile (gasp), and then the trail climbs more gradually. The trail for Woodland Lake and King Lake goes straight/right; turn left uphill for the Lost Lake Trail. Continue to bear left for Lost Lake. When you reach the lake, bear left and go around the south side. Avoid the north side below avalanche chutes that have buried and killed people. The south side of the lake is safe. Travel around it far enough to see the spectacular views of Chittenden Mountain (10,860 feet), Bald Mountain (11,342 feet), South Arapaho Peak (13,397 feet), and Jasper Mountain (12,923 feet).

LOST LAKE TRAIL

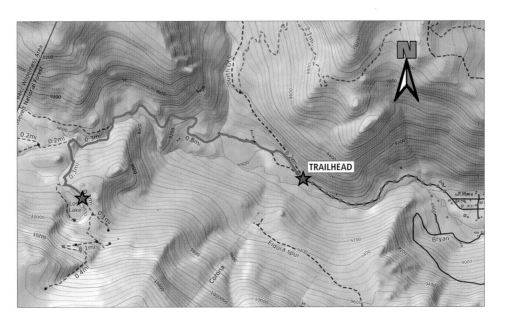

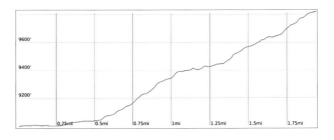

36. **Woodland Lake Trail**

ROUND TRIP	10 miles
DIFFICULTY	Difficult
SKILL LEVEL	Intermediate
HIGH POINT	10,800 feet
ELEVATION GAIN	1,800 feet
AVALANCHE DANGER	Low to none
MAP	Latitude 40° Boulder Nederland Trails
CONTACT	Boulder Ranger District, Roosevelt National Forest, 303-541-2500

COMMENT: The Hessie Valley is a beautiful riparian area of Middle Boulder Creek, just west of the town of Eldora. You will see rock formations, peak views, and moose if you are lucky. It is a good route for family excursions, since skiing just part of the trail is worthwhile. Either plan to arrive early or visit during the week to avoid crowds and garner a close-in parking spot.

This trail has some narrow steep sections so mid-width skis would be better than skinny skis, though skinny skis are fine for most of the route. You will want a major Front Range storm before visiting since much of the trail and road are sun exposed.

GETTING THERE: From Nederland, go south through the roundabout onto Peak to Peak/Highway 72 for around 1 mile and turn right onto CR 130. In approximately 2 miles you will see the turnoff on the left for CR 140 uphill for Eldora Mountain Resort; don't turn, go straight. The town of Eldora is another 2 miles west, and the Hessie Trailhead is beyond the closed or impassable road on the west side of town. Parking is limited. Pay attention to the No Parking signs and don't block residents' access to their driveways, or you will be towed.

THE ROUTE: Your distance to the trail might vary a bit depending on where you can park. In any case, you will have at least a 0.75-mile stroll or ski on the Fourth of July Road to reach the Hessie intersection. You will see the north side of the Eldora Mountain Resort to the south. At the fork, the Fourth of July Road goes straight uphill; you will bear left downhill on the Hessie road/trail. It is another 0.7 mile to the Hessie townsite sign that notes you are at 9,000 feet. Continue straight ahead on the level trail as you enter trees. You will see a collapsed cabin on the right; bear left. In about 0.3 mile you will cross Middle Boulder Creek on either the footbridge or the frozen surface. You will then see signage for the various trailheads for numerous lakes that are all 1 mile away.

A snowy day on the Woodland Lake Trail.

Now the real fun begins as the trail begins to climb more steeply in about 0.25 mile and switchbacks to the northeast before turning west-northwest. This part of the trail can be windswept with exposed rocks or have deep drifts to navigate. The steep slopes to the north pose a slight avalanche risk; they generally don't collect enough snow for large releases. The trail climbs 400 feet in less than a mile before leveling. Expansive views of the valley are your reward. You will enjoy a less steep 0.25 mile of trail in the trees and reach another stream crossing and trail intersection. (If some members of your party are breathless, this is a good turnaround point.)

You will see signs for the various lakes: 1.5 miles to Lost Lake, 4 miles to Woodland Lake, 5 miles to King Lake, 4 miles to Jasper Lake, and 5 miles to Devil's Thumb Lake. Bear left across the footbridge onto the Lost, Woodland, and King Lakes Trail. The other route to the right goes to Jasper and Devil's Thumb lakes. You will climb 200 feet in 0.3 mile (gasp), and then the trail climbs more gradually and levels. The trail for Woodland Lake and King Lake goes straight/right; Lost Lake Trail is left. Continue to bear right. Enjoy the spectacular view of Jasper Peak from the meadow.

Cross the next footbridge or the frozen stream and trek to the next trail intersection at just under the 2-mile mark and around 9,500 feet. Stay left for Woodland and King lakes. Enjoy great views and a pretty wetland lake in the next 0.25-mile climb, a place where you could declare victory and turn around if the snow conditions are unfavorable. The trail goes left back into the trees and then takes a sharp right northwest to another stream crossing; if it is mid-winter you might be able to skip the bridge. The trail levels at the Indian Peaks Wilderness boundary and climbs more gradually as it crosses more meadows next to the stream. There is a frozen waterfall on the right before a trail intersection with a sign indicating left for Woodland Lake.

At 9,600 feet, the trail climbs more steeply at 100 feet per 0.1 mile. You have a great overview of the glacial moraine. At 9,900 feet the trail levels again briefly and crosses a narrow footbridge to the south. It then turns west and back to the south sharply. You climb some steep switchbacks up to 10,000 feet, then decide if you want to ski down the switchbacks. You will continue up to 10,300 feet before leveling with another frozen water feature. Hopefully the wetland will be frozen and covered with deep snow. The trail turns south across a meadow, where you can enjoy a ridgeline view at 10,600 feet. You will then climb to an even more spectacular view of the ridge at 10,800 feet as you edge the frozen lake. Climb above the lake at 11,000 feet for an even better panorama.

WOODLAND LAKE TRAIL

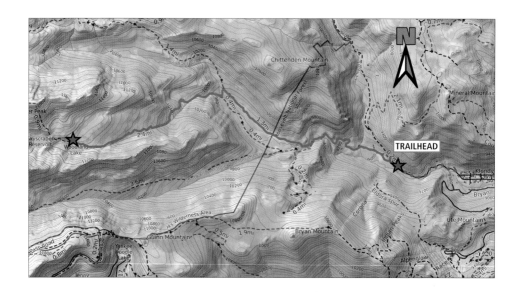

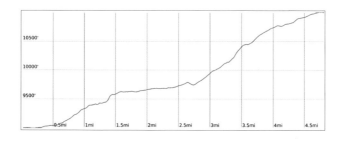

37. Jenny Creek Trail

ROUND TRIP	3.2 miles to Jenny Creek; 10.6 miles to Yankee Doodle Lake; 9 miles to Guinn Mountain Hut
DIFFICULTY	Moderate to Jenny Creek; challenging to Yankee Doodle Lake
SKILL LEVEL	Intermediate
HIGH POINT	9,700 feet at Jenny Creek; 10,900 feet at Yankee Doodle Lake; 10,900 feet at Guinn Mountain Hut
ELEVATION GAIN	650 feet to Jenny Creek; 1,450 feet to Yankee Doodle Lake; 1,600 feet to Guinn Mountain Hut
AVALANCHE DANGER	None
MAP	Trails Illustrated #102, Indian Peaks
CONTACT	Boulder Ranger District, Roosevelt National Forest, 303-541-2500
RESTRICTIONS	No dogs are allowed on the resort trails or on the adjacent USFS Jenny Creek Trail.

COMMENT: This popular trail begins at Eldora Mountain Resort next to the Nordic Center and is free of charge. (The resort trails require a trail pass.) The Eldora Nordic Center offers snack foods, beverages, and restrooms. Once you wind your way through the ski area, you will be traveling through a peaceful, thick lodgepole pine forest. You will be treated to the shining mountaintops of the Indian Peaks gleaming through the treetops on your roller coaster trail adventure. There are two Jenny Creek Trails: one is a short loop at the bottom of Deadman's Gulch within the Eldora Mountain Resort Nordic Center, and the other a U.S. Forest Service access trail that starts next to the beginner ski runs. The access trail can be hard-packed snow unless there has been a recent snowstorm.

You can ski this route on skinny, AT, or telemark skis. If you're going to the Guinn Mountain Hut, you will need telemark skis or AT skis with skins for the steep ascents and descents, or you will have to be a skinny ski expert. Eldora Mountain Resort is planning to eventually install an alpine ski lift at the bottom of Deadman's Gulch that will dramatically alter the nordic area and their Jenny Creek Trail.

GETTING THERE: From Boulder, take Canyon Boulevard/Highway 119 west for 17 miles to Nederland. Go left/south through the roundabout onto Peak to Peak Highway 72 for around 1 mile, and turn right onto CR 130. In approximately 2 miles, turn left on CR 140 uphill to Eldora Mountain Resort. Park outside the resort on the left

South Arapaho Peak soars in the distance above the Jenny Creek Trail.

where the access trail is marked. Then walk into the resort and turn left toward the Nordic Center where you will see the access trail next to the easiest ski run.

THE ROUTE: Go uphill next to the Tenderfoot magic carpet and Little Hawk beginner ski run. There is a Forest Service access sign next to the trail. About 50 yards uphill there is another USFS sign on the left, actually pointing downhill; don't take the trail on the left, but continue straight uphill west-southwest. Once the trail levels out at the top of the slope, go right/west around the back of the chairlift and continue uphill. You will be next to the downhill ski run. You will see the trail turning to the left/south, and there will be a blue Forest Service access sign. Watch for skiers coming down the steep hill at high rates of speed. Uphill another 100 feet you will see a large brown sign pointing you right/west for the Jenny Creek and Guinn Mountain trails. You will encounter one of the steepest hills, but the trail goes up much more gradually after it. There are brown USFS trail markers every 100 yards or so and some blue diamonds. You will climb gradually up to around 9,700 feet, high on a ridge above the Jenny Creek valley below with nice views before the trail descends down to the creek, bottoming out at around 9,500 feet.

    This is a good turnaround point, unless you want to make the long steep climb up Guinn Mountain to the Guinn Mountain Hut. When the trail reaches the creek bottom, it intersects with Jenny Creek Road and the Guinn Mountain Trail. Bear right/northwest to take the Guinn Mountain Trail, which climbs steeply uphill. It is another

2 miles one way in the trees to the hut. For Yankee Doodle Lake, take Jenny Creek Road another 2.7 miles one way. You will be paralleling and then intersecting the Rollins Pass Road that is heavily used by snowmobilers. The Guinn Mountain Hut is a better destination if you don't mind a very steep climb, because you can take shelter if a storm blows in or even plan to spend the night. The Guinn Mountain/Arestua Hut is maintained by the Colorado Mountain Club, and is on a first-come, first-served basis. You can check the reservation calendar on the CMC Boulder Group website by clicking on the reservations link at cmcboulder.org.

JENNY CREEK TRAIL

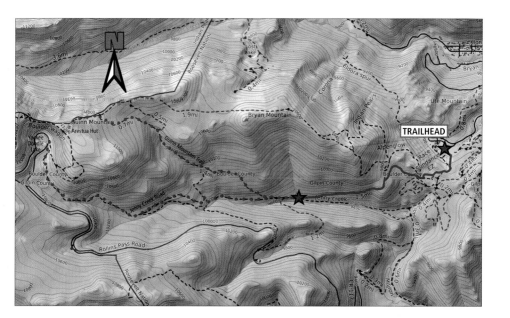

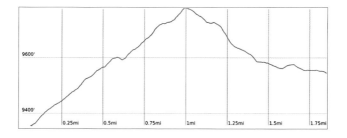

38. Rising Sun & Setting Sun Trails

ROUND TRIP	4.3 miles
DIFFICULTY	Challenging
SKILL LEVEL	Advanced to expert
HIGH POINT	10,030 feet
ELEVATION GAIN	834 feet
AVALANCHE DANGER	None to low
MAP	Eldora Mountain Resort and Nordic Center
CONTACT	Eldora Mountain Resort, 303-440-8700, eldora.com
RESTRICTIONS	No dogs are allowed on the resort trails or on the adjacent USFS Jenny Creek Trail

COMMENT: The Rising Sun and Setting Trails are part of the Eldora Mountain Resort Nordic trail system (trail pass required) and can combine for a spectacular, challenging loop. Sections of the trails are steep, so using AT or telemark skis and skins is advised. You could ski them on skinny skis if you are an expert and it is a powder day. If you are an expert skier who likes to ski in trees, go to the top of the Lonestar snowshoe trail and ski down through the trees, watching for the Setting Sun Trail.

You can also just ski part of the trails and have a shorter, less challenging excursion. Both trails travel very close to the Tennessee Mountain Cabin if you want an overnight stay. Reservations for this cabin are made through the Nordic Center. The Eldora Nordic trails are in a heavily forested area and are generally protected from wind. If you want a predictable environment, skiing within a ski area is a good option. You will pay for a day pass, and you will have well-marked trails with warming and snack facilities. The resort also rents skinny skis.

GETTING THERE: From Nederland, go south through the roundabout onto Peak to Peak Highway 72 for around 1 mile, and turn right onto CR 130. In approximately 2 miles, turn left on CR 140, uphill to Eldora Mountain Resort. When you enter the resort, turn left toward the Nordic Center.

THE ROUTE: The Rising Sun and Setting Sun trails are the most difficult cross-country ski trails at the ski resort. They gain over 800 feet while rolling up, down, and sideways. If you go clockwise, and are doing the entire loop, you will finish going downhill in the most scenic section. From the Nordic Center start on the Dixie/Beaver's Revenge Trails. Pick up a trail map at the Nordic Center to see the alternative routes. The map is oriented with north on the bottom and south on the top. When you reach the top of the Beaver's Revenge Trail, look on the left for the Rising Sun Trail. You will climb at least 1 mile before the Lonestar snowshoe trail separates off to the right; continue straight to the intersection of the Rising Sun and Rob's Shortcut Trail.

If you want to see the cabin, detour off on Rob's Trail. The Rising Sun Trail turns sharply to the right and goes downhill and then uphill to the intersection with the Setting Sun Trail. Go straight for the Setting Sun Trail or take a sharp right to continue downhill on Rising Sun. Setting Sun is the best descent. The middle section of Rising Sun traverses uphill after 0.25 mile. The Setting Sun Trail descends through a wooded stretch and then offers spectacular views of the Continental Divide with James Peak to the southwest and the Arapaho Peaks to the northwest. This is a great place for a snack break. You will eventually intersect the Rising Sun Trail and then end up on the uphill Sawmill Trail, intersecting with the Twisted Tree and Ja Sure ski trails. Turn right and climb the short hill up Twisted Tree for another nice descent down to the Gandy Dancer Trail. Take Gandy Dancer back to 17th Avenue Trail and the Nordic Center.

RISING SUN & SETTING SUN TRAILS

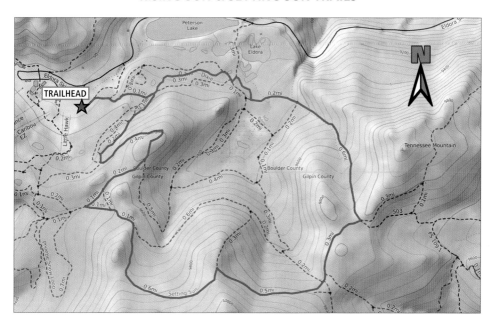

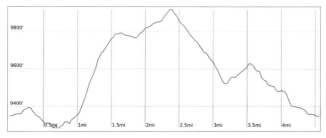

39. Caribou—Anchor Mine

ROUND TRIP	3 miles; alternate route 3.85 miles
DIFFICULTY	Easy to moderate
SKILL LEVEL	Novice to expert
HIGH POINT	10,500 feet
ELEVATION GAIN	450 feet; alternate route 580 feet
AVALANCHE DANGER	Low to moderate
MAP	Latitude 40° Boulder Nederland Trails
CONTACT	Boulder Ranger District, Roosevelt National Forest, 303-541-2500

COMMENT: The trails surrounding the historic Caribou townsite start at over 10,000 feet, which means every time you break out of the trees you are treated to a new, spectacular view. Beginning at the parking lot, with its view east of Mount Thorodin and the sweeping meadow that once was home to thousands, and continuing west, you are treated to spectacular views of the Indian Peaks. Caribou was famous for more than silver, though, and tales of its fierce winds continue today. Fortunately, you can avoid most of the wind if you stay in the trees.

The first part of this route can be an enjoyable out-and-back for a novice/intermediate skier. Venturing beyond the cabin can be a fun route for those who don't mind a very steep climb for some very rewarding powder turns. The views from the lower slopes of Bald Mountain are also spectacular if you don't suffer from vertigo. This is a route for advanced intermediate to expert skiers with telemark or AT skis, good climbing skins, and avalanche gear (beacon, shovel, probes). It is generally around a 20-degree slope, but there is steeper avalanche terrain nearby. Don't ski it during times of high-avalanche danger and don't go too far south into the avalanche zone.

For the most part, the trails that fan out from the Caribou townsite are not especially difficult, although they can be windswept and rocky in spots. But even if you have to take your skis off and walk small sections, the views are worth it. Mid-width skis are best for these trails, and if you arrive after a major storm and before the winds come, you're in for a treat.

GETTING THERE: You will need four-wheel-drive and good snow tires to get to the trailhead for these trails. From the Nederland roundabout, follow Colorado Highway 72 west for 0.5 miles. Turn west on the unpaved, rough, and rarely plowed County Road 128 (Caribou Road) and follow it 5 miles to Five Points (identified by the five-way intersection). This is a loosely organized parking area.

THE ROUTE: The access road is due west from the parking lot, while the road down-hill to Rainbow Lake Road is at 1 o'clock. Go straight down the road, which becomes very exposed to sun and wind and might be snow-free for the first 0.25 mile. Once you re-enter the trees, the coverage is usually good. Where County Road 128J or FS 505-1 goes left, stay right. The road descends into a drainage and across a creek that can be exposed early or late in the season. It then climbs for around 1 mile before reaching a gate. Go around the gate and bear right, staying on the road. This part of the trail is on private property; please be respectful. You will reach the Anchor Mine cabin in less than 1 mile. This can be a good spot to turn around for your trip back.

If the snow conditions are good and you're interested in making some turns, stay away from the cabin and bear right uphill and then turn right and edge along the bottom of the steep, treed slope until you reach the clear slopes on the west. Turn west and climb up the very steep hill while edging next to the trees. After 0.25 mile you can trend to your left, traversing south through the trees and then west and up as high as you want to go. Or just go straight up as far as you wish for a shorter ski. The snow usually gets sketchy within 0.5 mile, and you will reach a rocky band. If there is deep powder, you can try to go higher, but it is often windblown, crusty or snow free the higher you go. Ski as many laps as you want and then retrace your route for even more fun skiing on the way back.

CARIBOU: Once thriving boom town

The mining camp of Caribou sprang to life after word got out about "belts of rich silver ores" in the mountains north of Central City in 1869. By 1871 stages arrived regularly with passengers and mail, and during the harsh winters, sleighs brought passengers from Nederland. In its first years the thriving community of Caribou had 60 businesses and 400 people, supported by 20 producing mines. At its peak, Caribou was home to 3,000. The silver crash of 1893, three fires, and epidemics of scarlet fever and diphtheria decimated the once booming town, and after 35 years of glory, hardly anything remains of this important mining camp in Colorado history.

A picture-perfect sunny day on the trail above Caribou townsite.

OTHER TRAILS TO EXPLORE: If you turn onto 128J/505-1, the trail continues on a moderate climb for the next 1.5 miles. In 0.75 mile, take a right at the trail intersection. As the trail continues to climb, watch for motionless ptarmigan and snow hares darting through the snow in the open areas. In a little over a 0.5 mile, turn west-southwest. It can be difficult to find the trail here, but continue in the same general direction until the trail turns to the right and heads up a very steep hill. This is a good spot to turn around, but first soak in the incredible view across the valley of Eldora Mountain Resort and the peaks beyond. Once you've found your way, the trip back is always easier, but don't forget that the last part to the parking area is uphill.

Another route is to circumnavigate Caribou Hill and the massive mines that made Caribou famous on 128J and one or more of the 505 roads, but often parts of this route are windblown and rocky.

CARIBOU—ANCHOR MINE

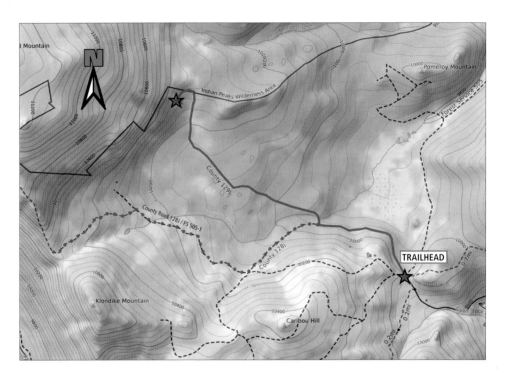

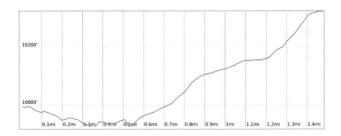

40. **Caribou 4WD Road**

ROUND TRIP	4.5 miles
DIFFICULTY	Easy
SKILL LEVEL	Novice
HIGH POINT	9,991 feet
ELEVATION GAIN	320 feet
AVALANCHE DANGER	Low to none
MAP	Latitude 40° Boulder Nederland Trails
CONTACT	Boulder Ranger District, Roosevelt National Forest, 303-541-2500

COMMENT: This is an easy trail when the sun is out and the wind isn't blowing. It follows a road, although at times the skiable portion is very narrow. This is a good route for a large group with varying abilities; it's a gradual descent, and you can turn around wherever you want. Don't forget the sunscreen and snacks. You can use skinny skis for this route.

GETTING THERE: You will need four-wheel-drive and good snow tires to get to the trailhead for this trail. From Nederland, follow Colorado Highway 72 west for 0.5 miles from the traffic circle. Turn west on the unpaved, rough, and rarely plowed County Road 128 (Caribou Road) and follow it 5 miles to Five Points (identified by the five-way intersection). This is a loosely organized parking area.

THE ROUTE: From the parking area, follow the sign for the Caribou 4WD route to Rainbow Lakes (Forest Road 505). This is a popular route for four-wheelers in the summer, but in the winter the gates are closed to vehicles. You will gradually descend until you come to a crossing of Caribou Creek, or until you decide to turn around.

Keep in mind that the entire trip back will be an uphill excursion and slower than your trip out. Just after you start on the trail, you will pass a crane in a wide peat bog area on the west side of the road. At 0.7 mile, you will come to the intersection with FS 116J.1, which goes to some mine tailings. Stay to the right and continue on the four-wheel-drive road. You will be following Caribou Creek through an open area and then into the forest, where the road narrows, all the time continuing to descend. At 4.5 miles, you will come to the creek crossing. This is a good spot to turn around if you haven't already, and start your trek back uphill to the parking area.

CARIBOU 4WD ROAD

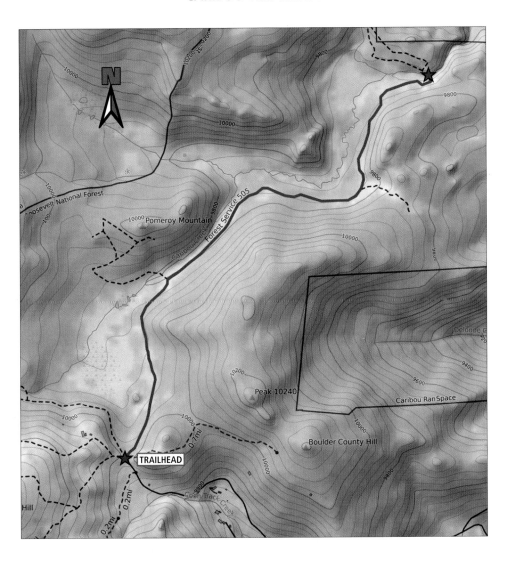

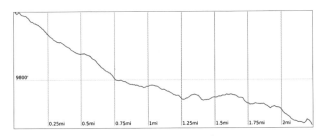

Chapter 7

ROLLINSVILLE

"We are all one in nature. Believing so, there was in our hearts a great peace and a welling kindness for all living, growing things."

— Luther Standing Bear, *Land of the Spotted Eagle*

Rollinsville is a mountain town that was created to serve not only the numerous mines and miners, but also as a railroad stop on the way to the famous Moffat Tunnel that bores under James Peak and the Continental Divide to Winter Park. It is now the entryway to the Moffat Road and the popular trailheads 10 miles west at or near the east portal of one of the highest (9,239 feet) and the longest (6.2 miles) railroad tunnels in the world. You are likely to see coal and freight trains plying their way through the expansive and beautiful mountain valley, or even Amtrak's California Zephyr going to or from the West Coast. The tunnel was holed through in 1926 in a blast triggered by U.S. President Calvin Coolidge. The first railroad traffic went through in 1928. It is still a very busy, often clogged route for Union Pacific and Burlington Northern-Santa Fe trains.

The Mammoth Gulch, Rogers and Heart Lake, and Forest Lakes trails are on the way to or at the East Portal of the tunnel. Two of the trails are highly scenic routes to high-mountain lakes, while Mammoth Gulch features spectacular views of the riparian and glacier-carved valley.

Rollinsville is 4.5 miles south of Nederland.

View of the Continental Divide from Mammoth Gulch Road.

41. Rogers Pass Lake & Heart Lake

ROUND TRIP	8.2 miles
DIFFICULTY	Moderate to challenging
SKILL LEVEL	Novice to the meadow; intermediate/advanced to Rogers Pass and Heart Lakes
HIGH POINT	11,340 feet
ELEVATION GAIN	2,100 feet
AVALANCHE DANGER	None to low
MAP	Trails Illustrated #103 Winter Park, Central City, Rollins Pass, Boulder County Trails, Colorado Front Range Recreation Topographic Map
CONTACT	Boulder Ranger District, Roosevelt National Forest, 303-541-2500
RESTRICTIONS	You will be in the James Peak Wilderness Area, so no open fires are permitted, and dogs must be kept on leash. This is for their safety, as you might encounter fast downhill skiers.

COMMENT: Ski any portion of this popular trail, and you will have an enjoyable trek in a stately old-growth forest with a few ridge-top views along the way. You will need a long day to make it all the way through part of the James Peak Wilderness to Rogers Pass Lake and Heart Lake, but they are magnificent jewels, cupped by the soaring mountaintops of the Continental Divide. The trail has many steep sections, making it an intermediate to advanced ski trail. You will need AT or telemark skis with climbing skins unless you just ski 1 mile to the first meadow and turn around. This is a very popular trail on weekends with lots of dogs. It is marked with intermittent blue diamonds.

GETTING THERE: From Nederland, go left/south through the roundabout onto Peak to Peak Highway 119 south for 4.5 miles to Rollinsville; turn west/right on narrow, gravel Gilpin CR 16 and drive 8 more miles to the Moffat Tunnel and the East Portal Trailhead. The road is plowed, and there is a large parking area and pit toilet restrooms.

THE ROUTE: Go around the right/north side of the tunnel on the South Boulder Creek Trail (#900). You might have to shed your skis to get over a couple of footbridges early or late in the season. The snow is often thin for the first mile of the trail because of sun and wind exposure early and late in the season, but fine mid-winter. Once you enter the thick tree cover you will have good consistent snow. At 1.2 miles, you will

The East Portal trailhead.

reach the intersection with the Forest Lakes Trail; continue straight ahead. In another 0.3 mile, you will reach a fork in the trail as it steepens. In about 0.25 mile, the trail turns sharply right uphill on a switchback that goes north/northeast; many people miss this turn. At around another 0.4 mile you might see the Crater Lakes Trail (#819) on the right; continue straight ahead. You will see another false trail on the right as the trail levels briefly and then climbs steeply to 10,000 feet, crossing a tributary of South Boulder Creek and turning due south.

Take a minute to enjoy the old-growth forest of stately trees, many of which are draped in Spanish moss. Look to the left and you can see the snow-capped high ridge-line tracking west, often with spindrift looking like wispy clouds being blown over the top. You will be protected from the wind by the thick tree cover. A somewhat less steep section will catapult you up to 10,300 feet, where there will be a stream crossing and the trees will open up with more views to the south of the high ridge as well as the ridge to the north. You will pass through a lot of pretty glades as the trail climbs more gradually over the next mile to around 10,400 feet. You can enjoy another sunny break in the trees with a small meadow on the right. The trail goes south and levels, and goes temporarily downhill. Then the trail swings west, and the next mile to Heart Lake is much steeper, climbing 700 feet (gasp). Look for potential side trails to the lakes that are both at just over 11,000 feet. Heart is at 11,300 feet and Rogers Pass is at 11,100 feet. Take a long lunch break, and enjoy the fast ride down.

ROGERS PASS LAKE & HEART LAKE

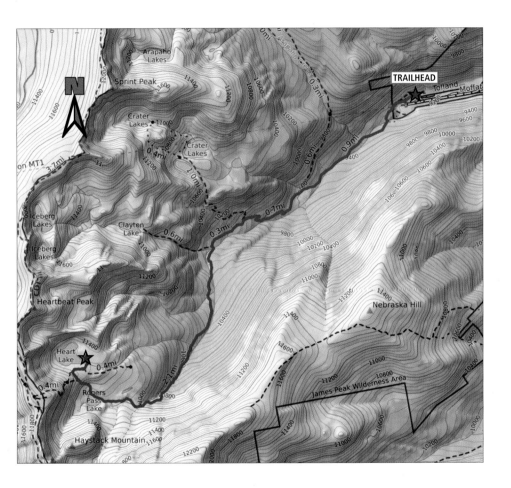

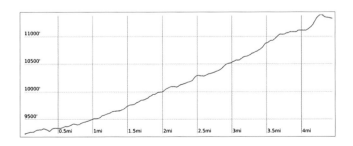

42. Forest Lakes Trail

ROUND TRIP	6.5 miles to lower lake; 7.0 miles to upper lake
DIFFICULTY	Moderate
SKILL LEVEL	Intermediate to advanced
HIGH POINT	10,820 feet at lower lake; 11,020 feet at upper lake
ELEVATION GAIN	1,400 feet at lower lake; 1,620 feet at upper lake
AVALANCHE DANGER	None to low
MAP	Boulder County Trails, Colorado Front Range Recreation Topographic Map
CONTACT	Boulder Ranger District, Roosevelt National Forest, 303-541-2500
RESTRICTIONS	You will be in the James Peak Wilderness Area, so no open fires are permitted, and dogs must be kept on leash. This is for their safety, as you might encounter fast downhill skiers.

COMMENT: Forest Lakes is a scenic jaunt to two high-mountain lakes with good views of the Continental Divide for the last 1.5 miles. Skiing any portion of this route will be rewarding. This is a much easier and shorter route than the trek to Rogers Pass Lake and Heart Lake. You will want AT or telemark skis to ski it. It requires advanced ski skills, since it is a fast and steep descent. It opens up to views and sun earlier than the Rogers Pass/Heart Lakes route, but that also means portions of the south-facing route melt off faster. This trail is not as well-marked with blue diamonds as the Rogers Pass/Heart Lakes route.

GETTING THERE: From Nederland, go left/south through the roundabout onto Peak to Peak Highway 119 south for 4.5 miles to Rollinsville; turn west/right on narrow, gravel Gilpin CR 16; drive 8 more miles to the Moffat Tunnel and the East Portal Trailhead. The road is plowed and there is a large parking area and pit toilet restrooms.

THE ROUTE: Go around the right/north side of the tunnel on the South Boulder Creek Trail (#900). You might have to shed your skis to get over a couple of footbridges. The snow is often thin for the first 1 mile of the trail because of sun and wind exposure early and late season, but it will be fine in mid-winter. Once you enter the thick tree cover you will have much better snow. At 1.2 miles, you will reach the intersection with the Forest Lakes Trail (809); go northeast/right, having climbed around 400 feet. The trail is initially an old road that traverses a steep slope, climbing 300 feet

Tracks on the Forest Lakes trail.

in around 0.75 mile. You will climb 200 feet and cross Arapaho Creek in about 0.5 mile. There is a footbridge—use it if the creek is not completely frozen over. You will have intermittent views of the riparian valley as you climb through the thick trees. The road ends as the trail swings northwest and rolls more gradually uphill through a mixed forest. The trail breaks from the trees and has excellent views of the high-mountain ridgeline on your left from a pretty glade at around 10,000 feet. This section of the trail is a bit hard to follow with its multiple social ski trails, but you will have the ridgeline on your left for orientation.

Keep traveling northwest toward the lakes. The trail climbs more gradually for the next 0.75 mile. When you pass the intersection with the Arapaho Lakes Trail, you will be around 1 mile from the lower lake. You reach 10,400 feet gradually. The last 0.5 mile is steeper, as the trail climbs another 200 feet in short order. Enjoy the beautiful lake with the Continental Divide ridgeline as the backdrop. If you continue on to the upper lake, you might hear snowmobiles on the Rollins Pass Road, which is only 0.25 mile beyond it.

Some skiers like to ski the trees on the left side of the trail after you cross the bridge on the descent. Pick your route carefully since the trees can be very tight if you turn off too soon. Go at least 0.25 mile before taking to the trees.

FOREST LAKES TRAIL

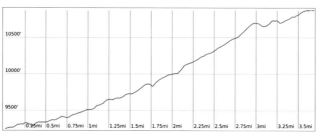

43. Arapaho Lakes Trail

ROUND TRIP	7 miles to lower lake; 7.5 miles to upper lake
DIFFICULTY	Challenging
SKILL LEVEL	Expert
HIGH POINT	11,220 feet at lower lake; 11,500 feet at upper lake
ELEVATION GAIN	1,700 feet to lower lake; 1,900 feet to upper lake
AVALANCHE DANGER	Moderate to high on the ridgeline above the lakes
MAP	Boulder County Trails, Colorado Front Range Recreation Topographic Map
CONTACT	Boulder Ranger District, Roosevelt National Forest, 303-541-2500
RESTRICTIONS	You will be in the James Peak Wilderness Area, so no open fires are permitted, and dogs must be kept on leash. This is for their safety, as you will encounter fast downhill skiers.

COMMENT: The Arapaho Lakes Trail is one of the best trails in the area for skiing through trees. It is a much steeper climb than Forest Lakes, but if you like tree skiing and don't mind tight trees requiring quick turns, you will love it. You will climb to the top of a ridge overlooking the second lake with a spectacular view of the 12,000-foot ridgeline of unnamed peaks. One is informally called Radio Beacon Peak. Most people don't descend to the upper lake from the overlook, and the slopes above it are highly hazardous for avalanches until spring consolidation. Skiing any portion of this route will be rewarding. This is a much shorter route than the trek to Rogers Pass Lake and Heart Lake. You will want AT or telemark skis to ski it. It requires advanced ski skills since it is a fast and steep descent on skis. This trail is not as well-marked with blue diamonds as the Rogers Pass/Heart Lakes route.

GETTING THERE: From Nederland, go left/south through the roundabout onto Peak to Peak Highway 119 south for 4.5 miles to Rollinsville; turn west/right on narrow, gravel Gilpin CR 16; drive 8 more miles to the Moffat Tunnel and the East Portal Trailhead. The road is plowed, and there is a large parking area and pit toilet restrooms.

THE ROUTE: Go around the right/north side of the tunnel on the South Boulder Creek Trail (#900). Until the creek is covered and frozen you might have to shed your skis to get over a couple of footbridges. The snow is often thin for the first mile of the trail because of sun and wind exposure early and late season, but it will be fine in mid-

Dappled sunlight on the trail.

winter. Once you enter the thick tree cover you will have much better snow. At 1.2 miles, you will reach the intersection with the Forest Lakes Trail (809); go northeast/right, having climbed around 400 feet. The trail is initially an old road that traverses a steep slope, climbing 300 feet in around 0.75 mile. You will climb 200 feet and cross Arapaho Creek in about 0.5 mile. There is a footbridge—use it if the creek is not completely frozen over. You will have intermittent views of the riparian valley as you climb through the thick trees. The road ends as the trail swings northwest and rolls more gradually uphill through a mixed forest. The trail breaks from the trees and has excellent views of the high-mountain ridgeline on your left from a pretty glade at around 10,000 feet. This section of the trail is a bit hard to follow with its multiple social ski trails, but you will have the ridgeline on your left for orientation. Keep traveling northwest toward the lakes. The trail climbs more gradually for the next 0.75 mile.

When you reach the intersection with the Arapaho Lakes Trail, you will be around 0.75 mile from lower Forest Lake. The trail levels and descends slightly to Arapaho Creek. The #819 Trail turns sharply left/west and ascends rapidly as the trees thicken. Keep the creek on your right as you ascend through the tall, thick, mixed forest of ponderosa and lodgepole pine. If you bear left you will reach the shore of the lower lake. Most skiers want to bear right to surmount the overlook of the upper lake and massif so they can take a few more turns on the steep slope. The Arapaho Lakes descent requires deep, mid-winter snow cover since it travels over fallen trees and stumps.

ARAPAHO LAKES TRAIL

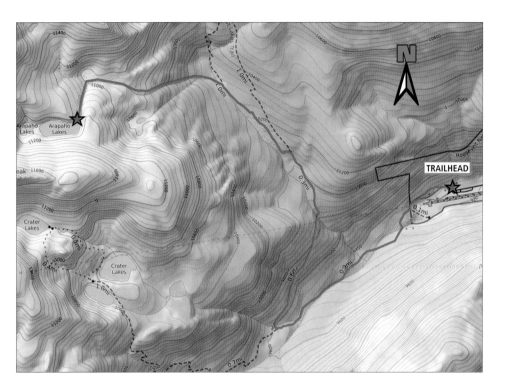

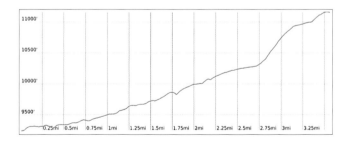

44. Mammoth Gulch Road

ROUND TRIP	3 miles to three-way intersection Route 1: 1.75 miles; Route 2: 3.75 miles; Route 3: 2.5 miles
DIFFICULTY	Moderate
SKILL LEVEL	Novice for the road; intermediate for Nebraska Hill
HIGH POINT	9,700 feet at intersection; 10,200 feet at Baltimore Ridge summit
ELEVATION GAIN	850 feet to 1,300 feet
AVALANCHE DANGER	Low to moderate
MAP	Trails Illustrated #103, Winter Park, Central City, Rollins Pass, Boulder County Trails
CONTACT	Clear Creek Ranger District, Roosevelt National Forest, 303-567-3000

COMMENT: What in summer is a four-wheel-drive road becomes a scenic route for skiing in the winter. You will see sweeping views of the Continental Divide ridgeline and James Peak. You might see Amtrak and other trains barreling by on the nearby east-west railroad tracks. The primary challenge is very limited parking and an aggressive sheriff who will ticket you. You will need a four-wheel-drive vehicle to park unless it is early or late season. Carpool, and have a backup plan to ski the East Moffat trails in case there is no off-road parking available. You can ski this route on any style of skis if you are an experienced skier, but it is not good for beginners. If you want to take some turns on the Nebraska Hill bowl that is northwest of the road, you will want AT or telemark skis; it is steep enough to avalanche. If you stay on the road and have good skills, skinny skies are adequate unless the snow is deep and untracked.

GETTING THERE: From Nederland, go south through the roundabout onto Peak to Peak Highway 119 for 4.5 miles to Rollinsville; turn west/right on narrow, gravel Gilpin CR 16. Drive approximately 6 more miles to the whistle-stop town of Tolland. The Mammoth Gulch Road is the first road on the left/south after Tolland.

THE ROUTE: This route offers three fairly straightforward out-and-back routes. You will gradually climb up around 800 feet on the road for about 1.5 miles before it starts to level out a bit. At the intersection, you have three choices.

1) Forest Trail 183: You can take this trail on the west side downhill, losing around 200 feet of elevation into a very pretty meadow and mixed conifer/aspen area. Once you have bottomed out in the former reservoir in Mammoth Gulch, there are no trail

View from Mammoth Gulch road.

markers and routefinding becomes an issue. If you can carefully retrace your route, you can wander around as you please and then ascend back up to the main road/trail.

2) Go straight ahead toward the head of Mammoth Gulch, below Kingston Peak and James Peak. The road climbs gradually to around 10,000 feet over the next 2 miles, where you will reach avalanche terrain. Nebraska Hill is to the right. You can ski into the gulch, northwest of the road for low-angle, relatively safe terrain before you reach the steep slopes of Nebraska Hill, which can be hazardous. This is a good turnaround point unless you are a winter mountaineer with avalanche training. If you are, and avalanche danger is low, you can continue up valley to Echo Lake below James Peak. This Echo Lake is not the same as the Mount Evans Echo Lake.

3) Take the sharpest left and the steeper uphill option that stays on CR 4N. In 0.5 mile it climbs to another intersection, where you go left again if you want to summit Baltimore Ridge (10,260 feet), or climb another mile up to an intersection with Apex/Kingston Peak Road at 10,500 feet. Turning west on this road will lead you to James Peak, but Rollins Pass or St. Mary's Lake are the safer approaches for James Peak. St. Mary's Lake is accessed from I-70. (The description for skiing up James Peak in this book is from St. Mary's Lake.)

If you want more certainty, stay on the main trail/road in choice 2 above, which will continue to climb very gradually, with some level spots. Because the road eventually tracks under avalanche terrain and dead-ends in a drainage below James Peak, take a topographic map so you know when you are below the steep avalanche terrain. The top of this gulch is surrounded by avalanche slopes, which are best avoided unless the snow is very stable.

MAMMOTH GULCH ROAD

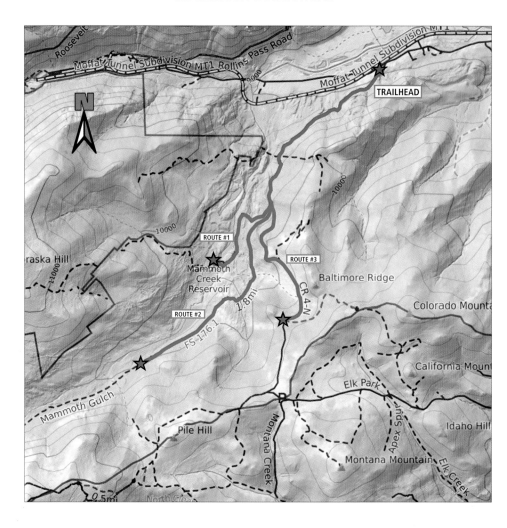

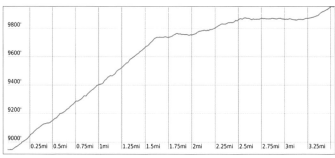

Route 3 (center)

45. **Raccoon Loop Trail**

ROUND TRIP	2.5 miles
DIFFICULTY	Moderate
SKILL LEVEL	Intermediate
HIGH POINT	9,400 feet
ELEVATION GAIN	500 feet
AVALANCHE DANGER	None
MAP	Golden Gate Canyon State Park, Colorado Front Range Recreation Topographic Map
CONTACT	Golden Gate Canyon State Park, 303-582-3707
RESTRICTIONS	Dogs must be kept on leash. A Colorado State Parks pass, daily or annual, is required to use this trail.

COMMENT: The Raccoon Trail is one of many beautiful trails in Golden Gate Canyon State Park. The trailhead is a grand overlook of the Continental Divide and Indian Peaks. This trail is one of the best choices in the park for skiing because it is over 9,000 feet high and protected by trees. This doesn't mean it always has enough snow, so check with the park or be prepared to carry your skis. Visiting after a major Front Range upslope storm is ideal. The worst case is a superb winter hike. If you start at the overlook, you will enjoy the aforementioned spectacular peak view. The trail then goes downhill and you will end on an uphill to get back to the overlook. If you start at the campground, you will end your trek on a downhill. This description starts from the overlook. You can use any style of skis if you are an experienced skier, but it is not for beginners.

GETTING THERE: From Nederland, take Highway 119 south for 10 miles to Gap Road/CR 2, which is 5 miles south of Rollinsville. There is a large brown state park sign as well as other park signage. You can access the trail from either Reverend's Ridge Campground or the overlook. For the overlook, continue uphill past the campground turnoff for another 1.5 miles; it will be on your left. The county road is plowed and there is a parking area with pit toilets.

From Golden, take Highway 93 north approximately one 1 mile to Golden Gate Canyon Road (Highway 46). Turn left onto 46 and drive for about 13 miles to the park. Continue on 46 to Highway 119. Turn right on 119 toward Nederland and then take another right in about 4 miles onto Gap Road/CR2. Follow the signs to Panorama Point.

View of the Continental Divide from Raccoon Loop Trail.

THE ROUTE: Start by enjoying the view from the visitor center deck; it is one of the best choices for photos. From the overlook parking area you have two choices for this loop: northeast/clockwise travel, or south/counter-clockwise. In both cases you will be going downhill at the start and uphill at the end.

I suggest a clockwise route since the initial downhill this direction is a bit more gradual. The trail is to the right of the deck and turns southwest through switchbacks. You will have some peak views as the trail rolls gently through the mixed forest to an intersection in about 0.7 mile. If you go left/straight you will be on the Elk Trail to Bootleg Bottom (1.2 miles); turn right/west-northwest and continue downhill in a pretty glade that Robin Hood would enjoy. You will bottom out in about 0.5 mile and the trees open up with a nice meadow on your left. You will see the side trail to the campground on your left; in 100 yards, take a sharp right and S-turn to stay on the Raccoon Trail. You will see a private cabin on your right. This is an excellent spot for photos of the rock formations silhouetted by the stately aspens. You will edge along the magnificent aspen grove and then encounter the steepest part of the trek.

The trail climbs 200 feet, quickly gaining part of the 500-foot climb that has just begun. This part of the trail is sun exposed and might have thin snow. The trail levels and then climbs steeply again. Turn around to enjoy the peak views behind you before climbing some more. After you have climbed almost 400 feet and another 0.5 mile, the trail levels, descends, and takes a sharp right/southeast turn through aspen trees. It turns right again downhill then goes left uphill to reach the park road. The trail parallels the road back to the overlook. If you see the side trail on the right, take it to enjoy more spectacular views for the last 0.25 mile.

RACCOON LOOP TRAIL

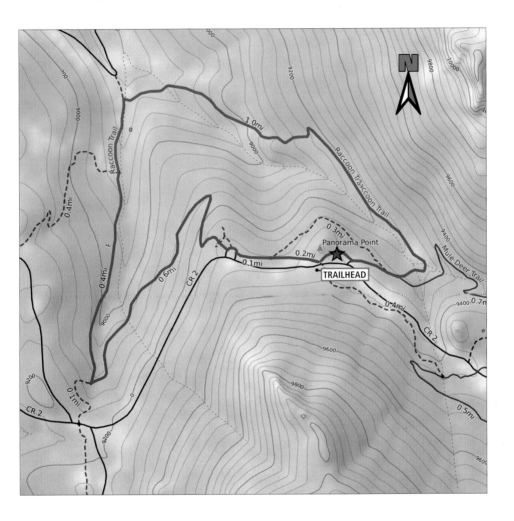

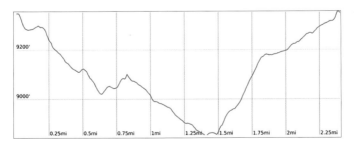

A marmot inspects visitors to his lair on James Peak.

North Central Colorado

Chapter 8

MOUNT EVANS AREA

"The horizon is bounded and adorned by a spiry wall of pines, every tree harmoniously related to every other; definite symbols, divine hieroglyphics written with sunbeams. Would I could understand them!"

—John Muir, *My First Summer in the Sierra*

Mount Evans (14, 264 feet) is one of highest mountains in the state and one of two that has a road to the top, which was built in 1930. Ironically, it is also the home of the Mount Evans Wilderness Area, an excellent place to recreate in the winter. It is an expansive and grand high-mountain environment that inspires easily accessible and safe winter recreation.

There are a variety of trails, but this book focuses on three of the most popular and easily usable options. Mount Evans is almost the twin of 14,060-foot Mount Bierstadt. They are connected by the impressive Sawtooth Ridge, and their combined massif is significant. The Sawtooth is not an easy winter route. Both peaks are discussed in this book. Skiing to the summit of Bierstadt is a potential route because it is a bit safer than attempting the summit of Mount Evans, since people have been killed by avalanches on the road near Mount Goliath. There are low angle routes to the summit with little danger, but don't go if you aren't an experienced winter mountaineer with avalanche training. Mount Evans was first successfully climbed on snowshoes by Albert Ellingwood in March of 1916; Mount Bierstadt was first ski-climbed in 1934. Mount Evans is approached from the north on I-70 out of Denver.

EARLY SKI HISTORY

In the early 1920s, Saint Mary's Glacier was a regular destination for Colorado's earliest skiers. In 1923, the Denver Rocky Mountain Ski Club organized the first annual Fourth of July Ski Tournament on the glacier. Lift-served skiing began at St. Mary's in the 1950s in Anchor Gulch, south of the lake and glacier. The owners and the name of the ski area changed several times, from Silver Lake, to Silver Mountain, to Saint Mary's Glacier Resort. Rope tows, T-bars, and other lifts served skiers on Wednesdays through Sundays until 1986, when the area, which never had enjoyed much success, was permanently shut down.

46. Echo Lake & Chicago Lakes Trails

ROUND TRIP	3 miles
DIFFICULTY	Easy to moderate
SKILL LEVEL	Novice
HIGH POINT	10,903 feet
ELEVATION GAIN	100 feet to restaurant; 363 feet to Mount Evans Byway
AVALANCHE DANGER	None for Echo Lake Moderate to considerable for Chicago Lakes Trail
MAP	Trails Illustrated #103, Winter Park, Central City, Rollins Pass
CONTACT	Clear Creek Ranger District, Arapaho National Forest, 303-567-3000

COMMENT: Echo Lake is an easy, almost flat family route around a sparkling frozen lake surrounded by sweeping views of soaring Front Range peaks. You can add a short, more challenging jaunt for a spectacular view on the first part of the Chicago Lakes Trail before avalanche danger turns you around. The short excursion on the Chicago Lakes Trail will deliver a superb view of the Mount Evans massif and its lofty neighbors. Unless the snowpack is completely stable, you don't want to wander too far on the seductive Chicago Lakes Trail because of the slide potential of the slopes above it. You can also extend this ski trip by continuing on the Echo Lake Trail to Mount Evans Byway. You can use skinny skis for these trails.

GETTING THERE: Take I-70 to Idaho Springs and then Exit 40 south for Mount Evans. Take Highway 103 south for 14 miles to the shoreline of Echo Lake. There is parking at the Echo Lake Picnic Area, or go 1 mile farther south to the entrance of the closed Echo Lake Campground, seasonal restaurant, and Mount Evans Byway road.

THE ROUTE: If you park at the picnic area, the trail goes counter-clockwise around the lake to the right from the picnic area and restrooms. These are the only available facilities open in the winter months. The best views of Mount Evans are from the starting point on the southeast side of the lake before you enter the thick trees. Snap a photo and head west. After 0.25 mile you will see a sign for the Chicago Lakes Trail going straight, while the Echo Lake Trail turns to the left.

If you want an additional spectacular view of the Evans massif, continue straight on the Chicago Lakes Trail for a short side trip. A short stretch of this trail is passable during low avalanche danger and a fun side trip. In another 0.25 mile you will round

The soaring cliffs of Mount Evans above the Chicago Lakes Trail.

the bend, break from the trees, and see the impressive cirques and peaks of Mount Roger, Mount Warren, Mount Spalding, and Mount Evans on the horizon. This is a good time to take a photo and turn around if you don't want to expose yourself to avalanche terrain. As the Chicago Lakes Trail continues, it is bordered on both sides by avalanche terrain, so don't attempt it when there is any danger of avalanches. Reverse course to the Echo Lake Trail and turn right when you intersect it.

The Echo Lake Trail follows a flat route away from the lakeshore under a pretty tree canopy that will protect you from the cold breeze. Very soon you will see a fork in the trail; go left. You reach an access to the Mount Evans Byway and the closed restaurant at 0.75 mile. You can continue up to the Byway (see the next route) if you want to extend your adventure. If you go right at the fork, you will go uphill, at first gradually, and then steeply, as the trail makes its way to the Mount Evans Byway at the 1.5-mile mark. You can also wander up to the rocky ridge and enjoy better views through the trees.

ECHO LAKE & CHICAGO LAKES TRAILS

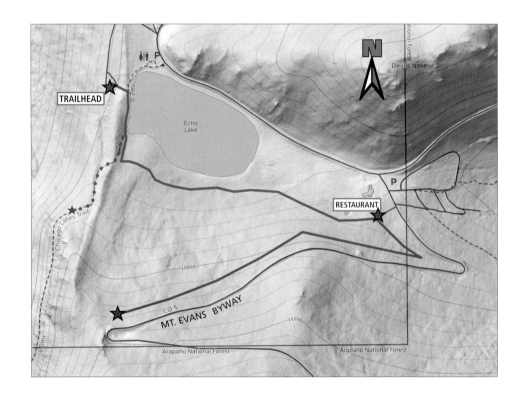

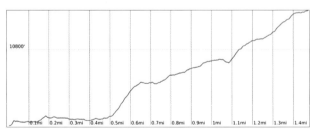

Echo Lake Trail

47. **Mount Evans Byway**

ROUND TRIP	5 miles to Mount Goliath
DIFFICULTY	Easy to moderate, challenging to the summit
SKILL LEVEL	Novice for partial route; intermediate/advanced for summit
HIGH POINT	11,598 feet
ELEVATION GAIN	1,000 feet to Mount Goliath rest area
AVALANCHE DANGER	Low to Mount Goliath; considerable to high near Mount Goliath Natural Area

COMMENT: This heavily traveled scenic highway is closed in the winter to motorized travel, making it a fun Nordic ski. It is a steady, though not steep, climb with ever-expanding views of Mount Evans and Mount Goliath. Parts of the road are sun-exposed and wind-swept and can be completely snow-free early or late season. If the snow is not good, try the tree-sheltered Echo Lake route. You can use any style of ski to ski up the wide road.

GETTING THERE: Take I-70 to Idaho Springs and take Exit 40 for Mount Evans. Turn on Highway 103 south for 15 miles to the south end of Echo Lake. There is parking at the entrance to the closed Mount Evans Byway, Echo Lake Campground, and seasonal restaurant.

THE ROUTE: This wide, paved road makes a nice roomy winter trail. Just go around the gate and as far as you desire. The first 2.5 miles are low-angle terrain with no avalanche exposure. The road starts off traveling in the trees southeast 0.25 mile to a hairpin turn where it begins to climb west a bit more steeply. You will gain around 400 feet over the first mile. When you reach the next turn you will see the 1-mile marker on the right side of the road. You will have some nice views of the peaks of Independence (11,450 feet) and Alpine (11,552 feet) to the west and Griffith (11,568 feet) and Alps (10,552 feet) to the north. If you want a good view of Grey Wolf Mountain (13,602 feet), Mount Spalding (13,842 feet), and part of the Mount Evans massif, round the turn and go right, off road, uphill, through the trees. Once you clear the trees you will see the massif if it is not too cloudy. If the snow is mediocre, you can descend near the mile marker down to the extension of the Echo Lake/Chicago Lakes Trail. The snow can improve with elevation. It is a very steep descent on the side trail to Echo Lake, a bit less so in the trees on the left, so be careful if you go that way.

The road continues surrounded by trees, for another mile to the 2-mile marker, gaining another 300 feet. In around 0.5 mile, you will reach the next turn, where the

The Mount Evans Byway.

road tracks southwest and you can see Mount Goliath (12,216 feet). It is a good place to turn around since you will be treading into potential avalanche terrain. If you are sure the snowpack is stable, you can continue on another 0.25 mile or so to the summertime nature center and Goliath Natural Area Trailhead. This is a good place to get out of the wind, have a snack, and enjoy the twisted krummholz trees. Don't go to the nature center, or up Goliath's slope unless you have had an avalanche class and can dig a snow pit to evaluate the risk. There was a recent avalanche fatality near the Mount Goliath Nature Center. You can stop short of the steep slopes of Goliath and have a fun, scenic jaunt. If you have winter mountaineering skills, you can continue on the road. It goes to the upper slopes of Goliath. Taking the Goliath Natural Area trail is not advisable since it treks directly below very risky avalanche terrain. Some experienced mountaineers ski the road all the way to the summit in the winter. If you have had an avalanche course, and are well prepared, this is a possible option on a clear day.

If you have a stable snow day and favorable weather, you can ski all the way to the summit. Some members of the Colorado Mountain Club do it safely every winter. The longer days of late spring would make it easier because of more daylight and stabilized snow. Avoid Goliath on high-hazard avalanche days.

MOUNT EVANS BYWAY

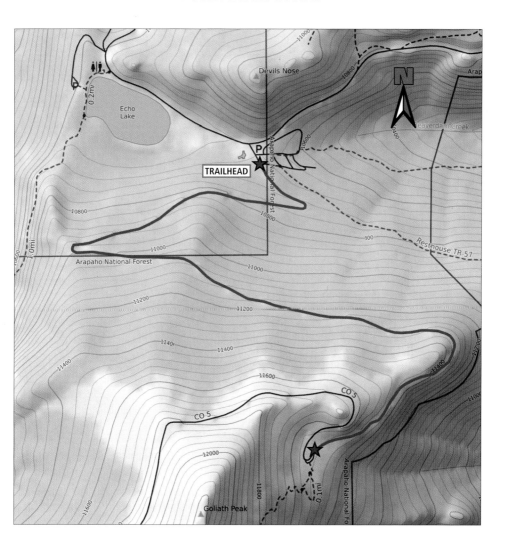

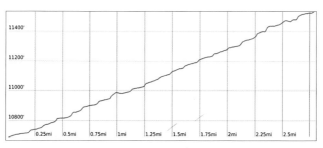

48. Saint Mary's Glacier & James Peak

OPTION 1		
ROUNDTRIP	4 miles to top of Saint Mary's Glacier
DIFFICULTY	Moderate
SKILL LEVEL	Intermediate for glacier; advanced for James Peak
HIGH POINT	11,200 feet
ELEVATION GAIN	600 feet

OPTION 2		
ROUNDTRIP	8.5 miles to James Peak
DIFFICULTY	Challenging
SKILL LEVEL	Intermediate to expert
HIGH POINT	13,250 feet
ELEVATION GAIN	2,700 feet

AVALANCHE DANGER	Moderate to considerable
MAP	Trails Illustrated #103, Winter Park, Central City, Rollins Pass
CONTACT	Clear Creek Ranger District, Arapaho National Forest, 303-567-3000

COMMENT: This is a very climbable glacier in a spectacular setting that is an easy drive from Denver. It is a permanent snowfield that most call a glacier, and, though it shrinks in the summer, there is usually enough snow for year-round use. You have a lot of recreational options when visiting Saint Mary's Glacier, especially if you have avalanche training. Many people enjoy the climb from the lake to the top of the glacier, taking in the nonstop round-trip views of the Front Range, and calling it a day. You can also do some laps on skis.

When you reach the area above the summit of the glacier, you can see an impressive panorama of James Peak and its Front Range neighbor, Mount Bancroft. Some find this sight to be an irresistible invitation and extend their adventure to the summit of James Peak. Avalanche danger on the slopes of the glacier and peak could be high, so check on conditions with the Colorado Avalanche Information Center or U.S. Forest Service before attempting the route. Heavy usage by other skiers doesn't necessarily mean it is safe. This area is not recommended for families with children, as it requires sound mountaineering skills to scale the glacier in the winter. You will need AT or telemark skis and skins to ski this route. If you are climbing James Peak, take an avalanche beacon and shovel and don't do it alone.

Near the summit of James Peak.

GETTING THERE: From Denver, take I-70 west about 30 miles to the Fall River Road/ Saint Mary's/Alice Exit 238. Follow the signs approximately 8 miles north to the Saint Mary's Glacier Area two paid parking lots. Both require a $5 fee, and no change is available. You will need to bring your own pen to write your license plate number on the fee envelope. Don't park along the road or block access to homes; the fine for parking on the street is heavy. There are restrooms in the parking lots.

THE ROUTE: Go south from the parking lot, then turn north and follow the drainage toward Saint Mary's Lake. On this approximately 0.5-mile trek you might have to carry your skis. You will gain about 200 feet to reach the edge of the lake. Go to the right along its eastern shore for around 1 mile to the foot of the glacier. This is as far as families or the inexperienced should go unless you just want to get your toes wet on the bottom of the glacier. If you have steep snow experience, climb up the slope another 0.3 mile, gradually turning northwest, and you will reach the mid-point of the glacier. After gaining another 250 feet, you will enjoy views of the rock outcrops. The ascent is not as steep for the next 0.5 mile, but you will climb up to approximately 11,200 feet to reach the top of the glacier and even better views. At 1.5 miles and 11,600 feet, you will reach a relatively flat saddle where you can enjoy James Peak views on a clear day.

To get to James Peak from the saddle, continue west and then northwest on a very obvious well-traveled route that is relatively flat and easy for about 1.5 miles. If it is socked in and/or snowing and you cannot see James Peak or there are no tracks to follow, reconsider unless you are an experienced mountaineer and have a topographic map and compass or GPS unit and are a good routefinder. Don't track too far to the northeast or you will climb a false summit and encounter steep slopes. Reach the foot of the peak at about 3 miles from the trailhead. From here the route steepens considerably, and you'll have to employ some routefinding skills. Once you reach the base of the peak, continue to follow the right-hand/northeast slope. Stay just below the ridge and you can angle your way to the summit in another 0.75 mile.

SAINT MARY'S GLACIER & JAMES PEAK

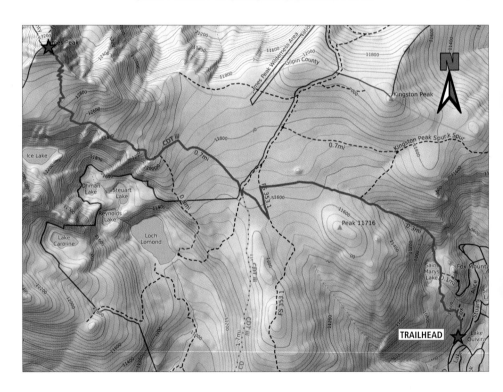

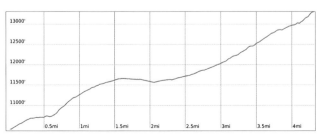

49. **Beaver Brook Watershed**

ROUND TRIP	6 miles, out-and-back
DIFFICULTY	Easy to moderate
SKILL LEVEL	Novice
HIGH POINT	9,250 feet
ELEVATION GAIN	650 feet, starting at 8,600 east gate, and 9,250 west gate
AVALANCHE DANGER	None
MAP	Trails Illustrated, Boulder-Golden
CONTACT	Clear Creek County Open Space, 303-679-2305, co.clear-creek.co.us/192/Open-Space

COMMENT: This pretty area near Evergreen features easy rolling hills interspersed with a beautiful high-mountain meadow, and a pleasing mixed forest of conifer and aspen. The trail is good for cross-country skinny skis and beautiful foothills views. The elevation is relatively low at 8,500 feet, so you will want to wait for a good Front Range foothills snowfall or two before exploring it. (If you arrive and the snow is lacking, continue uphill to the Chief Mountain or Echo Lake Trail.) The Beaver Brook Watershed trail isn't well known, so you won't see a lot of people. The main trail is a closed road and wide enough for ski turns. You can go west or north from Lewis Gulch or the Beaver Brook Reservoir. There are many trails to choose from, so look for tracks or break trail. The trail is not well marked, but the closed roads are easy to follow. The route can be extended toward Blue Valley or North Beaver Brook.

GETTING THERE: From Denver, take I-70 west and then go south on the Evergreen Parkway (CO 74) for 4.1 miles to Squaw Pass Road (CO 103). Go west/right on 103 for 3.7 miles to Old Squaw Pass Road (170) and turn right/north; the gate and trailhead is on the left/west side immediately after you turn.

From Idaho Springs, drive 10 miles on CO 103, look for the parking area on a curve on the north side of the road. The trailhead is unnamed at the west end. The west end is across from Witter Gulch Road (#475).

THE ROUTE: From the east end of the trail, you will descend gradually and then a bit more steeply the farther you get from the gate. When you reach a fork in 0.5 mile, bear left. The tree cover thickens and that usually provides better snow cover. The trail then curves into a southwest direction and rolls over a small ridge with views of Beaver

Beaver Brook trailhead.

Brook Reservoir. It descends as it passes meadows that adjoin the reservoir. It climbs another small ridge and travels west and south away from the reservoir, then descends into Lewis Gulch. When you intersect the road in Lewis Gulch you have gone around 1.2 miles; bear left. (If you want to extend your ski beyond 6 miles, take a soft right and climb north out of the gulch toward North Beaver Brook Road. Go as far as you wish through the open meadows and return.) For the main route, bear left after a large meadow toward Squaw Pass Road (103). (If you want to extend your outing from this intersection, go straight toward Blue Valley through the thick forest and climb out of the gulch.) You will go back into trees, and in 0.25 mile, cross another meadow. After another 0.3 mile you will reach the last large meadow that will take you to the west end trailhead at Highway 103.

BEAVER BROOK WATERSHED

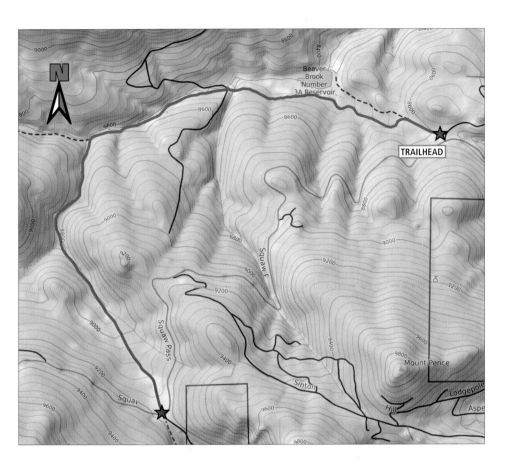

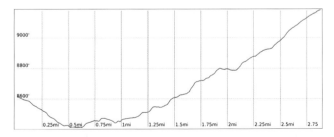

50. **Chief Mountain**

ROUND TRIP	4.5 miles
DIFFICULTY	Moderate
SKILL LEVEL	Intermediate
HIGH POINT	11,700 feet
ELEVATION GAIN	900 feet
AVALANCHE DANGER	Low
MAP	Latitude 40° Colorado Front Range Trails
CONTACT	Clear Creek Ranger District, Arapaho National Forest, 303-567-3000

COMMENT: This pleasant trek offers striking views of Mount Evans as well as Roslalie Peak, Rogers Peak, and Mount Goliath to the west, and Griffith Mountain, Saxon Mountain, and Alps Mountain to the north. It is one of the best panoramic views close to the Denver area. The starting elevation also means more reliable snow. The final climb of 200 yards to the summit is often too windblown and rocky for skis. You will want AT or telemark skis for this outing.

GETTING THERE: You can take I-70 to Idaho Springs Exit 240 toward Mount Evans and go to mile marker 18 on CO 103. Or, take I-70 to Exit 252 and go south on CO 74, the Evergreen Parkway, to Bergen Park. Then turn west on CO 103 toward Mount Evans. Drive 11 miles just past the Echo Mountain ski area and park on the north side of the road. The trail is on the south side of the road.

THE ROUTE: The trail climbs steeply southeast away from the road and then intersects the Old Squaw Pass Road. After crossing the wider road, you will see the continuing trail turning west and a sign that says "Chief Mountain 2 miles." The trail goes westerly after 0.25 mile, breaking out of the thick tree cover. The spectacular panorama to the northwest opens up as you climb on switchbacks near rock formations. The trail switchbacks southwest and then sharply north-northwest as it approaches the summit from the south. The trail levels just below the summit, and a rocky scramble will take you to the very top. It is usually wise to shed your skis for the final scramble. Enjoy the view of the Mount Evans Byway and massif, and Squaw Mountain to the east. On the way back, some people like to ski repeats through the trees back and forth to the Squaw Pass Road or CO 103. It can be fun if the powder is deep since there are well-spaced routes through the trees.

View from the Chief Mountain trail.

MAGNIFICENT AND DANGEROUS

Moose have now become a common sight in much of the Front Range. They were only transient visitors to Colorado until the Colorado Division of Wildlife introduced 24 in 1978 and 1979 from the Uintah Mountains of Utah and Grand Tetons of Wyoming to the Never Summer Range near Rand and Gould, Colorado, north of Rocky Mountain National Park. They are now roaming from the San Juan Mountains to Steamboat Springs and through most of the Front Range. It is best to admire these large animals from a distance, as moose kill more people than bears. They are around seven feet tall, can weigh up to 1,600 pounds, can run up to 35 miles per hour, and are not dog friendly.

CHIEF MOUNTAIN

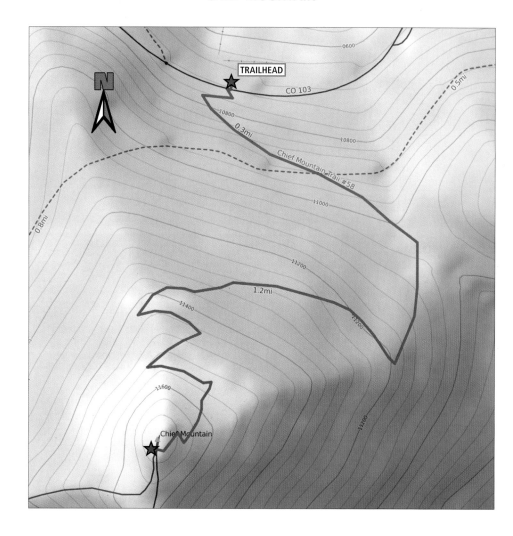

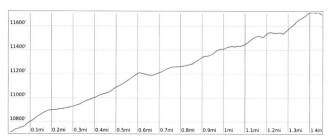

51. Jones Pass & Butler Gulch Trails

ROUND TRIP	Jones Pass: 5.8 miles (short of summit) Butler Gulch: 6 miles
DIFFICULTY	Easy to challenging
SKILL LEVEL	Novice for Jones Pass; Intermediate for Butler Gulch
HIGH POINT	11,000 feet
ELEVATION GAIN	720 feet
AVALANCHE DANGER	Low to high; can be avoided. Check with USFS, CAIC.
MAP	Trails Illustrated #103, Winter Park, Central City, Rollins Pass
CONTACT	Clear Creek Ranger District, Arapaho National Forest, 303-567-3000

COMMENT: This beautiful mountain valley close to Denver does not require a drive over Berthoud Pass. There are several trails you can explore at this popular location near the Henderson Mine and Red Mountain. You can ski just a section of this trail and be very happy. You will have to share the Jones Pass Trail with some snowmobilers. If you want a quiet experience, and much less traffic on I-70, visit during the week. Go up Butler Gulch or continue up to the top of Berthoud Pass for snowmobile-free trails. Off-trail slopes in this area can be very hazardous avalanche zones; stay on the main trail and away from the slopes of Red Mountain, where people have been buried by avalanches in the past. Experienced skiers will want to use AT or telemark skis and skins for these routes. If you're experienced, you can survive with skinny skis.

GETTING THERE: From Denver, take I-70 west about 40 miles and exit at Empire/US 40 for Berthoud Pass/Winter Park. Drive west on US 40 through Empire toward Berthoud Pass for about 12 miles until you come to the first sharp hairpin turn to the right. Before the hairpin turn, exit to the left onto CR 144 for Henderson Mine. Drive to the Henderson Mine complex, and a small road on your right goes to the winter trailhead. To the left is a large lot where you can park. The road is closed at the trailhead that serves both the Jones Pass Trail and Butler Gulch Trail.

THE ROUTE: Travel west through the trees on the joint trail until the junction at approximately 0.3 mile.

Bear right for the Jones Pass Trail. On the Jones Pass Trail you will have some glimpses of the ridgeline as you travel northwest through the trees. At a little less than 0.5 mile, you break out of the trees and enjoy the panorama of the valley and soaring

Avalanche class trekking to the site of a fatality on Jones Pass Trail.

ridgeline. Avalanche run-out zones can be seen across the valley on the steep slopes of Red Mountain to the west. Gradually bear northwest and then north, following West Fork Clear Creek. At 1.25 miles cross the creek.

On the other side of the creek where the trail/road veers sharply southwest, stay about 120 feet lower than the trail in the flat meadow area rather than traversing the ridge. The trail travels west through a varied landscape of high-mountain meadows and trees, gradually curving southwest. At about 1.75 miles, when you reach another creek, turn around because the avalanche danger can be high beyond this point. You can go all the way to the summit of the pass, but this is only advisable in late spring after the snow has consolidated; check snow conditions with the Colorado Avalanche Information Center or U.S. Forest Service before you go.

Bear left for Butler Gulch. This is a somewhat less difficult and quieter trail. It is a bit of a tree tunnel initially, which makes it a nice option on a windy day.

The first 1.5 miles are relatively flat, with a few downhill sections. The first real climb starts here, but it's not too steep. The trail continues up a few switchbacks where there are several obvious lines for skiing the trees back down, or you can follow the trail back. If you continue above treeline, you arrive at several open bowls that are skiable in fresh powder if the avalanche danger is low and they haven't been scoured by the wind.

JONES PASS & BUTLER GULCH TRAILS

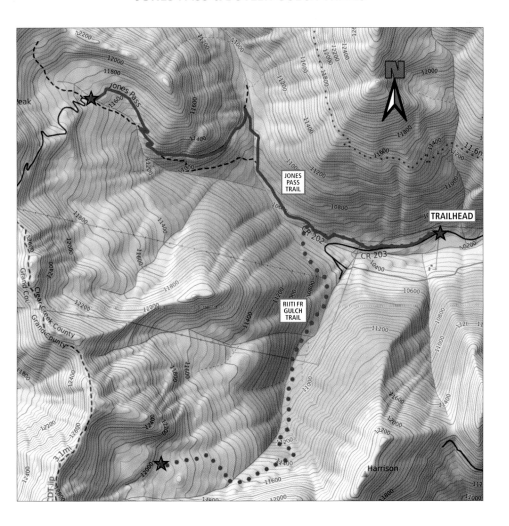

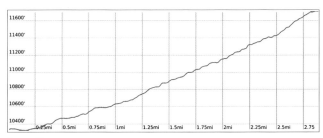

Jones Pass

Alpenglow on a Berthoud Pass trail.

Chapter 9
BERTHOUD PASS

*"It is a pity we have let the gift of lyric improvisation die out.
Sitting islanded on some gray peak above the encompassing wood,
the soul is lifted up to sing the Iliad of the pines."*

—Mary Austin, *The Land of Little Rain*

The trails atop Berthoud Pass offer spectacular, serene views. The easy access from Highway 40, however, means they don't necessarily offer complete serenity, but the 360-degree panorama is ample compensation. The top of the pass is a former downhill ski area that operated from 1937 to 2001, when it went bust. It has now become a de facto backcountry, earn-your-turns ski area. The base area elevation of over 11,000 feet means the snow is good early, late, and throughout the snow season. It is a large area, and there is more than adequate space for different winter sports enthusiasts.

Avalanche control is an ongoing effort by the Colorado Department of Transportation to protect the highway. This does not mean the entire area is always safe. Wear an avalanche beacon, take a shovel, and know how to dig and evaluate a snow pit. Check the Colorado Avalanche Information Center (CAIC) website so you know the general danger level before venturing onto the slopes. There are thousands of users, and there have been some avalanche fatalities in the general area because of foolhardy recreationists on the steepest slopes. Please stay safe.

Berthoud Pass can be reached from Denver via I-70 to US 40.

TODAY'S HIGHWAY STARTED AS A WAGON ROAD

Captain Edward L. Berthoud discovered his namesake pass when he mounted an expedition in the summer of 1861 to find a possible route over the Continental Divide for the railroad. His expedition of eight hardy souls included Jim Bridger, who, even though familiar with the area, did not previously know of the pass. Berthoud concluded the route wasn't suitable for the railroad and later surveyed it for a wagon road. In winter horse-drawn sleighs traveled the wagon roads in Colorado's high country. Today, U.S. Highway 40 follows his route. With its steep grades and the large number of switchbacks on the southern side, the pass is also prone to frequent avalanches. At least 55 avalanche paths have been mapped on the pass, some of them intersecting with the highway.

52. Eastside Trail–Continental Divide Trail–Colorado Mines Peak

ROUND TRIP	4 miles
DIFFICULTY	Moderate
SKILL LEVEL	Intermediate
HIGH POINT	12,200 feet
ELEVATION GAIN	1,000 feet
AVALANCHE DANGER	Low to moderate. Check the Colorado Avalanche Information Center website
MAP	Trails Illustrated #103, Winter Park, Central City, Rollins Pass
CONTACT	Clear Creek Ranger District, Arapaho National Forest, 303-567-3000

COMMENT: This trail offers a wide, easily followed route and a gradual climb to nonstop magnificent views. It originates next to the plowed parking area and heated restrooms on the east side of the Berthoud Pass Summit. Most of this route is low-angle and less likely to avalanche, especially on the Continental Divide Trail. The snow is rarely good above treeline because of exposure to sun and wind. Arriving immediately after a storm is the best strategy if you want to summit. Experienced skiers can use any style of ski, but AT or telemark skis with skins would be best because of the descent, especially if you ski all the way to the top of the peak.

GETTING THERE: From Denver, take I-70 west. Take Exit 232 for US 40, Empire, Berthoud Pass, and Winter Park. Travel 14 miles to the summit of Berthoud Pass. Park in the large lot on the east side of the summit.

THE ROUTE: The Continental Divide Trail is on the south side of the parking area. If you are facing the steep hill, with the restrooms on the left/north, the trail is on the right. From the south side of the parking lot, go southeast into the trees. It is a wide trail that was probably a service road or catwalk for the ski area. You will see a sign on the right side of the trail. The trail travels east gradually uphill for about 0.25 mile before turning sharply to the north and continuing uphill. After 0.5 mile, it intersects other northbound trails and a former ski run.

A Nordic trail continues on the other side of the ski run. Instead, turn sharply to the southeast and continue to follow the very long switch-backing trail uphill and

The view from the summit of Colorado Mines Peak.

out of the trees. As you clear the trees the panorama begins to unfold to the west. You will see the south side of Berthoud Pass and the Grays-Torreys massif to the southwest.

Continue to follow the trail/road as far as you wish before turning around as it widely switchbacks and slowly climbs. It is sometimes obliterated by deep snow. If it is, make your own switchbacks up toward the cell towers and former ski area facilities on top. With every traverse and turn you will have amazing views in every direction. The former ski area facilities are at 12,200 feet. The summit offers an even more commanding view of the Continental Divide to the north and Mount Evans to the south. You don't have to reach the summit of Colorado Mines Peak for a thoroughly enjoyable outing. You will have lots of company from backcountry skiers and snowboarders.

If you do want to go all the way to the summit, continue to follow the switchbacks. Eventually you will see the facilities on top of the peak. A great panorama awaits you on top. You also will have a good view of the trails on the west side of the pass. The snow can be very windblown and crusty up here because of wind and sun. Decide if you want to go for a second adventure.

EASTSIDE TRAIL–
CONTINENTAL DIVIDE TRAIL–
COLORADO MINES PEAK

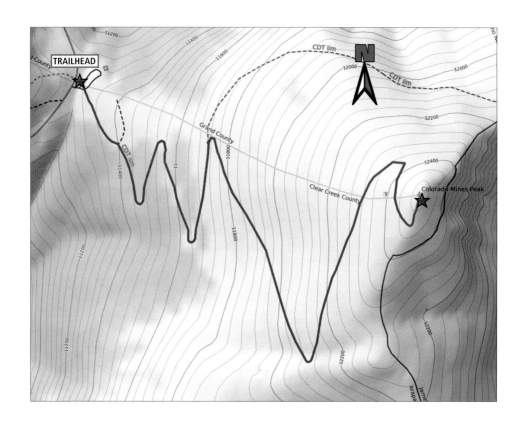

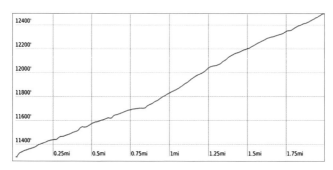

53. Westside Trail

ROUND TRIP	3 miles
DIFFICULTY	Moderate
SKILL LEVEL	Intermediate
HIGH POINT	12,000 feet
ELEVATION GAIN	800 feet
AVALANCHE DANGER	Low to moderate; check with the Colorado Avalanche Information Center or U.S. Forest Service
MAP	Trails Illustrated #103, Winter Park, Central City, Rollins Pass
CONTACT	Clear Creek Ranger District, Arapaho National Forest, 303-567-3000

COMMENT: This trail originates across from the plowed parking area with heated restrooms on the east side of the Berthoud Pass summit. It offers a wide, easy-to-follow trail and gradual climb to magnificent views. You will encounter more skiers and snowboarders on the west side of the pass, but you can avoid collisions by staying in the trees on the south side of the open terrain. You can go beyond this trail for more safe skiing, but stay off of the steep ridgeline. Use AT or telemark skis to ski this terrain.

GETTING THERE: From Denver, take I-70 west. Take Exit 232 for US 40, Empire, Berthoud Pass, and Winter Park. Travel 14 miles to the summit of Berthoud Pass. Park in the large lot on the east side of the summit.

THE ROUTE: Cross the highway to the west, put on your skis, and bear left/south uphill, rather than going up the steep terrain to the right/north. You can edge your way through the intermittent trees on the south side of the hill. There is an additional trail that goes southeast, but it tracks under some steep slopes so it's less safe. Go straight uphill to the west instead. You will generally find the snow to be more powdery in or near the trees. **Watch out for tree wells hidden by drifted snow: don't get too close to tree trunks because sometimes a well of air or loose snow can form, and if you fall in, it is almost impossible to get out without assistance. They can collapse suddenly, and throw people into the tree, causing injury and suffocation.**

You will find this steady but gradual climb does offer some less-steep sections, so creating your own switchbacks to take advantage of flat spots is a good idea. The

The Westside Trail on Berthoud Pass.

higher you climb, the better the view of the east side of Berthoud Pass and the terrain to the west. Go as high as you want, enjoy the vista, and then switchback your way back down to the parking lot. If you reach the top of the first lower hill/ridge, you can safely wander around to the west and north. There is another trail that travels northwest. Stay away from the steepest terrain to the west. Don't ski on it or under it unless you are an avalanche and ski expert.

WESTSIDE TRAIL

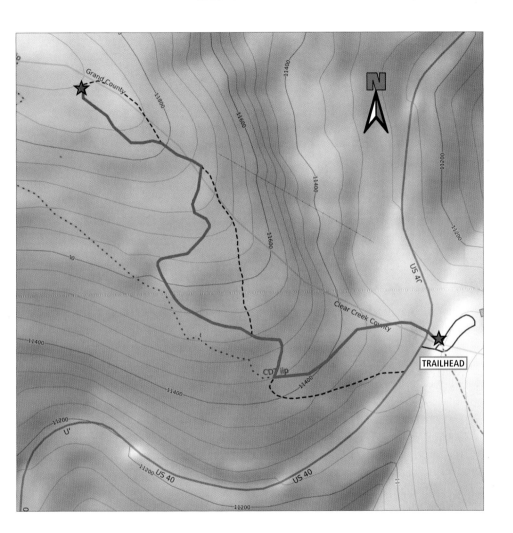

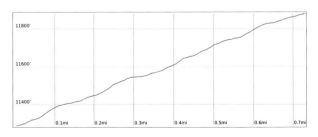

54. Second Creek Trail

DISTANCE	2 miles round-trip to the hut 3 miles round-trip to the end of the trail
DIFFICULTY	Challenging
SKILL LEVEL	Intermediate
HIGH POINT	11,342 feet at the hut
ELEVATION GAIN	713 feet to the hut
AVALANCHE DANGER	High, but can be avoided
MAP	USGS Berthoud Pass Quadrangle; USFS Forest Visitor's Map: Arapaho National Forest
CONTACT	USFS, Clear Creek Ranger District, 303-567-3000 Vasquez Peak Wilderness, Sulphur Ranger District, 970-887-4100 10th Mountain Division Hut System, 970-925-5775
NOTE	Dogs must be leashed when you cross into Vasquez Peak Wilderness, and they are not allowed inside the hut.

COMMENT: The high-elevation Second Creek Trail starts at 10,600 feet, just north of the summit of Berthoud Pass, and climbs up to a 10th Mountain Division Hut at the edge of the Vasquez Peak Wilderness. Strong backcountry skills are required for this short, steep trail. The hut is located at treeline, and whiteout conditions can make routefinding difficult, but the reward is some truly spectacular scenery. The Second Creek Basin receives about 500 inches of snow each year, and the top-of-the-world views are outstanding, but be aware that the weather can change instantly at these high elevations, and you are exposed to whatever the weather gods wish to send you when you are skiing above treeline. Also take note that the terrain around the Broome Hut is prone to avalanches. AT or telemark skis with skins are best for this trail.

The hut is open to day skiers with a restroom and sitting area. The public area of the hut is separated from the private area, which can be reserved through the 10th Mountain Division Hut System. The Broome Hut replaced a dilapidated A-frame built in the 1950s. It took fifteen years to raise the necessary $400,000, and two and a half years, to build with more than 6,000 hours of volunteer labor. It opened in 2013.

GETTING THERE: From I-70, take Exit 232 for Rocky Mountain National Park and Winter Park. Drive 17.8 miles over Berthoud Pass to the fourth hairpin turn from the summit on the left/west side of the road. The trailhead is marked with a sign for Second Creek Trail.

Ski tracks on the Second Creek Trail.

THE ROUTE: The trail starts in the trees, and the way is marked with colored poles or plaques on some of the trees. As the forest begins to thin, the trail leaves the creek and you climb a steep hill toward a large rock outcropping. Head toward a tall dead tree on the left side of the trail, and soon the hut and the cirque above it will be visible. The trail levels out some as you approach the hut. You will have climbed 700 feet in 1 mile from the highway to the hut. The views of the Continental Divide, Second Creek Basin, and the stunning but avalanche-prone Second Creek Cirque behind the hut are breathtaking. This is a fine spot to eat lunch and turn around for the quicker, downhill trip back to the trailhead. If you're not quite ready to go back, the trail continues west another 0.5 mile into the Vasquez Peak Wilderness area before ending abruptly at the edge of open tundra at 1.5 miles.

SECOND CREEK TRAIL

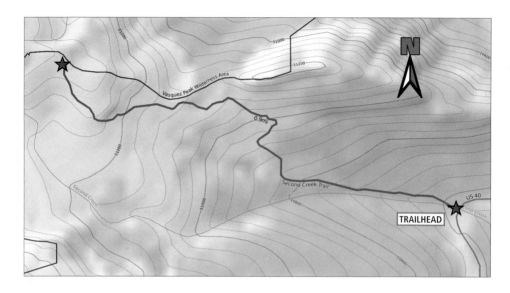

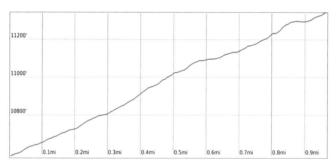

ARE YOUR GAITERS ON THE WRONG FEET?

The goal when putting on your gaiters is to get the buckles to the outside so that they don't catch on each other as you are snowshoeing. I don't know how many times I have put my gaiters on the wrong feet, said a few choice words, taken them off and started all over again. It doesn't help that my now ex-hiking partner looks at me and says, "So, got your gaiters on the wrong feet again? HAWHAWHAW?" When you look at your gaiters before putting them on it is fairly hard to figure out right from left unless, in a stroke of brilliance and foresight, you have written RIGHT and LEFT on the appropriate gaiter.

Chapter 10

WINTER PARK AREA

"In the nineteenth century, Fritjof Nansen wrote that skiing washes civilization clean from our minds by dint of its exhilarating physicality. By extension, I believe that snow helps strip away the things that don't matter. It leaves us thinking of little else but the greatness of nature, the place of our souls within it, and the dazzling whiteness that lies ahead."

—Charlie English

Devil's Thumb Ranch and Snow Mountain Ranch offer some of the best cross-country skiing in the state. They are not free, but they are well worth the price of admission. The trails are groomed and vary from family-friendly gliding across open meadows to challenging climbs and fast descents through more challenging terrain. Both ranches have full service Nordic centers with rentals and lessons. Both offer on-site accommodations and restaurants/coffee shops, and multi-day skiers can stay in nearby Winter Park, Tabernash, or Granby.

The ranches are located near Winter Park and Tabernash. Devil's Thumb is a private ranch, and Snow Mountain is owned by the YMCA of the Rockies.

Skiing the groomed tracks at Devil's Thumb Ranch.

55. Lactic Grande

ROUND TRIP	5 to 8.4 miles
DIFFICULTY	Challenging
SKILL LEVEL	Expert
HIGH POINT	9,550 feet
ELEVATION GAIN	1,050 feet
AVALANCHE DANGER	Low to none
MAP	Devil's Thumb Ranch Trail Map
CONTACT	Devils Thumb Ranch and Resort, 970-726-5632

COMMENT: This is one of the best expert ski trails in the state. You will climb over 1,000 feet from the base of the resort and enjoy spectacular views of Byers Peak and Winter Park Ski Area while winding your way through stately stands of aspens and conifers. If you catch it on a powder day, try to ascend very early before it's groomed for an amazing powder run, but watch out for the groomers. Climbing is easier after it is groomed. The trail features steep climbs and steep descents. Skinny skis are adequate.

GETTING THERE: From Denver, head west on I-70. Take Exit 232 onto Highway 40. Follow Highway 40 for approximately 30 miles through Empire, over Berthoud Pass, and past Winter Park and Fraser. About 2 miles past Fraser, take a right on County Road 83. Take the right-hand fork and follow it 3 miles to the ranch.

THE ROUTE: From the Nordic Center, go straight out to the south toward the Ranch Walk Trail and downhill to the first intersection. Go left/east on Blue Extra to the first right onto the Radcliff Trail. Take Radcliff uphill to Blue Extra and turn right/south toward the Sawmill Loop Trail. Bear left uphill onto Sawmill and then take the first right uphill toward the Waxwing Trail, and then left onto the Waxwing Trail. You will see sweeping views of the valley as you climb steeply northeast up to the entrance to Lactic Grande on the right. If it is early in the season, the entire route might not be open all the way to the south-facing part of the trail. If that is the case, go out and back as far as you can and return to the Waxwing Trail, and you will still have a great outing. If you take the Waxwing Trail down to the northeast, you will enjoy a steep, hairpin-turned descent to the Little Cabin Trail. Take Little Cabin to the north side of the Sawmill Loop and take it to Blue Extra. Return to the Nordic Center on Blue Extra.

If the entire Lactic route is open, continue to the south, climb to the top, and take in the view of Byers Peak to the west. Then enjoy an exciting descent to Disco. Take a

A view of Byers Peak and trails at Devil's Thumb Ranch.

sharp right on the Disco Trail, if you want to minimize additional climbing, turn left on Blue Extra and take it down to the Meadow Trail. Take Meadow north/right and turn left when it dead-ends to go back to the Nordic Center. If you want a bit more climbing, go left on Disco and then descend to Double Pole and back to Blue Extra.

Pick up a map at the Nordic Center or download at devilsthumbranch.com

56. Ranch Walk & Stage Route to Broken Barn or Meadow Trails

ROUND TRIP	4 miles
DIFFICULTY	Easy
SKILL LEVEL	Beginner
HIGH POINT	8,600 feet
ELEVATION GAIN	100 feet
AVALANCHE DANGER	None
MAP	Devil's Thumb Ranch Trail Map
CONTACT	Devils Thumb Ranch and Resort, 970-726-5632

COMMENT: This is a great beginners route on almost flat terrain, or a relaxing kick-and-glide warm-up for experienced skiers. You will also enjoy nice views to the east of the Continental Divide and a view of some of the highest peaks in Rocky Mountain National Park and the Indian Peaks Wilderness from the west. Skinny skis work well on these easy groomed trails.

HERRINGBONE UP THOSE HILLS

This quintessential cross-country ski technique is used on moderately steep hills that don't require side-stepping. Position your skis in a V-shape and dig your inside edges into the snow. Keep your poles behind you, and look uphill. Once you've mastered the technique, you can either walk or run uphill, and you'll leave that distinctive herringbone (like the bones in a fish) pattern in the snow.

The Continental Divide towers over the mixed forest and skiers at Devil's Thumb Ranch.

GETTING THERE: From Denver, head west on I-70. Take Exit 232 onto Highway 40. Follow Highway 40 for approximately 30 miles through Empire, over Berthoud Pass, and past Winter Park and Fraser. About 2 miles past Fraser, take a right on County Road 83. Take the right-hand fork and follow it 3 miles to the ranch.

THE ROUTE: Go south from the Nordic Center and bear left. Go downhill and then bear slightly right and ascend onto the Ranch Walk Trail. You will climb uphill gradually for almost a mile before the trail levels. You will pass the Broken Barn Trail on the left, go downhill and across a bridge to reach the Broken Barn/Stage Route intersection. Bear right/west to the Stage Route Trail as the trail climbs steeply uphill and turns west. This climb is the only advanced section of the trail. Take your skis off and walk up if you can't herringbone. The trail then levels out and goes right. Continue on Stage Route until you intersect Broken Barn, then turn left. Take Broken Barn to the Meadow Trail and turn right onto the Meadow Trail. Turn left at the next intersection and take the Meadow Trail back to the Nordic Center.

Pick up a map at the Nordic Center or download at devilsthumbranch.com

57. Snow Mountain Ranch

ROUND TRIP	Varies
DIFFICULTY	Easy to moderate
SKILL LEVEL	Beginner to intermediate
HIGH POINT	8,950 feet
ELEVATION GAIN	450 feet
AVALANCHE DANGER	None
MAP	Snow Mountain Ranch Trail Map
CONTACT	Snow Mountain Ranch, 888-573-9622

COMMENT: Snow Mountain Ranch sits on 5,200 acres just off Highway 40 between Tabernash and Granby. It offers over 120 kilometers of groomed trails for cross coun-try skiing, snowshoeing, fat biking, tubing, sleigh rides, and other winter outdoor activities. You can cross-country ski on their groomed trails from mid-November until mid-April. The terrain can accommodate everyone from the first-time skier to the elite racer. If you ski with your dog on the dog-friendly loops next to the Nor-dic Center, remember that leashes are required. Skinny skis are adequate for these groomed trails.

GETTING THERE: From Denver, head west on I-70. Take Exit 232 onto Highway 40. Follow Highway 40 for approximately 30 miles through Empire, over Berthoud Pass, and past Winter Park and Fraser. About 8 miles past Fraser, take a left on County Road 53. Turn right onto Nine Mile Road and left onto County Road 5311.

THE ROUTE: Get a map of the Nordic trails when you purchase your ticket at the Nordic Center. The trails are divided into zones that are ranked according to dif-ficulty. For an easy kick-and-glide from the Nordic Center, head south to pick up the Pole Creek Trail. Turn right on Pole Creek to Gaskill. Turn left on Gaskill and climb up to the view at Columbine Point. Continue straight on Swenson, take another right on Wilson to Heckman, to a more advanced trail that will take you to another great spot for views and snacks. After a fun descent through the forest, take a right on Just, a left on Pole Creek, and a right on Wilson to return to the Nordic Center. If you want to skip the more advanced Heckman trail, you can choose one of the intermediate trails that will take you back to the Nordic Center.

On the trail to Columbine Point at Snow Mountain Ranch.

OTHER TRAILS TO EXPLORE: The Nordic Center has a bulletin board with maps of many different routes you can explore, or ask the friendly experts behind the counter for their suggestions.

Pick up a map at the Nordic Center or download at snowmountainranch.org

Chapter 11

GUANELLA PASS AREA

"With luck, it might even snow for us."

—Haruki Murakami, *After Dark*

This popular area south of Georgetown offers many recreational options that are close to Denver and do not require a trip through the Eisenhower Tunnel. A bonus is Georgetown itself, a turn-of-the-nineteenth-century mining village that features restored Victorian architecture and a wide variety of great coffee shops, dining, and lodging options. Allowing for a snack or meal in picturesque Georgetown will add to your appreciation of this once bustling region that was mined heavily for silver and gold.

Guanella Pass Road was built as a wagon road during the mining boom in the 1860s. The road is now paved but is not plowed to the top of the pass in the winter. The pass reaches an elevation of 11,666 feet, so snow is reliable all winter, although the road can be challenging after a major storm. It is safest to use a four-wheel-drive vehicle since the road is narrow and the sides can be piled high with plowed snow or not have shoulders. The winter parking lots are 1.7 miles and 200 feet short of the pass summit, adding 3.4 miles and 400 feet to the Bierstadt Mountain route.

View from the Naylor Lake Trail.

The pass is very scenic, with excellent views of fourteeners Mount Evans and Mount Bierstadt, and the jagged Sawtooth Ridge that connects them. You can also see the tops of two other nearby fourteeners, Grays Peak and Torreys Peak, as well as numerous 12,000-foot and 13,000-foot summits. Best of all, you can venture out into the winter wonderland on safe trails, and even ski up Bierstadt if you have winter mountaineering skills. If you don't, ski as far as you like and turn around after a couple of miles when the terrain gets steep. You will still enjoy the spectacular scenery.

The standard shortest route to Guanella Pass from Denver is to take I-70 west about 40 miles and take the Georgetown exit (Exit 228). Drive toward town and then turn right toward Georgetown at the first four-way stop. Look for signs to Guanella Pass. Climb west and then south out of town on Guanella Pass Road/Highway 381 to the pass about 12 miles. The pass can be a challenging road in the winter, but it is plowed and generally negotiable in a car with snow tires.

If the standard shorter route is closed, an alternate route is to take Highway 285 for 56 miles to Grant and turn north on Forest Road 118, which goes to Guanella Pass.

Photo courtesy National Park Service

BIGHORN SHEEP

Bighorn sheep are one of the most rare and striking animals to see in Rocky Mountain National Park. Their agility is remarkable, and they can perch on or sprint across very steep and treacherous terrain. They have hooves that are soft and flexible on the inside, allowing them to make astounding jumps and precarious climbs. They also have thick double-layered coats of hair that protect them from bitter windchills. Both males and females have permanent horns rather than seasonal antlers. They were almost hunted to extinction in the early 1900s, but now, thanks to the protection of Rocky Mountain National Park, they have recovered and there are 800 living in the park. You might see them in the park above Wild Basin on the Continental Divide, near the Mummy Range and Horseshoe Park, on the higher parts of Trail Ridge Road, or on Guanella Pass.

58. Naylor Lake

ROUND TRIP	3 miles
DIFFICULTY	Easy to moderate
SKILL LEVEL	Intermediate
HIGH POINT	12,000 feet
ELEVATION GAIN	540 feet
AVALANCHE DANGER	None to high
MAP	Trails Illustrated #104, Idaho Springs, Georgetown, Loveland Pass, USGS Mt. Evans, Montezuma
CONTACT	Clear Creek Ranger District, Arapaho National Forest, 303-567-3000

COMMENT: This is a short, fairly easy trail to a pristine mountain lake surrounded by soaring cliffs and high peaks. It is one of the best trails on Guanella Pass within easy driving distance of Denver. The only disadvantage is the possibility of snowmobiles or SUVs on the road to the trailhead, though they are sometimes helpful for packing down the deep snow. This is an intermediate ski trail. Mid-width, AT, or telemark skis would be more fun on the descent. Stop at Naylor Lake in the winter; the continuing route to Silver Dollar Lake is highly hazardous for avalanches in the winter. Note that Naylor Lake itself and its shoreline are private property.

GETTING THERE: From Denver, take I-70 west about 40 miles to the Georgetown exit (Exit 228). Drive toward town and turn right toward Georgetown at the first four-way stop; look for signs to Guanella Pass. Climb west and then south out of town on Guanella Pass Road/Highway 381 to the pass, about 12 miles. The pass can be a challenging road in the winter, but it is plowed and generally negotiable in a car with snow tires. Drive on Highway 381 to the winter closure gate and park in one of the two parking lots.

THE ROUTE: From the parking lots, go right on the road to the Naylor-Silver Dollar Lake trailhead. The trail is steep at first, but don't be discouraged as it mellows. In fact, at about 0.5 mile, the route levels somewhat and you follow a small frozen creek for a short distance. At approximately 0.6 mile you will reach the Naylor-Silver Dollar Lake Trailhead on the left; it is well-marked. From the trailhead, cross the frozen creek. The trail then leaves the drainage with some switchbacks, climbing to the right/west and winding through the pretty trees.

Skiers near Naylor Lake.

It then climbs out of an interesting hollow at about 1.25 miles and traverses along a narrow section with a small drop-off on one side, which makes it more difficult to get off track. Stay away from the drop-off. You are almost there. After another 0.5 mile of climbing and winding through the trees you will emerge to a spectacular view of Naylor Lake, with Silver Dollar Lake in the distance, and the surrounding rock wall cirque that towers above it. You will have a unique view of Mount Wilcox, 13,738-foot Argentine Peak, Decatur Mountain and Squaretop Mountain. From the lake you can climb the peaks in the summer, but in winter the avalanche danger is significant above the lake, so check conditions with the Colorado Avalanche Information Center, or by digging a snow pit, before climbing higher. If conditions are safe, you can wander around and up higher, avoiding the steepest terrain, before returning to the trailhead.

NAYLOR LAKE

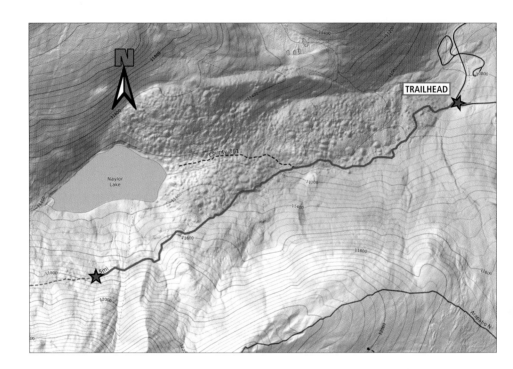

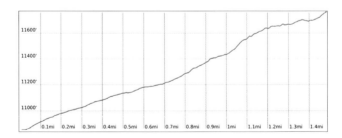

59. Mount Bierstadt

ROUND TRIP	3.3 miles to Scott Gomer Creek 10 miles to summit of Mount Bierstadt
DIFFICULTY	Moderate to challenging
SKILL LEVEL	Novice to base; expert for summit
HIGH POINT	11,669 feet at trailhead; 14,060 feet at Mount Bierstadt
ELEVATION GAIN	3,200-foot gain from parking areas to peak
AVALANCHE DANGER	None to high
MAP	Trails Illustrated #104, Idaho Springs, Georgetown, Loveland Pass
CONTACT	Clear Creek Ranger District, Arapaho National Forest, 303-567-3000

COMMENT: Mount Bierstadt, one of Colorado's highest peaks (topping out at 14,060 feet), is also one of Colorado's most accessible 14,000-foot peaks, as it is close to Denver. It is climbable in winter because much of the western side of the mountain gets blown free of heavy snow and there is a ridge on the northern edge of the western side that is relatively safe. If you plan to summit, start at dawn. Its upper slopes are not without avalanche danger, but you can also enjoy safe, shorter excursions in the grand high-mountain terrain at the base of the Evans-Bierstadt massif. The first 1.75 mile can be skied before encountering any danger, and the setting is magnificent. Simply start at the Guanella Pass winter road closure, which is 1.7 miles from the summer trailhead, and go as far as you like before turning around. Use your own judgment based on snow reports and the area you are crossing. To ski to the top you should be an expert ski mountaineer and excellent at evaluating avalanche danger. You will need deep snow to cover the footbridges or the wetlands. AT or telemark skis are necessary.

GETTING THERE: From Denver, take I-70 west about 40 miles to the Georgetown exit (Exit 228). Drive toward town and turn right toward Georgetown at the first four-way stop; look for signs to Guanella Pass. Climb west and then south out of town on Guanella Pass Road/Highway 381 to the pass, about 12 miles. The pass can be a challenging road in the winter, but it is plowed and generally negotiable in a car with snow tires. On Highway 381, when you break out into the open and see the striking view of the Bierstadt-Evans massif to the east, look for the Guanella Pass Trailhead for Bierstadt on the left/east side of the road 12 miles from Georgetown.

Wind-made snow waves on the summit of Mount Bierstadt.

THE ROUTE: The first part of the trail is virtually without avalanche danger, and it actually goes downhill to the east for 2.5 mile. Using this first section as an out-and-back trek is worth the trip, in combination with another nearby jaunt just for the view. At 2.5 miles you are near Scott Gomer Creek at around 11,400 feet. In crossing the creek you will encounter the infamous willows that befuddle many climbers. The newly designed trail includes several footbridges that make avoiding the willows easy. Unless there is recent snow, you might have to take off your skis to deal with the wooden bridges, or risk damaging your skis.

After you make it through the flat swamp, the trail climbs very gradually to the southeast for another 0.5 mile before you encounter steeper slopes and avalanche danger. But remember, the danger is relative to the conditions on the day you are climbing and can vary greatly. Make your way south around a pyramid-shaped rock and then climb southeast. After 0.5 mile of steep climbing almost due south, the trail settles down at about 1.5 miles to a steady incline heading southeast for a mile up the wide west ridge. The last 2.0 miles are often windswept, so skis might be optional because of exposed rocks. At about 2.5 miles the trail curves northeast for the steep final climb to the summit. The final pitch is very challenging on skis. This final stretch is often snow-free and icy so be cautious with your footing.

OTHER TRAILS TO EXPLORE: A trail on the west side of the highway from the Bierstadt Trail, the South Park Trail, is another short out-and-back with great views. It starts out on a short hill, travels about 100 yards or so on a flat area, and then descends to a creek before climbing again. After another 100 yards, it starts to meander and climb under avalanche zones and becomes unsafe to travel unless the snow is very thin or very stable.

MOUNT BIERSTADT

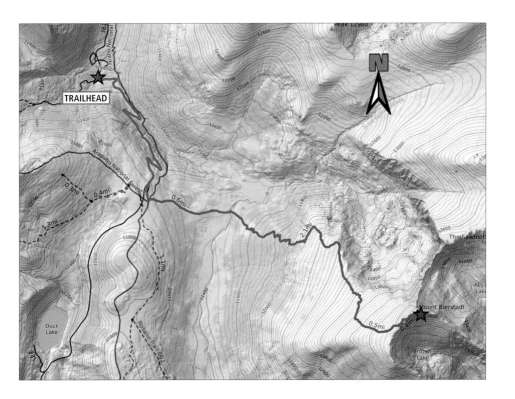

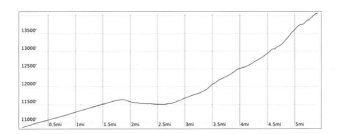

Nokhu Crags from the Colorado State Forest.

Northern Colorado

Chapter 12

POUDRE CANYON

"I frequently tramped eight or ten miles through the deepest snow to keep
an appointment with a beech-tree, or a yellow birch, or an old acquaintance
among the pines."

—Henry David Thoreau, *Winter Visitors*

Poudre Canyon is one of the Front Range's real treasures. One of the longest and most spectacular canyons in the state, it offers some of Colorado's best skiing. Its upper reaches around Cameron Pass are among the most reliable for early and late-season snow.

There is also a summer campus of Colorado State University in the lower reaches of Poudre Canyon. It is surrounded by Roosevelt National Forest and features the majestic mountain backdrops of the Cache la Poudre Wilderness, Comanche Peak Wilderness, and Rocky Mountain National Park. It is generally less heavily used than the Cameron Pass area, and some of the closer trails are a real treat. But some start at low elevations (8,000 feet) and usually are not reliable until midseason unless it is an early snow year. While most of the trails are closed to snowmobiles, the roads are not, and snowmobile traffic on the closed roads is variable.

Cameron Pass is the summit of Highway 14, at 10,276 feet, and one of the most popular destinations for cross-country skiers. You might also encounter some overlap with snowmobilers approaching from the Lake Agnes area. Most of the trails in this area start at an elevation of at least 9,000 feet. This generally means snow conditions are great, but windchills are potentially dangerous, so bring lots of warm clothing layers. Fortunately, these trails are generally well-protected by stately pine trees that act as windbreaks, and there are a lot of relatively warm, sunny, calm days. The pass is bordered on the south by Rocky Mountain National Park's aptly named Never Summer Mountains, crowned by the jagged Nokhu Crags, and on the north by the Medicine Bow Range. To the west is the Colorado State Forest and the stark beauty of North Park, offering additional access to the Rawah Wilderness.

From Fort Collins, go about 10 miles north on US 287 and exit west onto Highway 14 at Ted's Place.

60. Crown Point Road

ROUND TRIP	0.3 miles to spur road; 7 miles to FR 142; 12 miles to Browns Lake Trailhead
DIFFICULTY	Easy to moderate
SKILL LEVEL	Novice to beginners
HIGH POINT	10,500 feet (Browns Lake Trailhead)
ELEVATION GAIN	Up to 1,100 feet
AVALANCHE DANGER	None
MAP	Trails Illustrated #112, Poudre River, Cameron Pass
CONTACT	Canyon Lakes Ranger District, Roosevelt National Forest, 970-295-6700

COMMENT: This is an easy, scenic route along a wide, unplowed road with a gradual incline. You can take worthwhile shorter trips to a spur road, FR 142, or a longer trek to the Browns Lake Trailhead. In any case, you will have nice views of Poudre Canyon and the plains from the higher reaches, even in the first couple of miles. Crown Point Road is not plowed, so how far you can drive depends on the depth of the snow and the clearance of your four-wheel-drive vehicle. If you are not driving a four-wheel-drive vehicle, you can still have a fun trip, starting about 1 mile from Pingree Park Road. It will be more scenic if you can ski 3 to 4 miles up the road where some of the very best high-mountain scenery starts. You can, of course, turn around at any point, and choose the distance and trekking time that best suit you, given your starting point. Experienced skiers can use any style of ski for this route.

GETTING THERE: To reach Poudre Canyon, take US 287 north from Fort Collins about 10 miles and exit west onto Highway 14 at Ted's Place. This Scenic Byway winds through the Poudre Canyon alongside the largely unfettered Poudre River. The Pingree Park Road/CR 63E turnoff is on the left/south side of Highway 14 approximately 27.5 miles west of the entrance to the canyon at Ted's Place. Pingree Park Road is a well-maintained dirt road that is plowed all winter, but it might not be plowed immediately after a snowstorm. From Highway 14, take Pingree Park Road south for 4 miles. At a sign for Crown Point Road, turn right/west. After heavy snowfall, Crown Point Road is closed approximately 5.5 miles or less from Pingree Park Road and offers skiing from that point.

THE ROUTE: Starting 5.5 miles from the intersection with Pingree Park Road there are good views in the first mile. There are some sunny lunch or snack spots in the trees

Crown Point Road is a skiers and snowshoers only route in winter.

on the right. Just beyond the initial road switchbacks you can see a good view from the main road before you enter a tunnel of trees. Once you exit the switchbacks there are a couple of side trails on the left. The first one, a spur road at 1.5 miles, is a short dead-end route that offers nice panoramic views into the Comanche Peak Wilderness. It is an out-and-back side excursion if you are not planning to try the entire route to the Browns Lake Trailhead.

After that, the main route becomes a tall lodgepole-pine tree tunnel for a couple of miles. You are on the north side of the mountain, and if it is mid-winter, your exposure to the sun will be limited until you break from the trees at 3 miles. In approximately 3.5 miles you reach FR 142 on the right. This intersection is a good place for a break and snack.

From there, Crown Point Road swings more westerly, catches a lot of late-after-noon sun, and affords more views. If you are not too tired and have plenty of time to make the return downhill trek, continue 2.5 miles to the Browns Lake Trailhead. It is the best scenery on the route. (If you are really ambitious and exceptionally fit, you could go partway or all the way down to Browns Lake, but this is only advisable under ideal conditions.)

On the return, you have striking views of the top of Poudre Canyon and the plains far below. You should be able to make much better time because you are descending 1,000 feet back to your car.

CROWN POINT ROAD

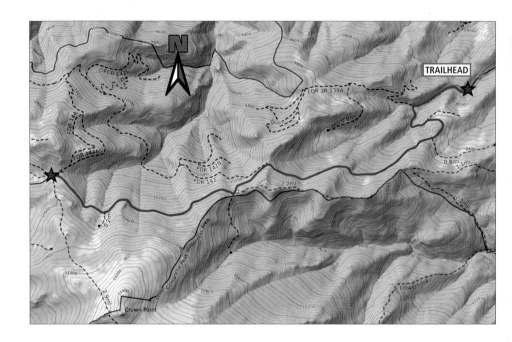

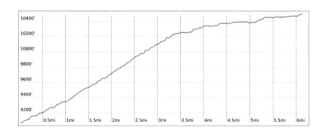

61. Signal Mountain Trail

ROUND TRIP	5 miles to beaver ponds; 10.5 miles to Signal Mountain
DIFFICULTY	Easy to challenging
SKILL LEVEL	Intermediate
HIGH POINT	9,000 feet at beaver ponds; 11,200 feet near Signal Mountain
ELEVATION GAIN	450 feet to beaver ponds; 2,700 feet to Signal Mountain
AVALANCHE DANGER	None to low, except on final slope to summit
MAP	Trails Illustrated #112, Poudre River, Cameron Pass
CONTACT	Canyon Lakes Ranger District, Roosevelt National Forest, 970-295-6700

COMMENT: This little-used trail offers protection from winter winds and a tour of a magical river arroyo. The trail is down at stream level along Pennock Creek and is fairly level for the first few miles, with nice views across the stream. The trail climbs gently before it steepens and pushes you to a final challenging assault of Signal Mountain. It offers a ski through a beautiful riparian area that features a mixed old-growth forest of aspen, pine, fir, and spruce and striking rock outcrops. It makes a nice out-and-back trip of any length, although climbing Signal Mountain is a serious all-day adventure. There is also a south access to this trail near Glen Haven that is immediately a steep climb.

From Pingree Park, the trail climbs gradually for the first mile or two then becomes a steep ascent. If you are going for the summit use AT or telemark skis. You can use Nordic skis for the first 2 miles.

GETTING THERE: To reach Poudre Canyon, take US 287 north from Fort Collins about 10 miles and exit west onto Highway 14 at Ted's Place. This Scenic Byway winds through Poudre Canyon alongside the largely unfettered Poudre River. The Pingree Park Road/CR 63E turnoff is on the left/south side of Highway 14 approximately 27.5 miles west of the entrance to the canyon at Ted's Place. Pingree Park Road is a well-maintained dirt road that is plowed all winter, but it might not be plowed immediately after a snowstorm. From Highway 14, take Pingree Park Road south approximately 10 miles, about 0.5 mile beyond the turnoff for Pennock Pass. The trailhead is on the left/east side of the road 2 miles before the CSU Campus. Park alongside the road.

THE ROUTE: The trail drops down from the road to a stream and then climbs up the other side of the drainage, winding its way through the thick forest. It drops again

View from Signal Mountain Trail.

to reach Pennock Creek at 0.5 mile. When the trail meets an old road, bear right. At approximately 1 mile, cross Pennock Creek on a footbridge that goes left/east across the creek and might require removing your skis. If it has been very cold and the stream is solidly frozen, you might be able to just walk across the stream, but don't take any chances.

The trail then begins to climb, gaining about 300 feet up and over a small ridge at 8,800 feet at around 1.5 miles. It climbs steadily and gains another 200 feet, rising to 9,000 feet in the next 0.5 mile or so as you parallel the stream on your right. The beaver ponds at about 2.5 miles mark the halfway point; here the trail leaves the main Pennock Creek drainage, crosses a smaller stream, and begins to climb more steeply as it leaves the streambed. There is a striking rock spire that can be a lunch or turnaround point, depending on your ambitions. The trail continues to climb, crossing the stream again at about 3.75 miles. At about 10,400 feet and 4.5 miles, it reaches a bit of a saddle that is still obscured by trees, where you might see an old road. Look to the right to pick up the faint trail.

Continue to climb toward treeline. This section is difficult to follow with good snow cover. At treeline you might encounter some windswept tundra. The summit of Signal Mountain is up to the right at a little less than 5.25 miles; South Signal Mountain (14 feet lower) is a 0.5-mile ridge walk farther on. The view from the summit ridge is superb, with a great panorama of the canyons, foothills, and plains below. You can also see Longs Peak in the distance.

SIGNAL MOUNTAIN TRAIL

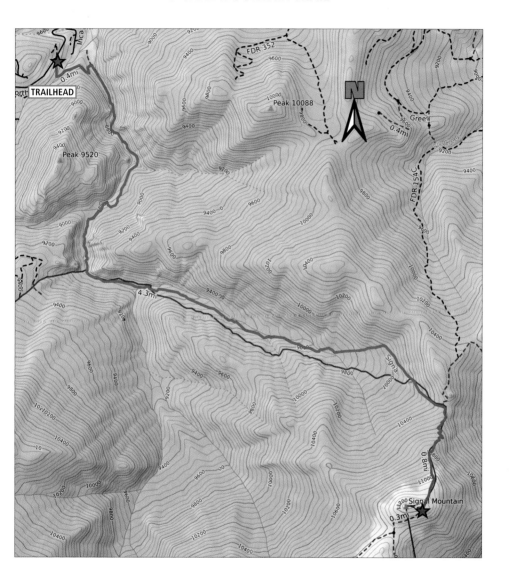

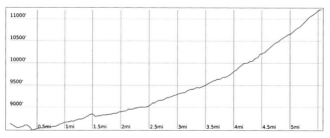

62. **Stormy Peaks Trail**

ROUND TRIP	3 miles to wilderness boundary; 6 miles to RMNP boundary; 10 miles to pass
DIFFICULTY	Easy to challenging
SKILL LEVEL	Intermediate
HIGH POINT	9,600 feet at wilderness boundary; 10,400 feet at RMNP boundary; 11,700 feet at pass
ELEVATION GAIN	572 feet to wilderness boundary; 1,372 feet to RMNP boundary; 2,672 feet to pass
AVALANCHE DANGER	None to low
MAP	Trails Illustrated #112, Poudre River, Cameron Pass
CONTACT	Canyon Lakes Ranger District, Roosevelt National Forest, 970-295-6700

COMMENT: The Stormy Peaks Trail features almost nonstop views of the impressive mountain backdrop as you climb out of the valley and gradually make your way above treeline. The trail travels through the stark beauty of a burn area and eventually climbs into a forest that is primarily lodgepole pine, but it also includes fir and spruce trees. The trail climbs into Comanche Peak Wilderness and then Rocky Mountain National Park. Dogs are not allowed in the park. The trail is not well-marked, so a topographic map and solid routefinding skills with a compass are necessary. It climbs gradually for the first mile or two then becomes a steeper ascent. If you are going for the summit you should be at least an intermediate skier and use AT or telemark skis. You can use Nordic skis for the first 2 miles.

GETTING THERE: Take US 287 north from Fort Collins about 10 miles and exit west onto Highway 14 at Ted's Place. This Scenic Byway winds through Poudre Canyon alongside the largely unfettered Poudre River. The Pingree Park Road/CR 63E turnoff is on the left/south side of Highway 14 approximately 27.5 miles west of the entrance to the canyon at Ted's Place. Pingree Park Road is a well-maintained dirt road that is plowed all winter, but it might not be plowed immediately after a snowstorm. From Highway 14, drive Pingree Park Road south 18 miles to the end of the road at CSU's Pingree Park Campus and park.

THE ROUTE: The trail starts off through a rocky area. It might be exposed if there hasn't been a recent snowfall. Just as the trail goes into tree cover, after about 0.25 mile, it takes a sharp left turn uphill on a short set of switchbacks to the top of the low ridge on the left/south side of the trail. You will see a lone, burned tree stump on the right; turn left uphill. The trail and switchbacks might be buried, and are unmarked, so this short climb is easy to miss. After you have climbed to the top of the ridge and if you prefer a shorter jaunt with an expansive view, consult your topographic map and turn northeast to climb the 9,360-foot-high hill called Denny's Point, and call it a day. You might see a sign for it if it isn't buried. You can also visit Twin Lake Reservoir via a back-door route by bushwhacking southeast for a 1-mile round-trip. Don't attempt these jaunts without a topographic map.

On the main trail, you will soon enjoy a very nice view of the campus and most of the Pingree Park area. You can see the sweeping cirque that frames Emmaline Lake above the valley to the northwest. The trail isn't easy to follow, so watch for tree blazes. Stay on the west side of the ridge when in doubt. You soon reenter the area that was burned. The stark contrast of the burned trees against the white snow is dramatic. The trail parallels Pingree Park as you travel southwest with magnificent views of the Comanche Peak massif. After a mile or so you enter a tree tunnel that lasts for more than 0.5 mile until you reach the Comanche Peak Wilderness boundary at approximately 1.5 miles. As the trees thin, you have your best view yet of Comanche Peak, Emmaline Lake, and Mummy Pass off to the north. This is a good place for a snack— or a good place to turn around.

Once you enter the wilderness area, look for tree blazes: wilderness trails are not well marked. The trail gets steeper on a series of steep switchbacks; several rocky sections and stream crossings might require you to remove your skis in early season. In about 0.25 mile you have a superb view of the U-shaped, glacier-carved "park" that is in the canyon below Ramsey Peak (11,582 feet) and Sugarloaf Mountain (12,101 feet). You pay for this view by gaining another 200 feet of elevation. In the next scant mile, the trail gains 600 feet, and at just under 3 miles you reach the Rocky Mountain National Park boundary. Enjoy more views of the glacier-carved box canyon below and get a good view of the Stormy Peaks above.

From here the trail veers due south; it is poorly marked. Stay parallel to the Stormy Peaks drainage. Frequently check the landscape so you can orient your direction. After 0.25 mile there is a sign for the Rocky Mountain National Park Stormy Peaks campsite. At 4 miles you emerge into a wonderland of high-mountain snow, windswept meadows, and dramatic rock outcroppings at 11,000 feet. It is worth the additional effort to go another mile and mount the pass (or even climb the Stormy Peaks, 12,148 feet).

STORMY PEAKS TRAIL

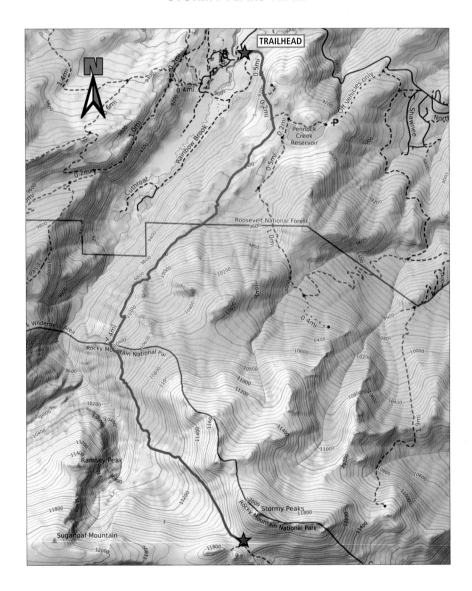

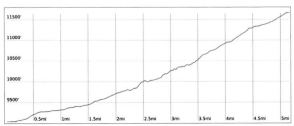

63. Cirque Meadows & Emmaline Lake

ROUND TRIP	6.5 miles to meadows; 10.6 miles to lake
DIFFICULTY	Easy to challenging
SKILL LEVEL	Intermediate
HIGH POINT	9,800 feet at meadows; 11,000 feet at lake
ELEVATION GAIN	900 feet to meadows; 2,100 feet to lake
AVALANCHE DANGER	None except near lake; can be avoided
MAP	Trails Illustrated #112, Poudre River, Cameron Pass
CONTACT	Canyon Lakes Ranger District, Roosevelt National Forest, 970-295-6700

COMMENT: This trail offers nice views of Pingree Park, the Stormy Peaks, and the dramatic backdrop of Fall Mountain and the Comanche Peak Wilderness framing a high-mountain lake. The first mile of the trail makes a nice family out-and-back; going all the way to Emmaline Lake makes for a challenging day. Cirque Meadows is a nice intermediary stop along the way. This trail is rewarding regardless of the distance traveled. The Tom Bennett Campground road might not be plowed, adding an additional 1 mile to the trek. You can use skinny skis to Cirque Meadows.

GETTING THERE: Take US 287 north from Fort Collins about 10 miles and exit west onto Highway 14 at Ted's Place. This Scenic Byway winds through Poudre Canyon alongside the largely unfettered Poudre River. The Pingree Park Road/CR 63E turnoff is on the left/south side of Highway 14 approximately 27.5 miles west of the entrance to the canyon at Ted's Place. Pingree Park Road is a well-maintained dirt road that is plowed all winter, but it might not be plowed immediately after a snowstorm. From Highway 14, drive Pingree Park Road south about 17.5 miles to the turnoff for Tom Bennett Campground. Continue past the campground to the first left. Park at the entrance to the unplowed road. The closure gate is around 0.3 mile from the main road.

THE ROUTE: The unnamed, unsigned trailhead is just up the road from the Tom Bennett Campground. Tom Bennett Campground might not be plowed, adding close to an additional 0.5 mile each way to your trip. Go past the campground on the main road and then look for the first road/trail on the left. The first 1.5 miles of the trail are out in the open on an old unmarked logging road called Cirque Road that travels through an old burn area. It is exposed to sun and might not have sufficient snow cover for skis. Don't be discouraged if you have to carry your skis because you are

The soaring cirque above Emmaline Lake.

likely to encounter excellent snow when you reach the trees. You will have a view of the Stormy Peaks and the other burn area to the south. You will also have a good view of CSU's rebuilt campus. It is closed in the winter, so no facilities are available. The trail climbs steadily. Enjoy the view before you reach the trees. At a little over 2 miles, the trail crosses Fall Creek. At about 2.4 miles, you will reach the intersection with the Mummy Pass Trail to the left; stay to the right. If you only want to go to Cirque Meadows and back, a side excursion up the Mummy Pass Trail could be a nice add-on.

Just past the trail intersection you enter the trees and good snow conditions. The trail winds, rolls, and switchbacks through a long tree tunnel with occasional glimpses of the valley below. Past a backcountry campsite the trail climbs steeply until you break into the open to re-cross the creek at Cirque Meadows, just past 3 miles. Enjoy the backdrop of the Comanche Peak glacier-carved cirque and the rust colors of the willows. This is a great photo opportunity or place for a snack break. You will find a picnic area just beyond the meadow. You have climbed around 900 feet to reach the meadows. If you want to reach the lake, you have another 1,200 feet and 4 miles of skiing. Check the amount of daylight left and the energy left in your legs.

After the meadows, you reenter the trees and the real climb begins, as you gain elevation over the next mile up above the creek. At about 4.4 miles, the trail climbs more steeply to once again closely follow the creek a scant mile to the wintertime magic of Emmaline Lake. The steepest climb is around 0.5 mile from the lake.

OTHER TRAILS TO EXPLORE: Mummy Pass Trail, and a cross-country route up Comanche Peak, are a couple of other moderate to challenging gems. The Mummy Pass Trail is an excellent outing for advanced skiers.

CIRQUE MEADOWS & EMMALINE LAKE

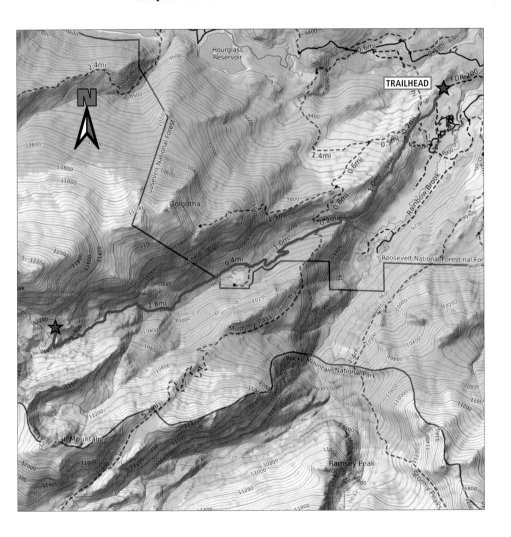

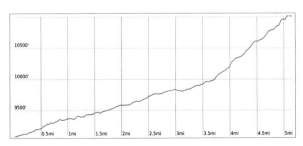

64. Big South Trail

ROUND TRIP	6 miles to viewpoint; 13.5 miles to Flowers Trail
DIFFICULTY	Moderate to challenging
SKILL LEVEL	Intermediate
HIGH POINT	9,000 feet at viewpoint; 9,400 feet at Flowers Trail
ELEVATION GAIN	560 feet to viewpoint; 960 feet to Flowers Trail
AVALANCHE DANGER	None to low
MAP	Trails Illustrated #112, Poudre River, Cameron Pass
CONTACT	Canyon Lakes Ranger District, Roosevelt National Forest, 970-295-6700

COMMENT: As you near the upper reaches of Poudre Canyon and Cameron Pass, this is the first trail you encounter that has reasonably good snow cover. Big South Trail is located just past Poudre Falls, which can be dramatic in early winter as the waterfall freezes into unpredictable shapes and the sun glistens on combinations of ice and water. The Big South Trail offers similar winter ice sculptures in its first 0.5 mile. This trail is best used in midseason conditions because the elevation is lower (8,440 feet) and snow can be sketchy early in the winter. The Big South Trail follows the south fork of the Poudre River (called the Cache la Poudre River) as it descends from its origins in the high western reaches of Rocky Mountain National Park and the Comanche Peak Wilderness. With the exception of spring runoff and June rise, when the Poudre swells to a roiling river, this section is a fairly narrow stream. Most of the trail is in the Comanche Peak Wilderness, where wilderness rules apply. This is usually a challenging skinny ski route because of the side slopes so mid-width skis would be better.

GETTING THERE: To reach Poudre Canyon, take US 287 north from Fort Collins about 10 miles and exit west onto Highway 14 at Ted's Place. Drive west and then south on Highway 14 for approximately 48 miles. The parking lot is on the left/east side of the road 1 mile past the turnout for Poudre Falls.

THE ROUTE: The beginning of the trail is very rocky because it is a compact canyon of frozen waterfalls, beautifully contorted ice, and snow-crested trees and boulders. The first part of the trail climbs slowly through the trees and over the rocky shore. After the first 0.5 mile, you enter the wilderness. The trail stays on the east side of the river, rolling, climbing, and dropping through the scenic small arroyo created by

PHOTO BY JOE GRIM

One of the steep slopes above the Big South Trail.

the river. It then climbs more steeply over a section of rocks that can be tricky early or late in the season if the snow cover is thin. This is the point, at about 1 mile, where you find out if there is enough snow to make the trek. If you are able to surmount this section, which features a bit of climbing and a need for care if you have children in the party, you will be able to continue. The trail travels through more rocky sections and breaks out of the trees for some nice views. In a very snowy year, this section of trail can be a vertical snowfield that is difficult to navigate. In this case, stay close to the streambed. If the river is frozen solid, you can venture onto to it at times. When you reach approximately 2.4 miles, you cross a bridge over May Creek. In a long 0.5 mile, you have a nice overlook of this branch canyon and the surrounding ridge lines at 3 miles. This viewpoint is a good place for a snack break and photos; turn around here for a nice, shorter outing.

The trail then descends back into the arroyo and crosses another drainage, meandering through the trees and becoming much flatter. The trail climbs and descends for the next 1 mile, with occasional vistas. Some wide sections of the river can be used for travel if it's frozen solid in mid-winter. At 5 miles the canyon opens up and offers 360-degree views of rock outcrops, meadowlands, and a stately, pristine old-growth forest. It's another 1.75 miles to the junction with the Flowers Trail and a washed-out footbridge across the river.

BIG SOUTH TRAIL

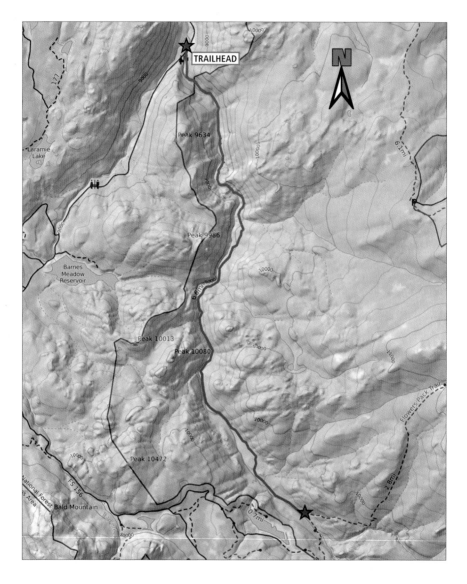

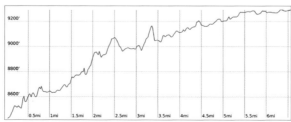

65. Blue Lake Trail

ROUND TRIP	4 miles to Fall Creek; 9.5 miles to Blue Lake
DIFFICULTY	Moderate to challenging
SKILL LEVEL	Intermediate
HIGH POINT	9,600 feet at Fall Creek; 10,800 feet at Blue Lake
ELEVATION GAIN	100 feet to Fall Creek; 1,700 feet to Blue Lake
AVALANCHE DANGER	Low to moderate above lake; easily avoided
MAP	Trails Illustrated #112, Poudre River, Cameron Pass
CONTACT	Canyon Lakes Ranger District, Roosevelt National Forest, 970-295-6700

COMMENT: As you near the upper reaches of Poudre Canyon and Cameron Pass, one of the most popular Poudre Canyon trails offers easy, short round-trip excursions or a moderate to challenging all-day adventure, depending on snow conditions and how far you go. It's 4.75 miles one way to the pristine mountain lake surrounded by towering mountains, and a 1,700-foot rolling elevation gain for extra fun. Unfortunately, the first couple of miles of this trail are the least interesting because of the thick lodgepole pine tree cover, but you will see some views along the way of the hills and reservoir. However, the lodgepole pine forest offers good protection from the wind, so this is a good trail for days with heavy windchill. Don't ski all the way to the lake if heavy snow is predicted unless you are prepared to spend the night. Blue Lake, a popular overnight destination for winter or summer backpackers, is in a magnificent setting among some of the highest peaks of the Medicine Bow Range, including its monarchs, 12,951-foot Clark Peak and 12,127-foot Cameron Peak. You can also summit Clark Peak from Blue Lake without a lot of avalanche danger if you are very ambitious or very fast and fit.

Experienced skiers can use any type of ski, but the curvy descents are easier on wider skis. The rolling trail makes it a bit difficult for skins. Attempting Clark Peak from this approach would take a very long day, expert skills, and AT or telemark skis.

GETTING THERE: To reach Poudre Canyon, take US 287 north from Fort Collins about 10 miles and exit west onto Highway 14 at Ted's Place. Take Highway 14 west 60 miles to the Blue Lake Trailhead parking area on the right/west side of the road. It is well-marked but doesn't have any facilities. If you reach Long Draw Road or Zimmerman Lake Trailhead, you missed it.

THE ROUTE: The trail starts at the edge of the parking lot, traveling right/north downhill for 0.5 mile, and then across Sawmill Creek and alongside Joe Wright Creek,

PHOTO BY ERIC ERSLEV

Looking to the high ridgeline from Blue Lake.

then it veers gradually northwest. The trail gradually climbs about 300 feet in the first mile. You can see Chambers Lake in the distance through the trees, and there are even a couple of view spots if you want a photo. It levels out to a steady roll through the trees for the next 1 mile and, as you enter the Fall Creek drainage, it opens up a little bit. The trail rolls quite a bit for most of the trip but climbs steadily farther on. These first 2 miles are under the thick cover of lodgepole pines until you cross Fall Creek and reach a nice small meadow area. This is a good spot to turn around for a shorter trip, or you can try to make it to the wilderness area boundary, where the trail gets much steeper.

At about 2.75 miles you will reach the Rawah Wilderness boundary; the trail is unmarked after this, but the beauty of the scenery increases dramatically. After this, you start the steady, steeper climb to almost 11,000 feet. It is heavily used, so route-finding likely won't be a problem unless you are first on the trail. It winds its way northwest through a relatively thick forest, but there are also some nice meadows and streams at a little under 4 miles. After another long 0.75 mile and a short downhill, you reach Blue Lake. The surrounding summits are not visible from the lake because they are obscured by their steep, heavily forested shoulders embracing the frozen lake. The views as you descend to the lake are superb. If you want to summit Clark Peak too, you can head around the lake and then west and south up the steep slopes. Don't attempt it unless you have winter mountaineering experience and know avalanche danger is low.

BLUE LAKE TRAIL

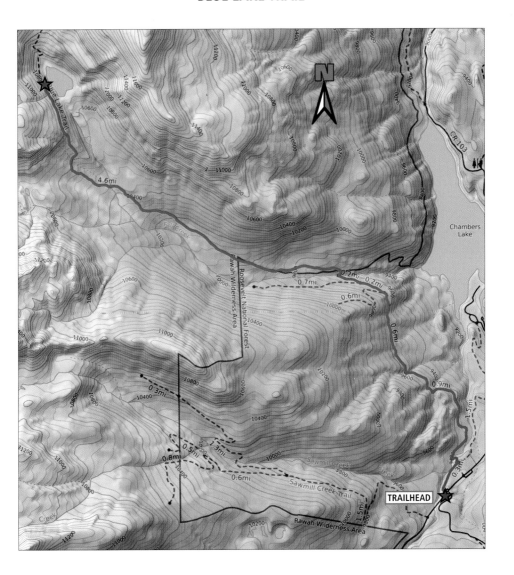

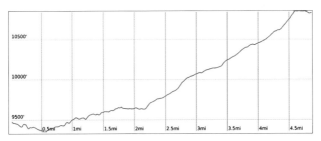

66. Sawmill Creek Trail

ROUND TRIP	3 miles
DIFFICULTY	Moderate
SKILL LEVEL	Novice to beginner
HIGH POINT	10,000 feet at trail fork
ELEVATION GAIN	500 feet to trail fork
AVALANCHE DANGER	None low; can be avoided
MAP	Trails Illustrated #112, Poudre River, Cameron Pass
CONTACT	Canyon Lakes Ranger District, Roosevelt National Forest, 970-295-6700

COMMENT: This relatively lightly used trail offers access to a high-mountain panorama of snow-covered peaks in the Rawah Range. Experienced skiers can use any style of skis on this steep old logging road. Advanced skiers like to wander off trail and uphill to the left/west side of the trail, climb steeply with skins and ski down through the trees back to the trail.

GETTING THERE: To reach Poudre Canyon, take US 287 north from Fort Collins about 10 miles and exit west onto Highway 14 at Ted's Place. Take Highway 14 west approximately 60 miles to the Blue Lake Trailhead parking lot on the right/west; the Sawmill Creek Trailhead is just beyond the Blue Lake parking lot. It is very easy to miss because it is marked by only a road and closed gate. From the Blue Lake parking lot, walk 200 yards west on the highway shoulder to the trailhead on the right. Do not park on the road because of almost daily work by snowplows. You could be ticketed, towed, or buried by a snowplow.

THE ROUTE: The Sawmill Creek Trail starts off in the trees on a gradual and then steep uphill following the old logging road. You can sometimes see blue diamond markers up fairly high on the trees, directing you away from dead-ends and incorrect logging roads, if they haven't blown down. After 0.5 mile or so traveling northwest, the trail turns sharply to the left/southwest and goes up a steep switchback. This is a very sunny section of trail and you will warm up considerably. There are nice views back to the southeast of the mountains and cliffs above Zimmerman Lake. In 0.25 mile, the trail turns back toward the Sawmill Creek drainage and travels primarily

The Rawah Range from the Sawmill Creek Trail.

west-northwest. At 1 mile, the trail levels somewhat and then goes slightly downhill 0.5 mile to reach a trail intersection at about 1.5 miles. Turn around here; it's a nice viewpoint for photos and a good place for a snack or lunch break. At this point, the nonstop views are quite spectacular, but the wind can become a factor.

SAWMILL CREEK TRAIL

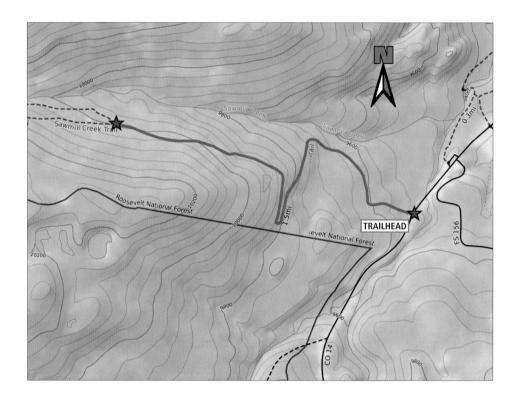

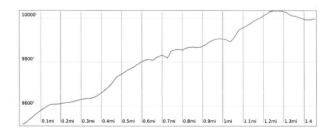

67. Trap Lake and Park & Iron Mountain

ROUND TRIP	6 miles to Trap Lake; 11.5 miles to Trap Park
DIFFICULTY	Moderate to challenging (Iron Mountain)
SKILL LEVEL	Intermediate
HIGH POINT	10,500 feet
ELEVATION GAIN	978 feet
AVALANCHE DANGER	Considerable; potential avalanche run-out zones in Trap Park near Iron Mountain; can be avoided
MAP	Trails Illustrated #112, Poudre River, Cameron Pass
CONTACT	Canyon Lakes Ranger District, Roosevelt National Forest, 970-295-6700

COMMENT: Trap Park, a draw or small canyon that is a beauty, offers varied scenery and a rolling trail. There are hills at first, followed by virtually flat terrain. It is worth the extra effort of a trip of its own, where you will have a great view of Iron Mountain and even climbing access to it, with some avalanche hazard. The trail rolls through a beautiful riparian area following the Trap Creek drainage for 2 miles or so, ending at the boundary of the Neota Wilderness. You will be at the foot of Iron Mountain. Avoid avalanche run-out zones on the mountain at times of high avalanche danger. You are likely to encounter snowmobilers on Long Draw Road, the approach to Trap Park. You can ski the slopes of Iron Mountain in the late spring after snow has consolidated and it is safe, if you are an expert skier. Experienced skiers can use any style of skis for this trail.

GETTING THERE: To reach the Poudre Canyon, take US 287 north from Fort Collins about 10 miles and exit west onto Highway 14 at Ted's Place. Take Highway 14 west 60 miles to the Blue Lake parking area on the right/west side of the highway. Less than 0.25 mile before the parking lot, just beyond the bulletin board, look for the Meadows/Long Draw winter trailhead parking lot. Long Draw Road itself is on the west side of the highway opposite the Blue Lake parking lot. You can park at the Blue Lake parking area, the Meadows/Long Draw winter trailhead, or at Long Draw Road.

THE ROUTE: The first part of this route along Long Draw Road can be obnoxious if there are a lot of snowmobilers on the road. The road itself can be pleasant with some

The ridge above Trap Lake on a snowy day.

nice views as it climbs. There is a side trail next to the road that you can use part of the way to avoid the snowmobiles. They are usually only intermittent in their use of the road. They might even save you some work by packing down the road when it is covered with loose powder. They are not allowed in Trap Park.

Follow Long Draw Road approximately 2.5 miles to the shortcut trail on the right to Trap Park, which is marked on a map. You can also continue on the road another 0.3 mile to the turnoff to Trap Park Trailhead. If you reach Trap Lake, which is next to Long Draw Road, you have gone too far. Trap Park begins in a small draw with very steep sides. The trail climbs over rocks and up onto a small ridge that provides a pretty overlook of the lake. The shortcut trail joins from the right at just under 3.5 miles. The main trail then descends to the creek and crosses it at 4 miles. The branch canyon opens up with spectacular views as the trail levels. At 4.75 miles a side trail climbs onto the north-facing ridge and offers another overlook. The main trail continues south another 1 mile along the right side of the creek. If you are ambitious, you can continue toward Iron Mountain.

This area is wetlands, so it has to have excellent snow cover unless you can stay on the unmarked trail. You will enjoy views of Iron Mountain until the trail enters thick tree cover. Don't attempt the climb unless you have winter mountaineering skills. Recently, an illegal snowmobiler was killed in an avalanche here when he got too close and high onto a lower slope.

TRAP LAKE AND PARK & IRON MOUNTAIN

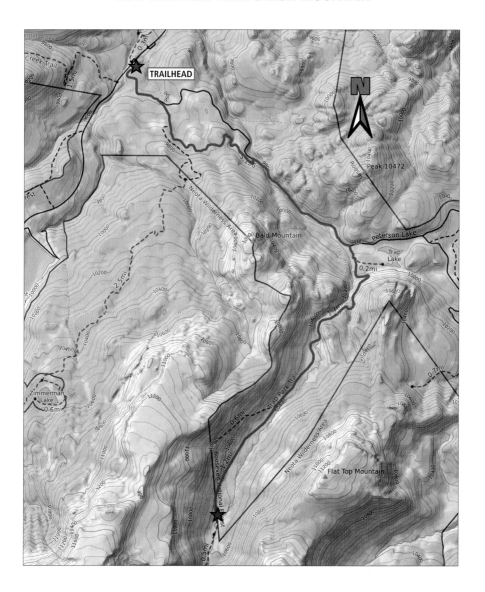

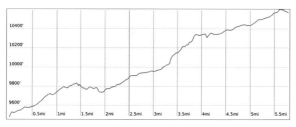

68. Zimmerman Lake & Meadows Trail

OPTION 1		
	ROUND TRIP	2.2 miles
	DIFFICULTY	Moderate
	SKILL LEVEL	Intermediate
	HIGH POINT	10,495 feet
	ELEVATION GAIN	476 feet

OPTION 2		
	ONE WAY	4.25 miles to Meadows/Long Draw winter trailhead
	DIFFICULTY	Moderate
	SKILL LEVEL	Intermediate
	HIGH POINT	10,495 feet
	ELEVATION GAIN	1,000 feet

AVALANCHE DANGER	None
MAP	Trails Illustrated #112, Poudre River, Cameron Pass
CONTACT	Canyon Lakes Ranger District, Roosevelt National Forest, 970-295-6700

COMMENT: Zimmerman Lake is one of the more popular winter destinations for snowshoers and skiers. A simple round-trip to the lake is a nice half-day (or less) activity that can easily be extended by taking the Meadows Trail north from the lake. Don't be discouraged if the parking lot is nearly full and the trail to the lake is crowded. Once you get to the lake you can have solitude. The short, gentle trail has views of the mountains in the Rawah Wilderness and Never Summer Mountains that form the northwest border of Rocky Mountain National Park. If you want an all-day adventure, add the Meadows Trail, which is best done one-way with a car shuttle at the Meadows/Long Draw winter trailhead. It is downhill starting from Zimmerman Lake. The Meadows Trail round-trip is only realistic during the short days of winter if you are fast, fit, and have routefinding skills. Just doing a portion of the Meadows Trail is also a nice out-and-back. The Meadows Trail enters the Neota Wilderness near Zimmerman Lake.

Experienced skiers can use any style of skis for this trail, because it is a rolling trail; waxable skis or pattern skis are better than skins for climbing and gliding.

On the trail to Zimmerman Lake.

GETTING THERE: Take US 287 north from Fort Collins about 10 miles and exit west onto Highway 14 at Ted's Place. Take Highway 14 west about 63 miles to the Zimmerman Lake Trailhead on the left/east side of the road a few miles before Cameron Pass. There are chemical toilets but no running water.

TIP: Although Highway 14 generally travels east-west, when you first enter Poudre Canyon, it dips dramatically to the southwest at Kinikinik. By the time you reach the Zimmerman Lake Trailhead, the road is actually more north-south than east-west.

THE ROUTE: The trail to Zimmerman Lake goes to the right/southeast out of the parking lot and then immediately left/east into the tall pine trees. It climbs gently for about 200 yards and then gradually steepens and narrows into a few switchbacks. The trail climbs almost 400 feet over the next 0.75 mile before exiting the trees and leveling out slightly into a tree-rimmed meadow. The trail widens on the right edge of the meadow. There is a view of the Medicine Bow Range from the top of the meadow. The trail continues to climb, then levels out as it goes left/north back into the trees. In another 0.25 mile you reach the west edge of the lake.

At the lake you have several options. You can climb a short hill to the right up to the surface of the lake or ski around the lake in either direction. The walk to the left/northeast is on a terra firma-supported trail; the walk to the right/southwest requires walking on the lake surface, which is not recommended unless it has been very cold. Do not attempt it in warm, early- or late-season conditions. You can simply survey the scenery, have a snack, and reverse course. You can also stay on the trail to reach the northeast edge of the lake. Continue north on the trail and at 1.1 miles reach a fork. The almost-flat right/easterly fork takes you to the north end of the lake for more loop trails; the Meadows Trail is straight and left/north. Once you reach the northeast corner of the lake you can bushwhack your way onto the hills above.

At the trail fork at 1.1 miles is the start of the Meadows Trail, which goes straight and left/north. Look for a brown wood sign at the beginning of the trail. There are other brown markers after the start of the Meadows Trail. The delightful Meadows Trail travels through part of the Neota Wilderness in open meadows. It goes over ridgelines that offer great views of the Medicine Bows and winds through old-growth forest of stately fir and spruce trees. It is a rolling trail with some small climbs and descents, but is generally downhill from Zimmerman Lake. It traverses and descends gently along the ridgeline for 1.5 miles, offering nice views of the Medicine Bow Range across the valley. Your best photo opportunity and a good place for a lunch break is at about 2.5 miles before you descend the ridge. At about 3 miles, the trail descends more steeply through the forest, which eventually gives way to an old clear-cut area where you enter a small meadow. At approximately 3.75 miles turn left and travel on Long Draw Road until you see the trail resume on the right. In another 0.5 mile, you reach the Meadows/Long Draw winter trailhead.

ZIMMERMAN LAKE & MEADOWS TRAIL

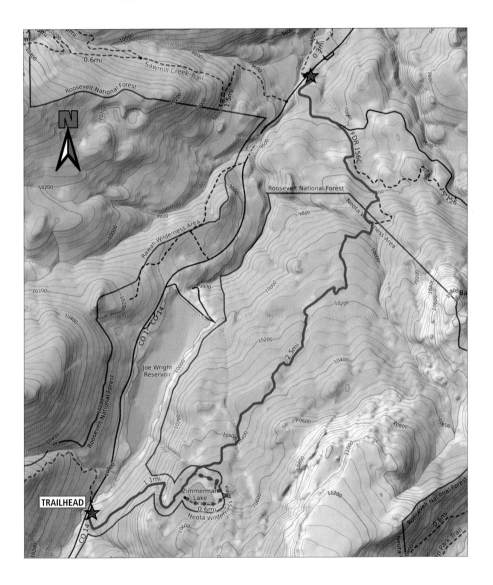

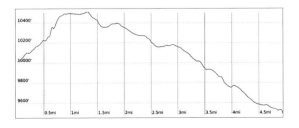

69. **Montgomery Pass Trail**

ROUND TRIP	3.5 miles
DIFFICULTY	Challenging
SKILL LEVEL	Advanced/intermediate
HIGH POINT	11,000 feet
ELEVATION GAIN	1,000 feet
AVALANCHE DANGER	Moderate to high near pass; can be avoided
MAP	Trails Illustrated #112, Poudre River, Cameron Pass
CONTACT	Canyon Lakes Ranger District, Roosevelt National Forest, 970-295-6700

COMMENT: This is one of the most rewarding and spectacular—but demanding—destinations in the Cameron Pass area that takes you high above treeline. It is a very popular area for telemark skiing and snowboarding because of the nice powder bowls northwest of the pass. The view from the pass is a panorama that includes the Nokhu Crags, Diamond Peaks, and the northern reaches of Rocky Mountain National Park. Going above the ski bowls is not recommended in times of high avalanche danger, though the trails to tree line below the bowls and the pass are fairly safe. This route to Montgomery Pass is much safer than the Diamond Peaks route that comes from Cameron Pass. There have been several avalanche deaths on Diamond Peaks.

You will need advanced ski skills and AT or telemark skis with skins to ski this trail. Skiing the bowls and the trail can be an exceptional powder day.

GETTING THERE: To reach Poudre Canyon, take US 287 north from Fort Collins for about 10 miles and exit west onto Highway 14 at Ted's Place. Take Highway 14 approximately 63 miles to the Zimmerman Lake Trailhead on the left side of the road before you reach Cameron Pass. The Montgomery Pass Trailhead is across Highway 14 and slightly to the right/north of the Zimmerman Lake Trailhead. It is well-marked but not easily visible from the road and can be spotted in the trees down the road from the Zimmerman Lake parking lot.

THE ROUTE: From the road, the trail climbs north gradually for the first 0.5 mile and then steepens following the Montgomery Creek drainage through trees. After about 0.5 mile, it veers to the left (slightly southwest). After 0.25 mile, it flattens out somewhat for another 0.25 mile, so you can catch your breath. It then steepens again. Overall it climbs west steadily at the rate of about 200 feet per 0.25 mile with alternating relatively flat and steep stretches. It is not extreme, but is not for the fainthearted or poorly conditioned, considering the elevation.

Ski bowls near Montgomery Pass.

At about 10,800 feet, at 1.25 miles, the trail starts to switchback steeply and opens up so you can see a small meadow ahead. There is a sign that shows that going straight uphill will take you to the ski bowl, while bearing right will take you toward the pass itself. The trail to the pass descends briefly before resuming its climb. The trail toward the bowl climbs very steeply for another 0.25 mile before mellowing somewhat. The next 0.5 mile to the top of the pass takes you out of the trees to spectacular, other-worldly views in all directions. Zimmerman Lake and Joe Wright Reservoir are to the east and north. The Medicine Bow Mountains and Clark Peak lie to the northwest, and the Nokhu Crags of Routt National Forest and Rocky Mountain National Park's Never Summer Mountains are to the southwest. It is often fairly breezy on top, and 10 degrees colder, but at least you don't have to worry about the afternoon thunderstorms of the summer climbing season. The worst you can face is a horizontal hurricane-force snow squall or whiteout; fortunately the latter is not a frequent occurrence. Depending on the weather, have a snack and then return down the trail or climb to the ridge top if avalanche danger is low.

You can ski south from the pass and traverse through the trees to the ski bowl area if there are no potentially dangerous cornices above. Stay low and don't make the trip if the cornices above are large due to avalanche hazard or if the avalanche ratings are above moderate. Be capable of digging a snow pit and evaluating it to be sure.

TIP: It's fun to enjoy skiing through the deep powder in the nearby bowls above the pass, or off-trail on the way down in the trees.

An alternate route down is in the Montgomery Creek drainage. You can make turns through the powder and float on top. This isn't advisable early in the season or if fallen timber and tree stumps are not covered by snow. Don't attempt this if you are alone.

MONTGOMERY PASS TRAIL

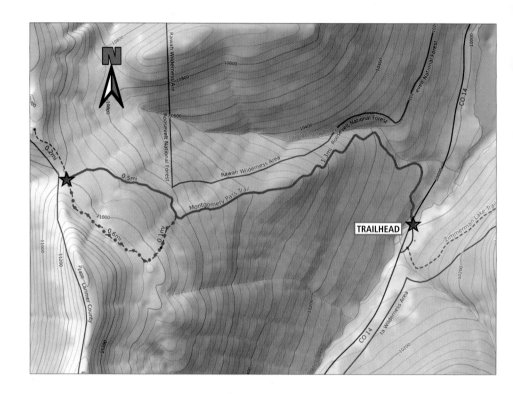

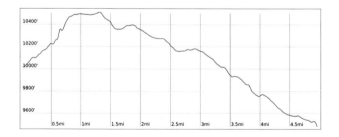

70. Cameron Connection Trail

ROUND TRIP	3.4 miles
DIFFICULTY	Easy
SKILL LEVEL	Novice to beginner
HIGH POINT	10,200 feet
ELEVATION GAIN	200 feet
AVALANCHE DANGER	None to low (one run-out zone)
MAP	Trails Illustrated #112, Poudre River, Cameron Pass
CONTACT	Canyon Lakes Ranger District, Roosevelt National Forest, 970-295-6700

COMMENT: This is a short, very scenic trail through an old-growth forest of spruce and fir that shares its trailhead with the Montgomery Pass Trail. It is often overlooked and is one of the easiest and most lightly used trails at Cameron Pass. It rolls gently through the tree cover with occasional views. It offers excellent shelter from prevailing winter windchill and, though it parallels the highway, is far enough from it to be completely buffered from its sound or sight. You can also start from the Cameron Pass summit parking lot or use two vehicles to make this a one-way trip. This trail is usable only in the winter because it crosses many streams and wetlands, so it is best to wait until mid-winter when the wetlands are frozen and covered. Experienced skiers can use any style of skis for this trail, skinny skis are usable because the trail is not steep.

GETTING THERE: To reach Poudre Canyon, take US 287 north from Fort Collins about 10 miles and exit west onto Highway 14 at Ted's Place. Take Highway 14 approximately 63 miles to the Zimmerman Lake parking lot, on the left side of the road, before you reach Cameron Pass. The Montgomery Pass Trailhead is across Highway 14, and slightly to the right/north of the Zimmerman Lake Trailhead. It is well-marked, but not easily visible from the road, and can be spotted in the trees down the road from the Zimmerman Lake parking lot. The Cameron Pass parking area is 1.5 miles west on the right/northwest side of the road. Blue diamonds mark the trail on the northeast side of the Cameron Pass parking area.

THE ROUTE: After parking in the Zimmerman Lake parking lot, go to the east end of the lot and cross Highway 14. The trailhead is hidden in the trees on the other side of the road next to the Montgomery Pass trail. Though the wind might be howling in the

Cameron Connection trailhead at Cameron Pass.

parking lot, you will be protected by trees on the trail. Sometimes the most difficult climb is getting up and over the drifted and plowed snow to the trailhead. From the Montgomery Pass Trailhead, turn left/southwest. You will see the sign for the Cameron Connection Trail. You will initially be paralleling Highway 14. The Cameron Connection climbs slowly and rolls gently southwest gaining 200 feet in about 1 mile, making it a good beginner's trail. The trail above Joe Wright Creek features beautiful spruce and fir trees that will shelter you from much of the wind most of the way on windy days.

At a little over 1 mile the trail nears the creek, following it more closely through three nice meadows with views of the Neota Wilderness near the pass. The meadow areas are the best places for photos. Reach the summit of Cameron Pass at about 1.7 miles. If you start at the Cameron Pass parking lot, the trail goes downhill at the start, and uphill for the finish, assuming you go out and back. If you want to extend your outing, go part way up the Montgomery Pass Trail and back. The first 0.5 mile is not that steep. If you want a significant aerobic workout, continue up to the steeper portions of the Montgomery Pass Trail before turning around, or go at a higher rate of speed on your way back. Since you will be at 10,000 feet, you will elevate your heart rate.

CAMERON CONNECTION TRAIL

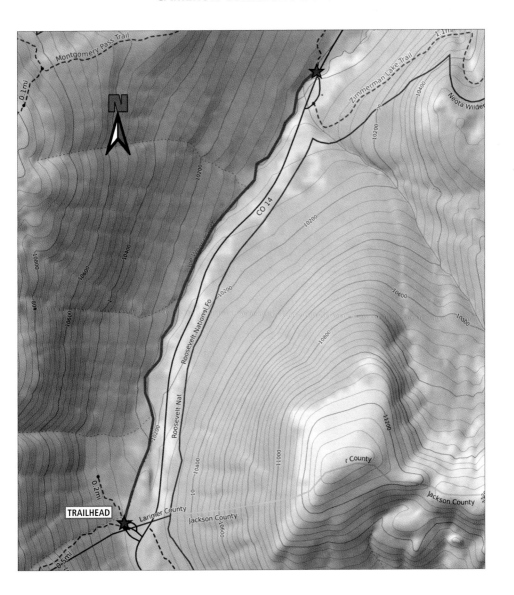

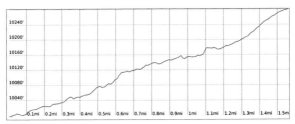

Thunder Pass view from Montgomery Pass bowls.

Chapter 13

COLORADO STATE FOREST

The sky opens above us, as clouds scud across the Divide
    in the setting sun.
The mountain ridgeline explodes with soaring spindrifts
    wind and snow descend to envelop us.
The trees sway, circle the trail,
    speak to us through the snow;
        on our finite planet,
        in our infinite universe.

—Alan Apt

The Colorado State Forest is made up of state trust lands that are, in this case, part of the Colorado State Park system. North of Highway 14, the state forest lies between the Routt and Roosevelt National Forests with the majestic backdrops of the Medicine Bow Mountains on its northern and eastern borders and the Never Summer Mountains of Rocky Mountain National Park on its southeastern border. Within the state forest are non-motorized and motorized trails. The Never Summer Yurt system and Michigan Reservoir cabins are available for rustic, overnight luxury.

Just driving west over Cameron Pass into Colorado State Forest is a treat because you get to enjoy several peaks on the northern border of Rocky Mountain National Park. First, you are greeted by the rugged splendor of the Nokhu Crags, with their rooster-top rocks and sparkling avalanche chutes. You can see Mount Richthofen peering over the Crags' shoulder, daring you to come back another day. Then you see the tail end of the Never Summer Mountains: Static Peak, Teepee Mountain, and, finally, Seven Utes. You also get to glimpse the edge of North Park and sample a piece of one of the least-developed recreational areas in the state, the Colorado State Forest.

71. Michigan Ditch, American Lakes, & Thunder Pass Trails

OPTION 1		
DISTANCE OF MICHIGAN DITCH TRAIL	Up to 5 miles
DIFFICULTY	Easy
SKILL LEVEL	Novice to beginner
HIGH POINT	10,249 feet
ELEVATION GAIN	200 feet
AVALANCHE DANGER	Low to none

OPTION 2		
ROUNDTRIP TO AMERICAN LAKES	9.8 miles (5 miles to trail junction)
DIFFICULTY	Easy to challenging
SKILL LEVEL	Novice to intermediate
HIGH POINT	11,240 feet
ELEVATION GAIN	960 feet
AVALANCHE DANGER	Low

OPTION 3		
ROUNDTRIP TO THUNDER PASS	10.3 miles (5 miles to trail junction)
DIFFICULTY	Challenging
SKILL LEVEL	Intermediate to expert
HIGH POINT	11,330 feet
ELEVATION GAIN	1,050 feet
AVALANCHE DANGER	Moderate to considerable

MAP	Trails Illustrated #200, Rocky Mountain National Park
CONTACT	Colorado State Forest State Park, 970-723-8366

COMMENT: This is one of the most popular trails in the Cameron Pass area because it has something for everyone. The almost-level trail is an excellent entrance to Thunder Pass and the Never Summer Mountains of Rocky Mountain National Park. It offers spectacular views of the Never Summer Mountains and Nokhu Crags across the Michigan River drainage, Diamond Peaks to the northwest, and North Park off in the distance to the southwest. It also features a gentle incline and very reliable snow. It can be savored by both beginners and backcountry adventurers who want to spend the night or surmount the pass. The trail is actually a Jeep road that is used to maintain the Michigan Ditch, which is part of the trans-mountain water storage system that funnels water from the western slope to the thirsty cities of the eastern slope. The ditch trail can be skied by beginners on skinny Nordic skis. It is more fun to use AT or telemark skis for Thunder Pass. The pass requires advanced skiing skills.

GETTING THERE: To reach Poudre Canyon, take US 287 north from Fort Collins about 10 miles and exit west onto Highway 14 at Ted's Place. Take Highway 14 west 65 miles to the top of Cameron Pass. Parking and toilet facilities are on the right/west side of the highway. The well-marked, gated trail is on the left/east side of Highway 14.

THE ROUTE: The almost flat Michigan Ditch Trail follows the road and Joe Wright Creek at first. If you are on a novice or family expedition, you can turn around in about 1 mile at some cabins. If you want more adventure and scenery, continue on the winding road. At about 1.25 miles, the highway turns west while the trail continues southeast. In another 0.75 mile, at a trail junction, continue straight. Reach the intersection with the trail to American Lakes and Thunder Pass in another 0.5 mile, at 2.5 miles.

From this junction, you can go to the right to continue following the Michigan Ditch Trail west around the bottom of the ridgeline of Nokhu Crags. This is an easy and short trek on a flat trail. You will cross to the south side of the drainage, stopping in less than a mile before reaching the avalanche chutes north of Nokhu Crags.

Or, at the junction you can go to the left on the American Lakes Trail, which climbs steadily toward the rocky panorama above treeline at 11,000 feet. This is a longer, more challenging route on a constantly climbing, rolling trail. There are some very steep stretches, but also some moderate to easy sections. You can essentially go as far and as high as you desire. Keep an eye on the time and allow enough daylight for your return. From the junction it is a little less than 2 miles to American Lakes. You reach the first lake at just under 5 miles, and a short distance later is the trail on the left to Thunder Pass. The trail straight ahead continues about 0.25 mile to the middle and upper lakes. The upper reaches of this trail offer very impressive views of the northern edge of the Never Summer Mountains, including the summit of Mount Richthofen.

The trail to Michigan Lakes.

The trail to Thunder Pass reaches its summit in another long 0.5 mile, at about 5 miles from the trailhead, unless you have included the lakes in your tour. If you make it to the top of Thunder Pass, you can see all the way down into the Colorado River drainage of Rocky Mountain National Park. Reaching the summit of Thunder Pass should only be attempted as an all-day adventure for the very fit and well prepared. You should have winter mountaineering gear with you. It is by no means dangerous, but is definitely a long, challenging day in high-altitude snow and cold, with some avalanche danger, especially if you venture off trail onto steep slopes.

MICHIGAN DITCH, AMERICAN LAKES, & THUNDER PASS TRAILS

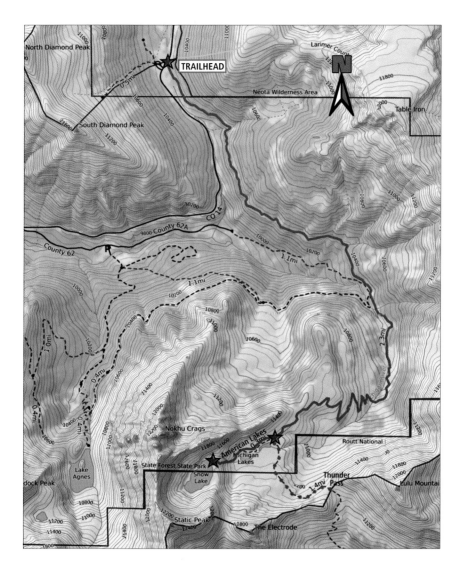

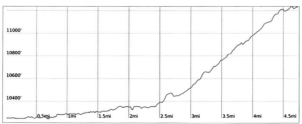

72. Lake Agnes

ROUND TRIP	5 miles
DIFFICULTY	Moderate to challenging
SKILL LEVEL	Intermediate
HIGH POINT	10,800 feet
ELEVATION GAIN	1,000 feet
AVALANCHE DANGER	Low to considerable
MAP	Trails Illustrated #200, Rocky Mountain National Park
CONTACT	Colorado State Forest State Park, 970-723-8366
RESTRICTIONS	A daily Colorado State Forest Pass is required for each vehicle. Carpool, since parking is limited.

COMMENT: This is a steep, popular, and spectacular trail. The first mile is shared with snowmobilers, but the last 1.5 miles are for snowshoers and skiers only. Experienced skiers can use any style of skis for this trail, but some of the steep descents on the return are more fun on wider skis.

GETTING THERE: To reach Poudre Canyon, take US 287 north from Fort Collins about 10 miles and exit west onto Highway 14 at Ted's Place. Take Highway 14 west 65 miles to Cameron Pass and continue 2.5 miles west of the pass. The trailhead is on the left/south side of Highway 14. You are likely to see several vehicles parked in the driveway and along the road.

THE ROUTE: The trail follows the campground road downhill into an open area where you have nice panoramic views of the Nokhu Crags and Iron Mountain. At the bottom of the road, in about 0.75 mile, the trail splits. Go right/south, uphill, crossing a footbridge. Going straight takes you up to the Michigan Ditch Trail and American Lakes on a route used by snowmobilers. Take the trail uphill into the trees where snowmobiles are not permitted. The trail is very steep in this section. Once you crest the hill at about 1 mile, the trail flattens out and comes out of the trees, so you can enjoy the stunning, panoramic view of the Never Summer Mountains. You will see the trail for the Agnes Creek Cabin/Nokhu Hut go downhill to the west; go straight unless you want to see it.

After about 1.25 miles, and 500 feet of gain, you will reach the summer trailhead and parking area. The view from this point is superb. If you have run out of gas, snap

Never Summer Mountains above Lake Agnes.

some photos and retrace your steps because the next section is very steep, gaining another 500 feet, and the trail can be buried in deep drifts, depending on your timing. In a good snow year, the trailhead outhouse will be almost covered by snowdrifts, so it is not open in the winter. The trail is marked with blue diamonds and travels to the left/southeast toward the Nokhu Crags. This area is the only section with avalanche hazard, unless you go to the south side of Lake Agnes. The route climbs steeply through the trees and it is sometimes difficult to follow the blue diamonds. If you lose the formal trail, head south toward the lake. Avoid getting too close to the Crags, especially if they are snow-covered. You will have to climb steeply over a hump that is higher than the lake and then descend 100 feet to the lake. You will reach Lake Agnes in a little under 2.5 miles. The lake is in a beautiful setting with a stunning ridgeline of the Never Summer Mountains as a backdrop. Stay away from the south side of the lake because of the avalanche hazard. There is no danger on the north side of the lake unless you wander over toward the Crags. Some skiers like to ski the bowls above the lake to the southwest. Do so only if you have excellent avalanche training and friends with beacons and shovels.

LAKE AGNES

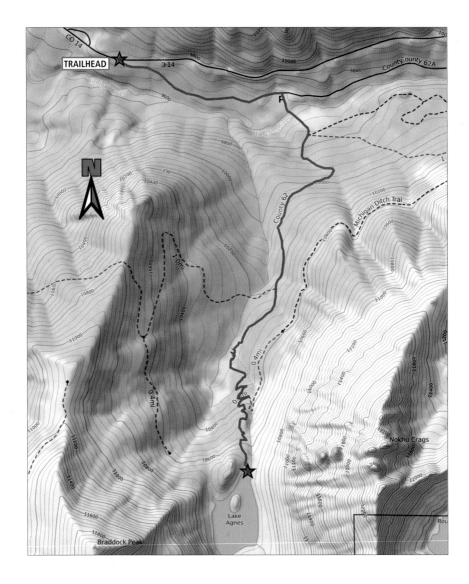

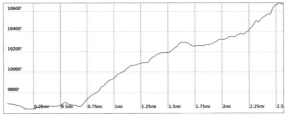

73. Seven Utes Mountain & Mount Mahler

OPTION 1		
ROUND TRIP TO SEVEN UTES MOUNTAIN	6.5 miles (2.75 miles to viewpoint)	
DIFFICULTY	Moderate to challenging	
SKILL LEVEL	Intermediate to expert, depending on conditions	
HIGH POINT	11,453 feet	
ELEVATION GAIN	2,000 feet	

OPTION 2		
ROUNDTRIP TO MOUNT MAHLER	8 miles (2.75 miles to viewpoint)	
DIFFICULTY	Moderate to challenging	
SKILL LEVEL	Intermediate to expert	
HIGH POINT	12,480 feet	
ELEVATION GAIN	3,000 feet	

AVALANCHE DANGER	Moderate to high at the upper portion; can be avoided
MAP	Trails Illustrated #200, Rocky Mountain National Park
CONTACT	Colorado State Forest State Park, 970-723-8366

COMMENT: These little-known mountains are nestled in Colorado State Forest at the edge of the Never Summer Range of Rocky Mountain National Park. They offer challenging trails with panoramic views of Mount Richthofen and the Diamond Peaks from the top of Seven Utes, and views of the Never Summer, Medicine Bow/Rawah, and Zirkel Ranges from the top of Mahler. Climbing these mountains in the winter is an adventure—with avalanche risks—that should be attempted only by very experienced skiers who are prepared. Knowing how to dig a snow pit and evaluate avalanche conditions is a recommended skill. Neither of these peaks should be attempted during times of high avalanche danger. Even beginners can have a very nice, satisfying shorter out-and-back trip that affords great views of the Diamond Peaks. If you can venture just a mile or two uphill on this gradually steepening trail, you will enjoy superb views of the Medicine Bow Range. And the closer you get to Seven Utes, the more impressive it is. The trailhead begins at the former site of a failed cross-country ski lodge that has since been torn down. There are no signs or markers for it.

Skiing this route to the summits is only for experienced skiers with AT or telemark skis and advanced ski skills, although less experienced skiers can enjoy an out-and-back short of the summits.

GETTING THERE: Take US 287 north from Fort Collins about 10 miles and exit west onto Highway 14 at Ted's Place. Take Highway 14 west 65 miles to Cameron Pass and continue west approximately 3.8 miles past the pass. Almost at the bottom of the hill, on the left/south side of the road, is a partially plowed drive angling to the southeast with a green gate. This is the former Seven Utes Lodge entrance. (If you reach the Ranger Lakes Campground, you have gone about 2 miles too far west.) Park in the driveway, or go down about another 0.25 mile to a turnout on the same side (south) and park there, then ski back on the road on the other side of the fence. The snow is likely to be deep enough for you to be able to step over the fence.

TIP: If you have trouble finding the trailhead, you can get directions at the State Forest Moose Visitor Center 2 miles west of the trailhead on Highway 14. It doesn't open until 9 a.m., however, so if you are planning an early start they won't be able to help you.

THE ROUTE: Take a look at your topographic map and the drainage you want to be in before starting; routefinding can be a bit tricky once you are in the trees and encountering lots of logging roads. The trail is just beyond the green gate, which is usually open. Go through the gate and take either of the next two trails you see on the right. They intersect after 200 yards. At first you go downhill for a short stretch, and gradually and then steeply uphill east and southeast on an old logging road. Ignore a trail going left/east near the crossing of the Michigan River, before the road steepens. There are no markers such as blue diamonds, but the trail is distinct even if you are the first one to use it.

Right after the trail gets significantly steeper, at about 0.75 mile, you intersect another wide, old logging road that is used by snowmobilers. Go to the left/east uphill on the road; you will see the continuing trail on the left as you round the very first hard right turn. It might not be well marked, so look carefully for it. Remember which drainage you want to be in—the one just east of Seven Utes Mountain—and the route will be more obvious. When you turn off the road, you will be on a narrow trail rather than an old road, with a 30- to 40-foot drop-off on your left. This continues for about 0.25 mile. There is a spectacular view of the Diamond Peaks behind you to the northeast. This 1-mile point is a good spot for a photo and snack break. This is also a good turnaround point for the inexperienced.

After approximately 200 yards, the trail crosses to the other side of the drainage, crossing the stream that is out of sight under the snow, unless your trip is too early in the season. The trail then goes east and south uphill and back into the trees, steepening considerably at a couple of big hairpins that straighten out at about 2 miles. It wanders around trees as you steadily make your way to treeline next to the drainage. You will see another ridge and peak to the right/west, which is Seven Utes. At intersecting

The mountains are (left to right): Nokhu Crags, Richthofen, and Mahler.

trails, bear to the right. When you emerge from the trees at about 2.75 miles, you can see Seven Utes to the right/southwest and Mount Mahler to the left/southeast. From this point you can choose to climb either.

The shorter, easier, and somewhat safer choice is Seven Utes. There is a trail going to the right/west across the top of the drainage cirque; that is your route over to Seven Utes. Once you cross the top of the drainage, pick the least steep route up to the saddle at about 3 miles and avoid areas that look like starting zones or runouts for avalanches. There are definitely avalanche hazards on this route, but you can avoid them. From the summit at 3.25 miles, enjoy views of the Never Summer Mountains or Rocky Mountain National Park and the Medicine Bow Mountains.

Mahler is a much higher summit that can be climbed from the same drainage as Seven Utes. There are many avalanche hazards on Mahler but it can be safely climbed if you stay on the southern shoulder of the mountain, pick your route carefully, and confirm reasonable snow stability with a snow pit. When you emerge from the trees at about 2.75 miles, where you can see Seven Utes to the right/west and Mount Mahler to the left/east, bear left/southeast. Continue uphill, bearing straight for a little more than 3 miles south and then go left, making your way away from the obvious avalanche zones and toward the right/south side of the mountain.

Avoid the dangerous potential avalanche zones dead-ahead on the west-facing slopes. The south ridge is not without some avalanche danger. From the south flank, carefully pick your way up to the top of the ridge saddle in a little more than 1 mile and then right (south and east) to the summit at 4 miles.

Enjoy views of the Nokhu Crags to the northeast, Richthofen a bit farther southeast, and the Never Summer Mountains and Zirkel Range visible to the south and west.

SEVEN UTES MOUNTAIN & MOUNT MAHLER

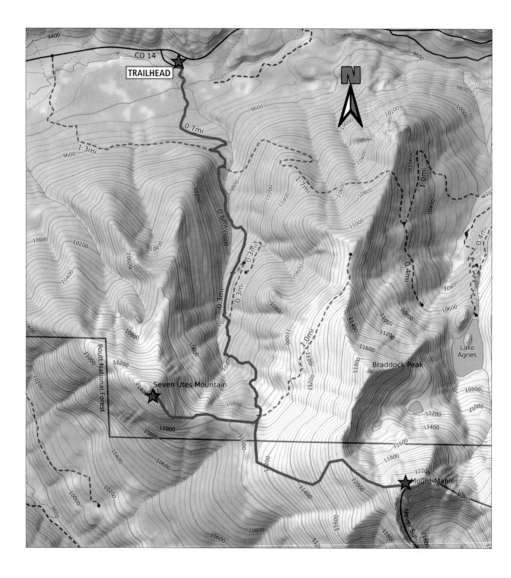

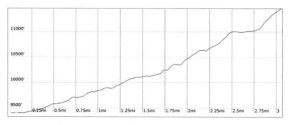

74. Ranger Lakes & Silver Creek

ROUND TRIP	3 miles to saddle; 10 miles to upper creek
DIFFICULTY	Easy to moderate
SKILL LEVEL	Novice to beginner
HIGH POINT	9,600 feet at saddle; 10,200 feet at upper creek
ELEVATION GAIN	300 feet to saddle; 900 feet to upper creek
AVALANCHE DANGER	None
MAP	Trails Illustrated #200, Rocky Mountain National Park
CONTACT	Colorado State Forest State Park, 970-723-8366

COMMENT: This easy-to-find trail starts at the Ranger Lakes Campground (closed in winter) on Highway 14, west of Cameron Pass. You can have an enjoyable and easy 3-mile round-trip jaunt to see the views, or continue on for more of a workout, although the rest of the trail is primarily a tree tunnel on what is a road in the summer until you climb over the ridge into the next drainage, where it opens up onto a spectacular valley surrounded by peaks. You might encounter snowmobilers on part of the trail/road.

Experienced skiers can use any style of skis for this trail, and it can be skied by beginners on skinny Nordic skis.

GETTING THERE: To reach Poudre Canyon, take US 287 north from Fort Collins about 10 miles and exit west onto Highway 14 at Ted's Place. Take Highway 14 west 65 miles to Cameron Pass and continue approximately 5.8 to 6 miles west of Cameron Pass to the Ranger Lakes Campground on the left/south side of the road. It is not heavily used, so you should be able to park in the entrance driveway. There is a recreational area parking lot another 0.8 mile west of the campground.

THE ROUTE: To find the trailhead, go downhill and keep the restroom on your right. Pass the campground loop road. You want the next trail on the right, which takes you west through the trees, and then alongside a somewhat open area that is tree-lined. It is almost flat at the outset and swings around Ranger Lakes, hidden in the trees, at about 0.5 mile. There are some trails on the left that go to Ranger Lakes if you want a short side trip to see the frozen lakes. The main trail then goes slightly downhill and emerges from the trees to give you a gorgeous view of the ridgeline of the Never Summer Mountains, Seven Utes Mountain, and Mount Mahler to the east. Cross the

Michigan Creek near Ranger Lakes.

Michigan River on a small bridge a little past 0.5 mile and enjoy the meadow and mountain views. This is a very good place for photos. The trail then reenters the trees and climbs uphill steeply for more than a mile, weaving through the thick trees with some meadow views. There is an intersection a little before 1.5 miles with confusing signs. Don't go left as the sign suggests for Silver Creek; bear right toward Illinois Pass. A little past the 1.5-mile mark, the trail crests a saddle with a few glimpses of the hills. Turn around here if you don't want to descend toward the Silver Creek drainage; it is another 2 miles to meadows.

Though the trail is in a beautiful and peaceful forest, you might encounter an occasional snowmobiler. At the intersection at 1.75 miles, turn left and follow the open, rolling trail into the Silver Creek drainage. Once you reach Silver Creek at 2.25 miles, follow it upstream and cross at about 2.75 miles. Wander through a beautiful meadow area to around 3.5 miles, where you can have a snack and reverse course, or continue to climb another 1.5 miles higher along the creek into the foothills of the Never Summer Mountains. You can continue for additional mileage or even set up a winter camp for the night.

RANGER LAKES & SILVER CREEK

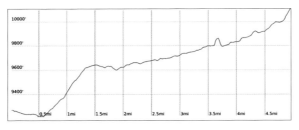

75. Grass Creek Yurt Trails

TRAIL LOOP	6 miles
ROUND TRIP TO END	9 miles
DIFFICULTY	Easy to moderate
SKILL LEVEL	Novice to beginner
HIGH POINT	9,200 feet on loop; 9,600 feet at end of trail
ELEVATION GAIN	200 feet on loop; 600 feet to end of trail
AVALANCHE DANGER	None
MAP	Never Summer Nordic Yurt System/Colorado State Forest
CONTACT	Colorado State Forest State Park, 970-723-8366; Never Summer Nordic, Inc., neversummernordic.com

COMMENT: This is one of the closest huts to visit, and it is near two nice trails: one a very easy loop trail, and the other an end-of-trail out-and-back that goes up a nice hill that can be used for repeated turns on skis. The setting is exceptional because of the backdrop of the Medicine Bow Mountains and Clark Peak towering above. You can also see the craggy Nokhu Crags along the way, gleaming in the distance in their own mountain world. Experienced skiers can use any style of skis for this trail, and it can be skied by beginners on Nordic skis.

GETTING THERE: To reach Poudre Canyon, take US 287 north from Fort Collins about 10 miles and exit west onto Highway 14 at Ted's Place. Take Highway 14 west 65 miles to Cameron Pass and continue west and then south over the pass 10 miles to Gould. Watch for signs on the right side of the highway for the State Forest campground and KOA. Turn right onto CR 41. Get a map from the unstaffed entrance station. Information is also available at the Moose Visitor Center south of Gould. Follow CR 41, a dirt and snow-packed road, approximately 4 miles east past the North Michigan Creek Reservoir and cabins to the parking area for the Grass Creek Yurt Trailhead on the left side of the road.

THE ROUTE: Cross the road to the trailhead. From the trailhead, travel east toward the yurt. At a trail junction in over 0.25 mile, continue straight/southeast. At about 0.75 mile, you will come to another trail junction.

If you want to trek on the loop trail, bear right and go directly past the yurt. (You can, of course, do the loop in either direction.) The trail will roll pleasantly and easily through the trees and in about 1.25 miles, after you have gone past the yurt, you will

PHOTO FROM NEVERSUMMER NORDIC, INC.

The Grass Creek Yurt.

climb more steeply up on top of a small ridge at 2.5 miles. Traverse the ridge and then turn left to meet the upper end of the loop at just past 3.5 miles. Go left to return to the trailhead, traveling the trail that parallels Grass Creek. In the summer, this is a road that affords a nice view of the yurt without passing too closely. At about 5.25 miles, complete the loop, and go straight 0.75 mile back to the trailhead.

If you prefer an out-and-back trek, take the trail straight ahead from the road where you parked, rather than traveling across the meadow and uphill to the yurt. The trail is a summertime road, so it is wide. You will roll pleasantly past pretty meadows and through a mixed forest. At a junction at 0.75 mile, take the left branch. If you want to practice jogging uphill and downhill on a gentle slope, this is a good place to do it. The trail continues to gradually climb up the draw for another 1.5 miles. At another junction a little past 2.25 miles, the other leg of the loop is to the right; go straight. As you continue straight ahead, you will reach Saw Mill Pile Hill, a steeper place to try hill activities if there is good powder. The trail continues uphill into thick trees. The end of the trail is about 4 miles out, giving you an 8-mile round-trip.

You can also combine the loop and the out-and-back, traveling up one leg of the loop and down the other on the way back for 9 miles total.

OTHER TRAILS TO EXPLORE: All of the other yurt trails are enjoyable outings: Ruby Jewel Trail and Jewel Lake below Clark Peak, Montgomery Pass Yurt Trail, and Dancing Moose Trail. You can ski all the way to Montgomery Pass with minimal avalanche danger.

GRASS CREEK YURT TRAILS

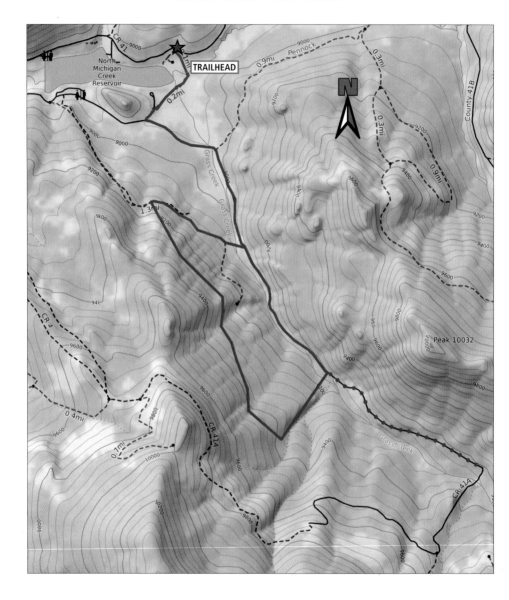

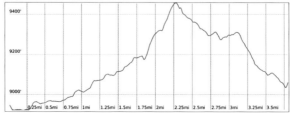

Chapter 14

STEAMBOAT SPRINGS AREA

"Winter is not a season, it's a celebration."

—Anamika Mishra

Although the Steamboat Springs area is a fair distance from the Front Range, it's impossible not to mention because it's one of the true winter wonderlands of the Rockies. Rabbit Ears Pass usually gets more than 300 inches of snow per year on average. Much of it is the "champagne powder" that has made the Steamboat Ski Resort famous and makes for a paradise on earth if you love cross-country skiing. You'll find deep, fluffy, powdery snow; snow draped fir trees; and ice crystals hanging in the air.

The trails on Rabbit Ears Pass usually see enough use to be packed down, making for easier travel. However, you might encounter very deep, unpacked snow on parts of the trails. Note that the great snow at Rabbit Ears Pass comes from rapidly changing and intense weather that can go from blue skies to blizzard in short order. Always check the forecast and be prepared for anything. Don't be dismayed by the droves of snowmobilers. The east end of Rabbit Ears Pass is reserved for snow motorists; the west end is for skiers and snowshoers. North Walton Peak Trail is the only trail where some overlap occurs.

A note on dogs at the pass: The West Summit Loop trails are heavily used, and dogs have been known to outnumber humans. The U.S. Forest Service requests that you leave your furry friends at home.

To reach Rabbit Ears Pass from Fort Collins, drive State Highway 14 west 65 miles to Cameron Pass, cross the Continental Divide, and continue 30 miles to Walden; then drive another 30 miles to US 40 at Muddy Pass. Rabbit Ears is a couple of miles west.

From Denver, take I-70 west 40 miles to Dillon, then take State Highway 9 north 38 miles to Kremmling, where you take US 40 north. It is 27 miles to Muddy Pass and the intersection with State Highway 14.

76. Walton Creek Loop 3A & North Walton Peak Trail 3C

OPTION 1		
	LOOP 3A	1.6 miles
	DIFFICULTY	Easy to moderate
	SKILL LEVEL	Novice
	HIGH POINT	9,600 feet
	ELEVATION GAIN	200 feet

OPTION 2		
	ROUND TRIP TO PEAK	6 miles
	DIFFICULTY	Moderate
	SKILL LEVEL	Novice to intermediate
	HIGH POINT	10,140 feet
	ELEVATION GAIN	640 feet

AVALANCHE DANGER	Low
MAPS	Trails Illustrated Rabbit Ears Pass, Steamboat Springs; USFS Rabbit Ears Pass Ski Route
CONTACT	Hahns Peak Ranger District, Routt National Forest, 970-870-2299
NOTE	The West Summit Loop trails are heavily used, and dogs have been known to outnumber humans. The U.S. Forest Service requests that you leave your furry friends at home.

COMMENT: This is the first set of cross-country ski trails you come to if you are traveling west on Rabbit Ears Pass. The Walton Creek trails are marked on the Forest Service map as 3A (campground loop), 3B (connector to the West Summit loops), and 3C (to North Walton Peak). There are no markings on the trails to tell you where you are in the system, but there is a detailed map at the trailhead, so it isn't too difficult to sort out. If you get confused, the best strategy is simply to reverse course to your car; keep track of the distance and time you have traveled in case you miss one of the trails.

The scenery is comely enough to support out-and-back travel too. Walton Creek Loop 3A is actually side-by-side loops that circle through the campground, the pretty creek drainage, and the wetlands area, with the usual array of picturesque, snow-

Skiers on the Walton Creek Loop trail.

draped blue spruce and fir trees. North Walton Peak Trail 3C is an easy route to follow because after the first 0.25 mile it is actually a summer road that is shared with snow-mobilers. (The other trails in this area are for non-motorized travel only.) Once you reach the road, the firmly packed surface makes for a fast ascent to the summit and sweeping views of Rabbit Ears Pass and part of the Yampa Valley in the distance to the west. Skinny skis are adequate, but midwidth skis are more fun on the peak.

GETTING THERE: From the State Highway 14 and US 40 junction at Muddy Pass, drive west on US 40 approximately 5 miles to Rabbit Ears Pass. The trailheads are approximately 18 miles east of Steamboat Springs. The trail parking lot is on the south side of US 40.

THE ROUTE: Walton Creek Loop 3A: Look for the knoll at the south end of the parking lot and go to the right/west; follow the power line for about 100 yards. Then turn left/southwest, cross Walton Creek (usually not visible), and go through the Walton Creek Campground. At 0.5 mile, reach a junction in the meadow just south of the campground (to the right is connector trail 3B to the West Summit loops); stay left. Walton Creek Loop 3A climbs steeply and at about 0.75 mile, tops a ridge. You then go downhill through an open area back to Walton Creek, passing through wetlands and willows before reaching another trail intersection at just past 1 mile; North Walton Peak Trail 3C goes to the right. Go left and follow Walton Creek mile back to the parking lot. (You can also combine the loop and the peak trail by going to the right here for a 6.5-mile trek.)

North Walton Peak Trail 3C: From the parking lot, take the trail that is closest to the Walton Creek trail marker and map, on the left/east side of the knoll. There is a trail on the right (the beginning of Loop 3A), which you should ignore. When you leave the parking lot, you go downhill to the southeast almost immediately, along Walton Creek. When you get to the bottom of the short hill, you are on the east side of a meadow that is a wetlands in the summer. There is a blue trail marker to your left that marks the trail's entry into the trees; proceed straight/left when you pass trail junctions in the first 0.5 mile. At about 0.6 mile, stay left when another trail comes in from the right (the other leg of Loop 3A). You travel through a small but very pretty valley while climbing gently uphill, winding through the trees.

At 1 mile, the trail dead-ends at North Walton Peak Road, which is shared with a few snowmobilers. Go to the right to reach the top of North Walton Peak. You will see two peaks with radio towers; North Walton Peak is the closest and least visible of the two. The firmly packed road surface makes for a fast ascent. The road is a bit of a tree tunnel at first, but the summit view is worth the trek. At about 1.5 miles the road veers sharply right/west and follows just below a ridgeline for 0.75 mile to a saddle at about 2.25 miles, then switchbacks south and west again before heading northwest the last 0.75 mile to the summit and sweeping views. Reverse course to return to the parking lot.

OTHER TRAILS TO EXPLORE: Connector trail 3B travels west, paralleling the highway and taking you to the West Summit trails parking area in about 3.25 miles. This is a nice option with a car shuttle.

SEE MAP ON PAGE 275

77. Fox Curve Loop 2B

LOOP	3.25 miles
DIFFICULTY	Moderate
SKILL LEVEL	Intermediate
HIGH POINT	9,600 feet
ELEVATION GAIN	200 feet
AVALANCHE DANGER	None to low (steep slope at start)
MAPS	Trails Illustrated Rabbit Ears Pass, Steamboat Springs; USFS Rabbit Ears Pass Ski Routes
CONTACT	Hahns Peak Ranger District, Routt National Forest, 970-870-2299
NOTE	The West Summit Loop trails are heavily used, and dogs have been known to outnumber humans. The U.S. Forest Service requests that you leave your furry friends at home.

COMMENT: Featuring a variety of scenery and usually superb powder, this loop can also be done as a very satisfying out-and-back of any length. It starts on a steep downhill, travels through a beautiful meadow and the edge of the forest, and then rolls up and down a couple of hills. Skinny skis are good for this trail.

GETTING THERE: From the junction of State Highway 14 and US 40 at Muddy Pass, drive west on US 40 approximately 6 miles. The trailhead is 17 miles east of Steamboat Springs. The parking area is on the north side of the highway.

THE ROUTE: Start at the west end of the parking lot. Go around the low fence to the right and you will see the trail going into the trees. Follow the loop clockwise (turn to the left) because it is much easier to follow. It also makes for a better out-and-back journey if you don't want to complete the entire loop. The trail tracks north and down the steep hill, descending into a meadow area. There are often several routes down to the meadow. When you reach the meadow, stay left and track west to reach the foot of the hill on the north end of the meadow, and then angle north. The trail travels north along the bottom of the east-sloping hill and goes into the trees at the northwest corner of the meadow. (You can use this hill for a fun side excursion in the deep powder if avalanche danger is minimal.)

The trail finishes its 200-foot descent, crosses Walton Creek at a side stream at just past 0.6 mile, and then climbs fairly gradually as it tracks northeast, into and out of the trees, following the stream drainage in a more heavily forested area. At about

1.25 miles, the trail turns southeast, gently climbing toward an open beaver pond area at 9,400 feet. After crossing the wetlands at 1.75 miles, the trail begins to climb steadily and somewhat steeply for 200 feet to surmount the 9,600-foot ridge at just past 2 miles. This is a good place for a snack or lunch because of the view. Descend from the ridge top, heading south. The last mile of the trail can be difficult to follow if you are breaking trail because it isn't well marked. At about 2.5 miles, curve to the west, continuing your 300-foot descent; at about 2.8 miles, stay on the ridgeline at about 9,300 feet and curve south to reach Walton Creek again at about 3.25 miles. Climb 100 feet to reach the parking lot.

SEE MAP ON PAGE 275

78. West Summit Loop 1B

LOOP	4.2 miles
DIFFICULTY	Moderate
SKILL LEVEL	Novice to intermediate
HIGH POINT	9,520 feet
ELEVATION GAIN	200 feet
AVALANCHE DANGER	Low (can be avoided; check conditions)
MAPS	Trails Illustrated Rabbit Ears Pass, Steamboat Springs, USFS Rabbit Ears Pass Ski Routes
CONTACT	Hahns Peak Ranger District, Routt National Forest, 970-870-2299
NOTE	The West Summit Loop trails are heavily used, and dogs have been known to outnumber humans. The U.S. Forest Service requests that you leave your furry friends at home.

COMMENT: The west end of Rabbit Ears Pass is a real treat for beginners or novices, although there are good intermediate-level trails here too. Trails here feature gradual climbs and beautiful vistas of the Yampa Valley, and are generally well marked. The very deep powder can at times make for challenging conditions, although the heavy usage usually means the trails are broken and well packed. Loop 1B is the easier of the two West Summit loops because Loop 1A has more ascents and descents.

GETTING THERE: From the State Highway 14 and US 40 junction at Muddy Pass, drive west on US 40 approximately 10 miles and watch for a large sign alerting you to

The author and friends on the West Summit Loop Trail.

the last parking area on the right. The trailhead is 13 miles east of Steamboat Springs. There are places to park on both sides of the road; use the pull-off on the north side of the highway. (The pull-off on the south side of the highway is for intermediate/expert trails 1C and 3B.) Skinny skis are adequate.

THE ROUTE: Go to the west end of the parking lot and look for a trail sign and a trail going to the right/north up a short hill. This is the 0.15-mile connector trail. Though the hill is a short one, it will immediately let you know that you are at 9,400 feet and that pacing yourself is important. At the top of the hill you can go left (west) or right (east). Either choice takes you into Loop 1A; for Loop 1B, go right.

The trail goes slightly downhill on a former road, paralleling US 40 for a very short stretch, then goes left through the trees. There are some small hills on both sides of the trail that are fun for jumping or rolling in the snow, which is only recommended if you are dressed in waterproof gear. In just under 0.5 mile, the trail descends to a wetlands area that is usually under several feet of snow in mid-winter. Here you reach a junction. Loop 1B's return leg is to the right; stay left on the 0.15-mile section of trail that overlaps for both loops.

The trail takes a sharp left through a beautiful meadow area that is rimmed by stately aspen and pine trees and then goes up the hill. Your goal is the beautiful grove of aspen trees at the top of the hill. If the willows are still exposed early in the season, angle northeast and then back northwest to avoid them. At the trail intersection at 0.6

mile, Loop 1A goes left; bear right on Loop 1B. (You can include a side trip left to the top of the ridge in 0.4 mile on Loop 1A first if you like.) Near this junction there's a great view of the Hahns Peak area to the west and north of Steamboat.

Turning right, continue to climb northeast through the trees and then reach some ridge-top meadow areas with nice views as you approach the high point at 1 mile. You then descend north 400 feet in 0.75 mile, skirting a wetlands area with a colorful mixture of aspen, pine, and red willows. The trail climbs northwest and at 2.1 miles, turns to the right/southeast to 9,300 feet, with some nice views of the wetlands and creek covered in a thick blanket of powder. At about 3 miles the trail heads southwest, climbing about 100 feet in 0.5 mile and then dropping again as you head west back toward the start. At 3.8 miles, reach the connector trail and turn left. The last 0.4 mile parallels US 40.

SEE MAP ON PAGE 275

79. West Summit Loop 1A

LOOP	3.5 miles
DIFFICULTY	Moderate
SKILL LEVEL	Novice to intermediate
HIGH POINT	9,700 feet
ELEVATION GAIN	400 feet
AVALANCHE DANGER	Low (can be avoided; check conditions)
MAPS	Trails Illustrated Rabbit Ears Pass, Steamboat Springs, USFS Rabbit Ears Pass Ski Routes
CONTACT	Hahns Peak Ranger District, Routt National Forest, 970-870-2299
NOTE	The West Summit Loop trails are heavily used, and dogs have been known to outnumber humans. The U.S. Forest Service requests that you leave your furry friends at home.

COMMENT: At the west end of Rabbit Ears Pass, the more difficult of the two West Summit loops—1A—offers a variety of ascents and descents. You have a broad, easy start followed by a gradual climb up to the ridgeline for great views. On a clear day, you will be treated to spectacular views of the Elk Valley to the north, the low hills of the Zirkel Range to the east, and the Flat Tops to the south. Skinny skis are adequate.

GETTING THERE: Follow the driving directions for West Summit Loop 1B.

THE ROUTE: Go to the west end of the parking lot and look for a trail sign and a trail going to the right/north up a short hill. This is the 0.15-mile connector trail. Though the hill is a short one, it will immediately let you know that you are at 9,400 feet and that pacing yourself is important. At the top of the hill you can go left/west or right/east. Either choice takes you into Loop 1A.

To do the entire Loop 1A, go right (counterclockwise) because the trail is easier to follow. The trail goes slightly downhill on a former road, paralleling US 40 for a very short stretch, then goes left through the trees. There are some small hills on both sides of the trail that are fun for jumping or rolling in the snow, which is only recommended if you are dressed in waterproof gear. In just under 0.5 mile, the trail descends to a wetlands area that is usually under several feet of snow at mid-winter. Here you reach a junction. Loop 1B's return leg is to the right; stay left on the 0.15-mile section of trail that overlaps for both loops. The trail takes a sharp left through a beautiful meadow area that is rimmed by stately aspen and pine trees and then goes up the hill. If the willows are still exposed early in the season, angle northeast, then back northwest to avoid them. At the trail intersection at 0.6 mile, Loop 1B goes right; bear left on Loop 1A.

Continue your climb northwest and then north up the hill and through the grove of aspen trees to reach the ridge line at 9,700 feet at just past 1 mile. On a clear day you will have spectacular 360-degree views. If there are beginners in your party, this is a good place to turn around.

Continue west and then south on Loop 1A to enjoy a ridge ski for more than 0.5 mile. The trail offers a nice variety of forested and open-meadow trekking. At about 1.75 miles, begin a significant downhill that descends to 9,400 feet at 2.3 miles. When you reach the telephone line a short climb later, watch carefully for the trail marker, because the trail turns sharply left. Descend 150 feet into a drainage and then regain it at a small saddle at about 3 miles. Descend 0.3 mile back to the connector trail and then climb gradually back to your car in 3.5 miles.

TIP: The easiest option for beginners is a short out-and-back to the left (clockwise) on part of Loop 1A. It has some very pleasing scenery and a good view of the Flat Tops, though it doesn't have the great views that doing the entire loop offers.

OTHER TRAILS TO EXPLORE: West Summit Loop 1C, on the south side of Rabbit Ears Pass across from Loops 1A and 1B, is not as scenic but is a moderate, much less crowded trail.

SEE MAP ON PAGE 275

WALTON CREEK LOOP 3A – NORTH WALTON PEAK TRAIL 3C
FOX CURVE LOOP 2B – WEST SUMMIT LOOP TRAILS 1A & 1B

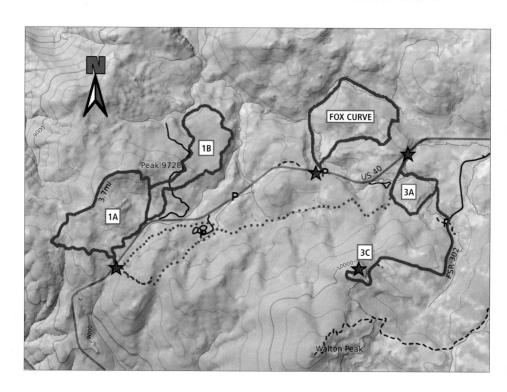

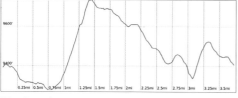

West Summit Loop 1A

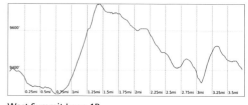

West Summit Loop 1B

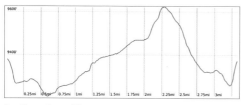

Fox Curve Loop 2B

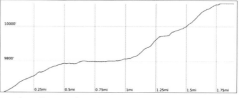

North Walton Peak Trail 3C

80. Spronks Creek & Chapman/Bench Trails

LOOP	4.8 miles
DIFFICULTY	Easy to moderate
SKILL LEVEL	Novice to intermediate
HIGH POINT	9,400 feet
ELEVATION GAIN	800 feet
AVALANCHE DANGER	Low
MAP	USFS Dunckley Pass Ski Trails
CONTACT	Yampa Ranger District, Routt National Forest, 970-638-4516

COMMENT: Nestled in the Dunckley Flat Tops, these lightly used trails offer a subtle beauty away from the hustle of Steamboat Springs and Rabbit Ears Pass. The Chapman/Bench Trail-Spronks Creek Trail loop is a very rewarding adventure for the reasonably fit if you take your time and brings lots of water; you will work up a good head of steam chugging uphill. The mountainside gets lots of late-morning sun in the winter, the kind that warms both the body and the soul, and it can get quite toasty. Dress in layers that can be deposited in a pack on the way up; when you reach the summit and start down the north slope and the wind whistles off the Flat Tops, you will want to fish those layers out and put them back on your rapidly cooling tendons, lest they talk back to you on the return trip.

The trail offers views of the Yampa Valley and, when you reach the heights of The Bench, superb views of the Dunckley Flat Tops and a beautiful high-mountain vale. The Chapman/Bench Trail, a steady, fairly steep climb that switchbacks uphill on an old road, is not recommended for small children or the marginally fit. Allow at least 3 hours; it might take you most of the day if the snow conditions are challenging. However, the Spronks Creek Trail is a relatively short but beautiful trail through a pretty aspen forest with nice views of the southern part of the Yampa Valley. You can do just this leg of the loop and retrace your route back to the trailhead for an easier route. Midwidth skis are best, but skinny skis are adequare for experienced skiers.

GETTING THERE: Take State Highway 131 to Phippsburg; when you are near the south boundary of Phippsburg, slow down and turn onto CR 16 to the west. Though this road is paved, you soon reach the unpaved Dunckley Pass Road at the first intersection; turn right. Dunckley Pass Road is closed in winter, but the closure is beyond the non-motorized trails for snowshoers and cross-country skiers. Watch for the last cattle guard before the closure. The trails are on the left, just beyond the cattle guard. There is a U.S. Forest Service stand with a map, and there are usually individual trail maps too.

THE ROUTE: From the trailhead, the trail rolls fairly gently downhill for the first 0.75 mile or so. At about 0.4 mile, there is an intersection (to the left is the Aspen Flats Loop Trail, your return leg, which continues to go downhill). The more challenging Chapman/Bench Trail goes to the right, continuing above Aspen Flats for 0.3 mile. At another trail junction at 0.7 mile (Spronks Creek Trail, your return leg, is to the left), stay right on the trail that goes charging uphill. After the trail stops switchbacking at about 1 mile, it climbs steadily through the very tall pine, fir, and aspens, cresting temporarily in a small meadow at a trail junction just past 1.25 miles. Before turning left here, go straight through the trees to the edge of the ridge and enjoy one of the better views in the Flat Tops. This is a good place to stop for photos and a rest break or snack. (You can retrace your steps to the trailhead from here for a good 2- or 3-hour out-and-back excursion of about 2.5 miles.)

Photo by Rasmus Svinding; Pexels

IF YOU SEE A BEAR

Black bears in Colorado hibernate. They snooze from mid-December to mid-March or April, with the males emerging first. Unlike humans, they lose fat, not muscle, while they sleep. They bed down in natural caves, snow caves, hollow trees, and logs. In colder climes some bears gather twigs and bark and just wait for Mother Nature to blanket them with snow. If you encounter a bear, back away slowly and speak softly. Do not run. Bears can run 35 miles per hour, so don't try to outrun one, and they can also climb trees. They are omnivores, but prefer nuts, berries, and plants. Just hope you don't look interesting, threatening, or tasty.

Back at the trail junction, the trail to the right (west then northwest) is the Chapman Cutoff Trail; instead, bear left (east, then south); it is immediately scenic. The trail goes downhill through the trees close to the western edge of the ridge line. At about 1.75 miles it bottoms out and reaches another trail junction (to the right is the Long Run Trail); continue straight/left, gradually veering east. Now you're on the Crosho Lake Trail, which meanders 0.75 mile east to another trail junction at 2.5 miles. The Crosho Lake Turnoff is to the right; keep going straight/left on the Crosho Lake Trail, which turns north downhill and at about 3 miles reaches a barbed wire fence.

Continue north to bottom out near the other end of the barbed wire fence at 3.25 miles, where the Spronks Creek Trail begins. Here, bear left (west) to make a climb back out to the trailhead. The draw is very narrow near the bottom, and deep snow can make it somewhat difficult to follow the actual summer trail. Just follow the drainage up the hill. You will be well rewarded for the effort by the colorful mixture of magnificent meadows, wetlands, and stately aspen, pine, and fir trees. The climb out is certainly easier than the climb up The Bench, but might seem longer or more difficult than it is because it is at the end of your trip. As you start ascending, stay on the left/south, side of the drainage; as the trail enters a small meadow at about 3.75 miles, stay on the left edge of the meadow. It can be difficult to follow if you are the first to break trail.

Just before 4 miles, you will encounter a trail intersection (straight ahead is the Chapman/ Bench Trail you started on); go to the right on the east side of the Aspen Flats Loop Trail. Bear right at all intersections to head back to the trailhead. It is a short, easy climb to a flat spot at 4.25 miles that provides a nice overlook of the aspen forest rolling to the valley below and of Rattlesnake Butte next to the Dunckley Pass Road. Once past the view, at about 4.5 miles, you encounter the other leg of the Aspen Flats Loop Trail—also the Chapman/Bench Trail you started on. You have nice views back toward Yampa; a good photo opportunity is just beyond the trail junction, on the right/east side of the trail. The trail rolls fairly gently uphill for the last 0.3 mile or so.

You can also do this return leg in reverse as a short out-and-back to Spronks Creek; when you bottom out at the fence line, simply retrace your route back to the trailhead for a 3.2-mile round-trip.

OTHER TRAILS TO EXPLORE: The trail to Crosho Lake is an easy side trip that can extend either the large loop or a Spronks Creek out-and-back.

The Long Run trail is an ambitious, challenging all-day adventure.

The Dunckley Pass Road/Chapman Cutoff Trail Loop winds considerably through thick tree cover and eventually tops out on The Bench. It is a steep, challenging route, and if it is early in the season and the snow cover is thin, it has a lot of fallen trees and stumps that are not covered by snow. Because of the thick tree cover, you won't see much until you top out. The proximity to Dunckley Pass Road means the musical whine of snowmobiles will reach your ears, reminding you of buzzing bees.

Wildcat Alley Trail is a nice short and easy loop side trip for Dunckley Pass Road.

SPRONKS CREEK & CHAPMAN/BENCH TRAILS

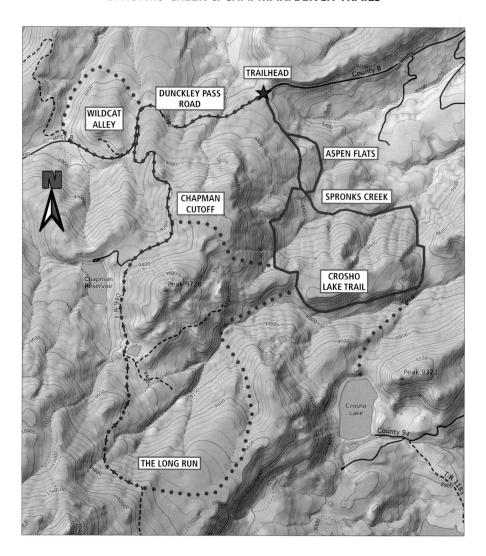

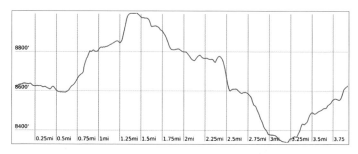

South Central Colorado

Chapter 15

COMO AREA

"I wish to preach not the doctrine of ignoble ease, but the doctrine of the strenuous life."

—President Theodore Roosevelt, speech before the Hamilton Club

One of the hidden treasures of the state, the unincorporated town of Como has a magnificent backdrop; it is the recreational gateway to Boreas Pass and the Gold Dust Trails, both of which are delightful ways to enjoy the scenic Tarryall Mountains, Tenmile Range, and Mosquito Range. Como is 9 miles north of Fairplay, on the northern end of scenic South Park. It was founded during the gold and silver mining boom that started in 1859. The scars of mining in the area are more readily visible when the snow melts. The town was named by Italian miners from Como, Italy, who worked locally looking for gold. There are presently no services in Como, other than a private Christian Camp and post office, though it is rumored that there is a general store. You can be sure of supplies in Fairplay.

The road to Como is plowed, and generally passable to passenger cars with good snow tires, but a four-wheel-drive vehicle is a good idea after major snowstorms. Be aware that the road may be passable in the morning, and not passable by afternoon because of drifting snow. Boreas Pass Road and the South Gold Dust Trails are the

THE DENVER, SOUTH PARK, & PACIFIC RAILROAD

The Denver, South Park, & Pacific Railroad operated in the Kenosha Pass and Como area traveling south from Denver in the late 1800s, to support miners during the gold and silver boom. It was a narrow-gauge railroad that generally followed the route of current US Highway 285. It reached Kenosha Pass in 1879 and eventually connected to Buena Vista and Gunnison. An engine from the railroad is on exhibit in the South Park Museum in Fairplay.

closest to Como. Boreas passed is closed to vehicles but open to snowmobiles during the winter.

If you are driving from Denver, you will reach Kenosha Pass before reaching Como; it is 10 miles north of Como. Kenosha Pass, at 10,000 feet, offers easy access to the popular Colorado Trail. It also offers a magnificent view of South Park and the 14,000-foot peaks of the Mosquito and Tenmile Ranges. This group of mountains is much more impressive when snowcapped and viewed from a distance than they are dotted by droves of people climbing them in the summer.

Kenosha Pass West looking at the fourteeners of the Mosquito Range.

81. Kenosha Pass — Colorado Trail West

ROUND TRIP	10 miles with a 0.8-mile side trip
DIFFICULTY	Easy to moderate
SKILL LEVEL	Intermediate
HIGH POINT	10,300 feet
ELEVATION GAIN	300 feet to viewpoint; Elevation loss up to 800 feet
AVALANCHE DANGER	None
MAP	Trails Illustrated #105, Tarryall Mountains, Kenosha Pass
CONTACT	South Park Ranger District, Pike National Forest, 719-836-2031

COMMENT: This very popular summer trail is also frequently used in the winter, but relatively lightly compared to many trails closer to Denver. This segment of the Colorado Trail on the west side of Kenosha Pass makes for short, easy out-and-back family excursions or more ambitious adventures. The first 2 miles of the trail is a very gradual climb, emerging out of the trees to a panoramic view of South Park, and the massive backdrop of the 14,000-foot wall of the Mosquito Range. On the way up the trail, you get some scenic glimpses of the Tarryall Mountains to the north, too. Avalanches are unlikely. The steep descent on the return makes wider skis a better option.

GETTING THERE: From Denver, go southwest on US 285. At about 65 miles you reach Kenosha Pass. Park on the west side of US 285 outside the Kenosha Pass Campground, which closes for the winter. The Colorado Trail is on the south/right side of the closed road as soon as you enter the campground.

THE ROUTE: Go through the main gated entrance that is straight ahead for the Colorado Trail (1776), and USFS Trail 849. If you go up the campground road, you will also see a sign for the Colorado Trail and the 849 trail that dead-ends on the ridge top to the south. Bear left, and follow the Colorado Trail 1776; it is well marked. The Colorado Trail heads northwest. At first you are in a very thick tree tunnel as you climb 150 feet, steadily but gradually, to about 0.5 mile, where you will cross a power line.

TIP: If you want to see views of South Park and the Mosquito Range more quickly, you can take the 849 trail that goes south and west from the main trailhead, or connect with trail 849 when you reach the power line by turning south/left uphill. You can

Looking across South Park from the Colorado Trail on Kenosha Pass.

enjoy some deep unpacked powder on this side trip, but this might also mean breaking trail and sinking down into the powder. The 849 trail is not well marked, and its route can be very confusing with multiple social trails. Just bear south and then west up the ridge. This side trip is approximately a 1-mile roundtrip, with some steep climbing to mount the ridge, where it dead-ends. After you top out in the view area at about 0.6 mile from the Colorado Trail, turn around and go back down 849 to the Colorado Trail. When you come back to the power line, you can use this open area as a connector between the trails to get back to the Colorado Trail and continue your trek to the west. From the 849 trail area, descend the power line to the north and then turn left/ west on the Colorado Trail.

If you stay on the Colorado Trail and skip the 849 side-trip excursion, you will climb gradually in the trees and gain another 150 feet over the next 1 mile before it levels off and then starts to go downhill to emerge from the trees. There is a stunning view of South Park and the Mosquito Range and a bench for a snack break. This part of the trail slants to the south so the snow can be very thin to nonexistent early or late in the season. After about 200 yards of downhill travel, it reenters more trees so the snow should improve.

Once you descend, the trail gently rolls. At just short of 1.5 miles the trail overlooks Baker Lake (private); if you turn around near here you will have about a 3-mile round-trip and about 400 feet in total elevation gain. In another 0.25 mile, the trail starts dropping down to Baker Lake's outlet stream, the low point of this route.

Continuing on from the Baker Lake overlook, you lose around 250 feet as you drop down 0.75 mile to the outlet stream, crossing it and then Guernsey Creek at 2.5 miles. Then you climb steadily but gradually, regaining those 250 feet and gaining another 250 feet in the next mile as you meander into and out of the trees. At about 3.75 miles you drop to cross another stream, rise again on the other side, and then at about 4.25 miles you descend 200 feet on the side of Jefferson Hill to Jefferson Creek Campground at around 5 miles (9,900 feet). As always, be cautious and turn around early if the weather is changing and a storm is blowing in.

KENOSHA PASS – COLORADO TRAIL WEST

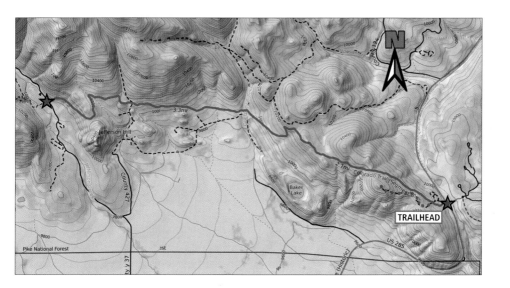

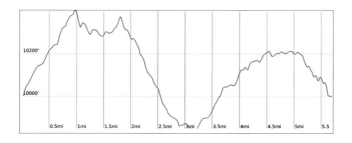

82. **Kenosha Pass — Colorado Trail East**

ROUND TRIP	3 miles
DIFFICULTY	Easy
SKILL LEVEL	Advanced beginner
HIGH POINT	10,350 feet
ELEVATION GAIN	350 feet
AVALANCHE DANGER	None
MAP	Trails Illustrated #105, Tarryall Mountains, Kenosha Pass
CONTACT	South Park Ranger District, Pike National Forest, 719-836-2031

COMMENT: This section of the Colorado Trail features sweeping views of South Park, magnificent aspen groves, and meadows. It is an easier excursion than the West Kenosha Pass option because it is more of a rolling trail and not as steep a climb. It is also easy to make this a short excursion of any length and enjoy nice views of South Park and the distant mountains. Experienced skiers can use any style of ski for this route.

GETTING THERE: From Denver go southwest on US 285. At about 65 miles you reach Kenosha Pass. Park on the west side of US 285 outside the Kenosha Pass Campground, which closes for the winter. The Colorado Trail is on the south/right side of the closed road as soon as you enter the campground, before you reach the 126 trail. There is a large sign and you will also see a smaller one as you look south.

THE ROUTE: The trail travels south and then southeast very gradually uphill. You will go through a livestock gate and then come to a bench and viewpoint in 0.3 mile. There are excellent views from the bench area if you want to take pictures of South Park. One hundred yards farther is a plaque about the multiple railroads that operated in South Park (it is only visible when the snow is not deep). You will enjoy an even more sweeping view of South Park with good photo opportunities below the power lines. This section of the trail is exposed to sun and wind, and the snow can be thin early or late in the season, so you might have to carry your skis for a while. The mountainside of aspen forest to the southeast offers the stark beauty of countless beige branches reaching for the winter sky. At less than a mile from the trailhead, you will enter a forest of predominantly aspen and enjoy its shelter from the wind. Views of the

Tarryall Mountains open up in another 0.5 mile. The trail very gradually climbs up to a high point of around 10,350 feet before leveling. When you are about 1.5 miles from the trailhead, the trail begins to descend. Unless you want a long, more ambitious excursion, this is a good turnaround point. Or, you can go another 6 miles one-way into Johnson's Gulch. You will enjoy even more mountaintop vistas on your return trip since you will be skiing toward the higher mountains of the Mosquito Range.

KENOSHA PASS – COLORADO TRAIL EAST

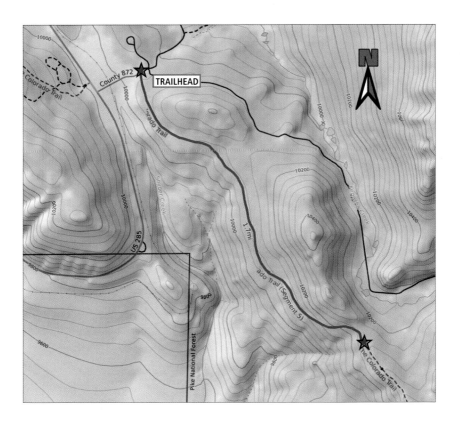

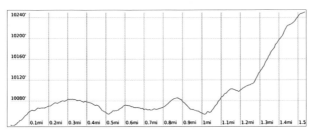

83. North Twin Cone Peak

ROUND TRIP	8.8 miles
DIFFICULTY	Moderate to challenging
SKILL LEVEL	Intermediate
HIGH POINT	11,300 feet
ELEVATION GAIN	1,300 feet
AVALANCHE DANGER	None to low
MAP	Trails Illustrated #105, Tarryall Mountains, Kenosha Pass
CONTACT	South Park Ranger District, Pike National Forest, 719-836-2031

COMMENT: This route follows FR 126, which is closed to cars but open to snowmobiles in winter, and meanders gradually up toward the summit of North Twin Cone Peak (12,323 feet). This little-used road is a good way to escape the crowds and enjoy a trail that is primarily tree-covered but offers some tree breaks and views of the Tarryall Mountains. The trail is not well marked for winter use, but it is a fairly obvious route because of the wide roadbed. Experienced skiers can use any style of ski.

GETTING THERE: From Denver, go southwest on US 285. At about 65 miles you reach Kenosha Pass. Park on the west side of US 285 outside the Kenosha Pass Campground, which closes for the winter. The trailhead is across US 285 from the Kenosha Pass Campground, but parking is available on both sides of the road.

COLD? PUT ON A HAT

When you are out in the cold without a hat, you lose from 7 to 10 percent of your body heat. The figures vary, but the heat loss is significant.

The rule is simple—always bring a hat, and if you're cold, put it on. Author Alan Apt wears a ratty old wool ski cap and has an ultra-lite stocking cap as a backup in his pack.

The Kenosha Pass trailhead.

THE ROUTE: From the highway, the route heads east across a meadow and then enters the mixed forest of aspen and evergreens. At about 0.6 mile, the trail rounds a small hill with a radio tower, offering some views of the Tarryall Mountains and gradually curving southeast to reach Kenosha Creek at 1 mile. There are breaks in the trees with nice views of the Lost Creek Wilderness Area. The road follows the creek closely for the next 1.5 miles, crossing it at about 1.25 miles. At about 2.5 miles the switchbacks begin in earnest from about 10,400 feet. You could turn around here for a pleasant 5-mile out-and-back, with only about 400 feet of elevation gain. The higher you go on the switchbacks, the better the view of South Park and the distant 14ers of the Mosquito Range.

The intense switchbacks take you up 900 feet in 0.75 mile, then at about 3.25 miles it settles down to more moderate but steady climbing that takes you up 400 feet in about 1 mile. You reach a good viewpoint at 11,300 feet at about 4.4 miles; turn around after enjoying the view of the Tarryalls, Lost Creek Wilderness, and South Park. If you continue on to the summit at 12,323 feet, you will have to climb another 1,000 feet.

NORTH TWIN CONE PEAK

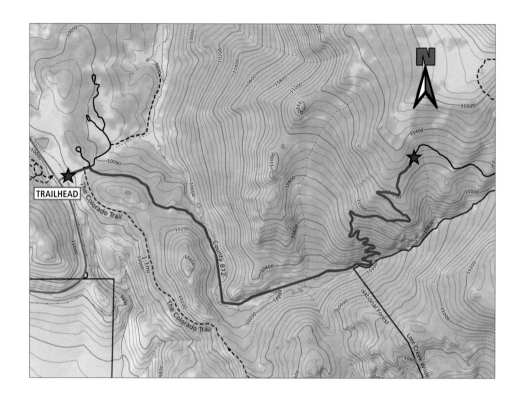

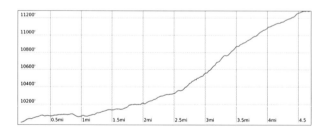

84. **Boreas Pass Road & Halfway Gulch**

ROUND TRIP	5 miles
DIFFICULTY	Easy to moderate
SKILL LEVEL	Novice
HIGH POINT	10,550 feet
ELEVATION GAIN	450 feet
AVALANCHE DANGER	Low to considerable
MAP	Trails Illustrated #109, Breckenridge, Tennessee Pass
CONTACT	South Park Ranger District, Pike National Forest, 719-836-2031

COMMENT: The road to Boreas Pass is a gradual then steep climb that offers superb views of South Park and the Tarryall Mountains. You might have to share the road/trail with snowmobilers. The road is usually well packed because of snowmobile use. With a little luck there will not be a major fleet of them starting off or returning when you are. Sections of the road are exposed to wind and sun and might be snow-free after warm weather. You can do an out-and-back of any distance if the snow is stable and there is no avalanche danger. You can even go up to the top of the pass and continue all the way to Breckenridge for a winter mountaineering overnight if the snow has consolidated and there is no avalanche danger. If the snow is unstable, then an out-and-back of 4 or 5 miles is recommended because the road travels next to slopes that are steep enough to produce avalanches. Keep your eyes on the north side of the road and turn around when the slope equals or exceeds 35 degrees. Experienced skiers can use any style of ski on this route.

GETTING THERE: From Denver, take US 285 approximately 75 miles to Como; at Como, take CR 33/Boreas Pass Road northwest. In approximately 5 miles there is a fork. Boreas Pass Road is on the north/right; the road you are on continues straight

---

THE ANCIENT GREEK GOD OF THE NORTH WIND

Boreas Pass is named after the ancient Greek god of the north wind. It can certainly blow here in the winter. The road was a spur line of the Denver, South Park & Pacific Railroad and went all the way to Breckenridge; a major engineering feat given the elevation and avalanches. Now it is a gravel road used by four-wheel-drive vehicles in the temperate months.

One of the non-stop views from Boreas Pass Road.

ahead and becomes CR 50. Park near Boreas Pass Road, which is closed in winter and isn't plowed. Sometimes it is usable by high-clearance four-wheel-drive vehicles for a short distance from the turnoff.

THE ROUTE: The trail heads east with great views of South Park ahead and the Tarryall Mountains behind. You will immediately have a nice overview of the riparian area. This part of the trail is south-facing, so it might be blown free of snow because of sun exposure. You might have to carry your skis for a while. When the trail rounds the 10,500-foot hill in a mile, you will have a partial view of South Park. The road then heads north, steadily gaining elevation and rounds another hill that is over 10,000 feet high in 0.5 mile. It quickly gains enough elevation to give you nonstop views of the surrounding mountain ranges and more of the South Park valley. At 1.5 miles, you reach Davis Overlook at around 10,300 feet; this is a good turnaround point if you are not ambitious or it is a family expedition. The road then heads northwest, gradually ascending over the next mile. As the road swings to the northwest, the views diminish for about 0.5 mile. You will see more views of Iron and Little Baldy mountains if you trek another 0.5 mile. At 2.5 miles, you reach Halfway Gulch.

Beyond Halfway Gulch the road curves north, and at around 3 miles there is considerable avalanche hazard for a mile. It is possible to cross the drainage and continue another 0.5 mile to enjoy the views, but at the 3-mile mark where avalanche danger begins, it is definitely time to turn around. A 3- to 6-mile round-trip on this road can be very rewarding for anyone, including families.

Attempt the pass only when the snow is consolidated and only if you are an experienced winter mountaineer with survival gear and skills. At 4.5 miles, the road reaches Selkirk Gulch then heads northwest to reach the pass summit in another 2.5 miles.

BOREAS PASS ROAD & HALFWAY GULCH

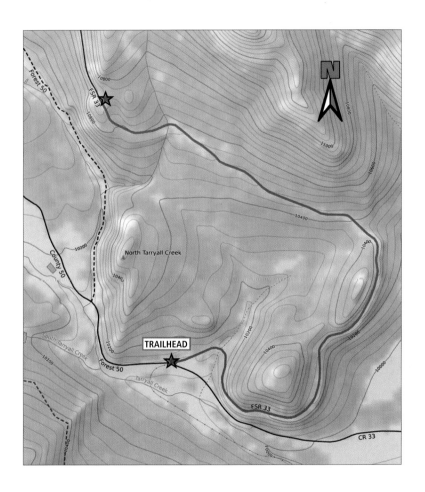

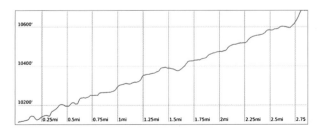

85. Gold Dust Trail South

ROUND TRIP	4 to 12.6 miles
DIFFICULTY	Easy
SKILL LEVEL	Novice to advanced beginner
HIGH POINT	10,600 feet
ELEVATION GAIN	600 feet
AVALANCHE DANGER	None
MAP	Trails Illustrated #109, Breckenridge, Tennessee Pass
CONTACT	South Park Ranger District, Pike National Forest, 719-836-2031

COMMENT: This very enjoyable trail, surrounded by a gorgeous aspen forest, is not heavily used and does not allow motorized traffic. It offers a scenic tour of the Tarryall Creek hills and valleys off the beaten path. This southern segment is good only in a snowy mid-winter; the snow is very spotty to nonexistent early and late in the season. This is a pleasant, meandering trail that rolls in and out of beautiful aspen and pine tree forests and over gentle terrain, offering tree-filtered views of the Tarryall Creek valley and surrounding mountains. It winds its way around the shoulder of Little Baldy Mountain, climbing very gradually to 10,600 feet before descending into the gravelly creek beds. It is described here as an out-and-back. Experienced skiers can use any style of ski on this route.

GETTING THERE: From Denver, take US Highway 285 approximately 75 miles to Como, exiting onto CR 33. In Como, when you turn off US 285 onto CR 33, follow signs to Camp Como. You will drive all the way through Como and then turn left on Church Camp Road (the last left in Como), and a little less than a mile. Park on the north side of the road near the entrance gate to the camp.

THE ROUTE: The trailhead is on the left/south side of the road; look for a brown Forest Service trail marker on the left very close to the fence for the camp. The trail is well marked once you find the trailhead. Follow the blue diamonds through thick aspen forest and wander through the stately trees, stark against the blue or snowy sky. You will be going gradually uphill, just south of the Church Camp boundary that is marked by the fence. As you go uphill you will be skirting above the camp and can see some of the buildings below through the trees. It doesn't take long to get out of sight of

Thick aspens on the Gold Dust Trail South.

the rustic camp. The trail then steepens considerably, climbing 300 feet over the next 0.5 mile before mellowing. It then takes 0.75 mile to climb the next 200 feet, to the high point of 10,600 feet, with nice intermittent views through the trees. At this point you will have traveled around the shoulder of Little Baldy Mountain at about 1.75 miles. This is a good place to reverse course unless you want to go down to the creek and then have to regain around 300 feet on the way back.

If you are ambitious, continue on if there is sufficient snow and the creek is frozen, and enjoy the great views as you roll over a small hill and then drop about 300 feet to cross scenic South Tarryall Creek at 3 miles. This is a good turnaround point since warm weather and exposure often make the creek impassable. If the snow is excellent, you can continue and go over 12 miles round-trip.

GOLD DUST TRAIL SOUTH

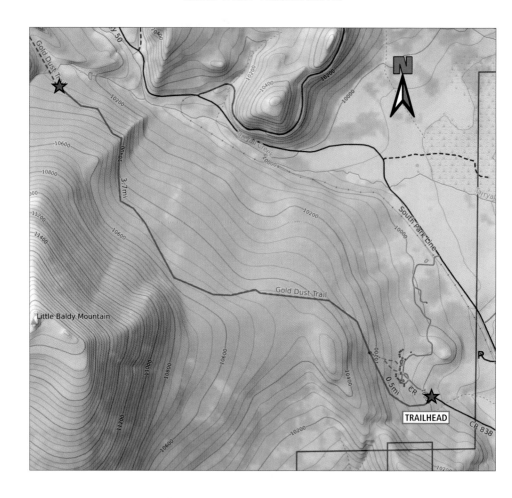

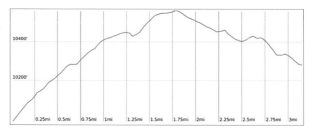

86. **Gold Dust Trail North**

ROUND TRIP	5 miles to trail junction; 7.5 miles to campground; 8.2 miles to pass road
DIFFICULTY	Moderate
SKILL LEVEL	Novice to creek; intermediate to Boreas Pass Road
HIGH POINT	11,482 feet
ELEVATION GAIN	500 feet to creek; 1,100 feet to Boreas Pass Road
AVALANCHE DANGER	Low to moderate near the pass
MAP	Trails Illustrated #109, Breckenridge, Tennessee Pass
CONTACT	South Park Ranger District, Pike National Forest, 719-836-2031

COMMENT: The northern segment of the Gold Dust Trail is an enjoyable, lightly used trail that does not allow motorized traffic and frequently has more snow than the southern segment. It is a bit more interesting and challenging because you have the option of making the exhilarating climb all the way up to the Boreas Pass Road, with avalanche hazard only as you get near to the road itself. It starts off as a narrow pine-tree tunnel and then opens up into a mixed forest of aspen and evergreens with very nice peek-a-boo views of Boreas Peak and North Tarryall Creek. As is almost always the case, the climb up takes considerably longer than the descent. Get an early start for the entire round-trip. Though the view from the Boreas Pass Road is well worth the effort, the round-trip is suitable for only the very fit and experienced because of the need for routefinding as you near the pass. A shorter out-and-back can be accomplished by novices. Most of the trail is well marked with blue diamonds. Experienced skiers can use any style of ski on this route.

GETTING THERE: From Denver, take US 285 approximately 75 miles to Como. At Como take CR 33/Boreas Pass Road northwest. In approximately 5.5 miles there is a fork; Boreas Pass Road is on the north/right; continue straight ahead, now CR 50. In 0.8 mile, reach the trailhead that is next to a large log cabin with a solar system. It is easy to miss the brown U.S. Forest Service sign on the south side of the road because it is set back from the road and parking is 0.3 mile west past the trailhead. The trailhead is signed, though not easy to spot from the road because of piles of snow.

THE ROUTE: The trail climbs northwest for the first 0.5 mile through a pretty mixed forest to offer some views back to the south and then climbs again through a narrow

The Tarryall mountains from the Gold Dust Trail.

draw before leveling out on a ridge top at around 10,660 feet. The trail then switch-backs broadly with a general north and west direction for 1.5 miles above an old water flume, so it's relatively flat. It then descends, crossing North Tarryall Creek at about 2.25 miles, and intersecting with CR 801, which is unplowed in the winter. If your ambitions have faded, this is a good turnaround point. You actually have two other options. You can follow the 801 trail coming in from the right/east down into the Selkirk Campground and then reverse course. Or, climb very steeply for 1 mile to the northwest on the Old Boreas Pass wagon road toward the Boreas Pass Road. The last 0.7 mile is a more gradual climb to reach the pass road for a total of around 4 miles.

The avalanche danger increases dramatically as you near the Boreas Pass Road because of the steep slopes of Boreas Mountain on the north side of the road. If you can dig a snow pit, and know that the avalanche danger is not high, proceed, enjoy the views, and reverse course. Otherwise turn around short of the pass to be safe.

GOLD DUST TRAIL NORTH

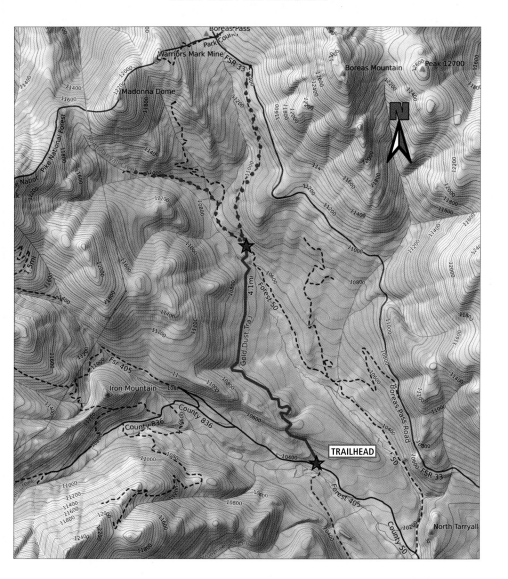

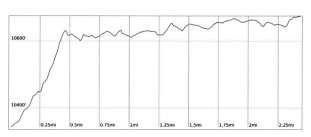

Chapter 16

LEADVILLE AREA

"Lately I have been learning when to give up, which is a kind of victory in itself. Why do I need a summit every time, when everywhere is the poetry of snow, of graupel, cornice, aspect, of champagne powder and breakfast crust, of sunrollers and punk, of crust, slab and drift?"

—Christopher Cokinos, *"The Tao of Pow: Learning to love winter,"*
High Country News, March 21, 2011

Leadville, the highest-altitude incorporated city in the United States, is a historic mining town surrounded by some of the most stunning scenery—and devastation—in the state. Colorado's highest mountain, 14,433-foot Mount Elbert, is to the southwest. The views of it and its neighbor, Mount Massive, would be the envy of any city. Unfortunately, Leadville is just a dozen miles south of the infamous open-pit mine at Climax, with its massive tailings pond. It is also surrounded by the scars of the gold and silver mines that scoured the area during the mining boom that started in 1878 and peaked by 1890, swelling the town to its largest population of 24,000 people. In spite of tailings that decorate the south end of town, the historic downtown is well worth a visit. It has been admirably rebuilt and refurbished and now offers a variety of dining and lodging options.

Don't be fooled by the somewhat funky state of Leadville and the surrounding area, where mine waste and tailings dominate some of the scenery. Though little of the surrounding terrain has not been mined or turned over, it still offers some spectacular and unique recreational opportunities. Tennessee Pass north of Leadville is replete with railroading history dating back to the narrow-gauge lines of the nineteenth cen-

10TH MOUNTAIN DIVISION

Tennessee Pass not only has railroad history, it was also a training site for the famous 10th Mountain Division during World War II. These hardy troops trained here for fighting in the Alps and had very high casualty rates during the war. Some returned to Colorado to open ski areas.

tury. Because of the mixed reputation created by mining, the trails around Leadville are not overrun by people. The very forgiving white carpet of snowfall does a thorough job of hiding the warts that are obvious during the warmer months.

Leadville is about 118 miles west Denver via I-70 and US 24.

A view from the Taylor Hill Trail.

87. Vance's Cabin

ROUND TRIP	5.5 miles
DIFFICULTY	Moderate
SKILL LEVEL	Intermediate
HIGH POINT	11,200 feet
ELEVATION GAIN	800 feet
AVALANCHE DANGER	None to low; can be avoided
MAP	Trails Illustrated #109, Breckenridge, Tennessee Pass
CONTACT	Holy Cross Ranger District, White River National Forest, 970-827-5715

COMMENT: One of the most accessible of the 10th Mountain Division huts, Vance's Cabin is less than 3 miles from the trailhead at Tennessee Pass. It is an easy trail to follow, featuring superb views of the Holy Cross Wilderness Area, Mount Elbert, Mount Massive, and Ski Cooper. There are some nice routes nearby for repeatable ski routes with skins. AT or telemark skis make the return descent more fun.

GETTING THERE: Leadville is on US 24, 23 miles south of I-70. From Denver, drive west on I-70 about 80 miles to Copper Mountain and take Exit 195, before Vail Pass, to Highway 91. Drive southwest about 23 miles to Leadville. Turn right on Highway 24 and go north 7 miles to Ski Cooper and Tennessee Pass. The Ski Cooper ski area is on the right/east side of the road. Pull into the parking lot. As you near the main lodge, look for a small one-story building on the right/south side of the road and the west side of the parking lot. It is the Nordic ski and snowshoe rental hut where you can get information about trail conditions and permission to park overnight.

THE ROUTE: The trailhead is a cat-tracked road across from the Nordic building, 100 yards from the main lodge on the left/north edge of the ski area.

Follow the road, Piney Gulch/Cooper Loop Nordic trail, downhill into the drainage toward Chicago Ridge, crossing Burton Ditch at about 0.3 mile, and reach the intersection with the turnoff for Vance's Cabin at about 0.6 mile. The 10th Mountain Trail is marked with some blue diamonds, but is not signed to the hut. To the right, the trail climbs higher, going south around Cooper Hill; take the trail to the left/north alongside the irrigation canal.

The trail then climbs gradually northeast along the edge of the trees and Burton Ditch into an open wetlands and meadow area where there is a trail junction at about 1.25 miles. The other leg of the Cooper Loop goes to the right/east. Go left (due

Looking west from Vance's Cabin trail.

north)—don't take the trail hard to the left (due west), which goes back down Piney Gulch to the highway. Shortly, you reenter thick tree cover and cross the confluence of the ditch and Piney Gulch. Follow the gulch upstream in a narrow drainage for 0.5 mile to another intersection at 1.5 miles. Here the trail to Taylor Hill continues straight/right to the northeast up the drainage. Take the hut trail to the left/northwest.

Begin the steep slog 600 feet up toward the shoulder of the ridge. The 10th Mountain Trail climbs sharply uphill to the northwest/north and then switchbacks. There are times when you have to look sharply to see the trail markers. There are widely spaced blue diamonds but because of the switchbacks they are easy to miss, especially if it is snowing. Once you reach the shoulder of the ridge in a little over 2 miles, the trail levels considerably and you have views of the mountains that surround the area. If it is early or late in the season you will have to detour around fallen trees.

In another 0.5 mile, the trail rounds the ridge and you come to a beautiful open meadow with spectacular views of the Holy Cross Wilderness Area to the west, Turquoise Lake to the south, and Mount Elbert and Mount Massive down valley. If you aren't staying at the hut, this is a good place to turn around because the trail goes steeply downhill to the left/west, edging the left side of the meadow and dropping in 0.3 mile to the hut. It is hidden below the lower left quarter of the meadow in the trees. The cabin has a nice deck with a superb view of Ski Cooper and the Holy Cross Wilderness.

VANCE'S CABIN

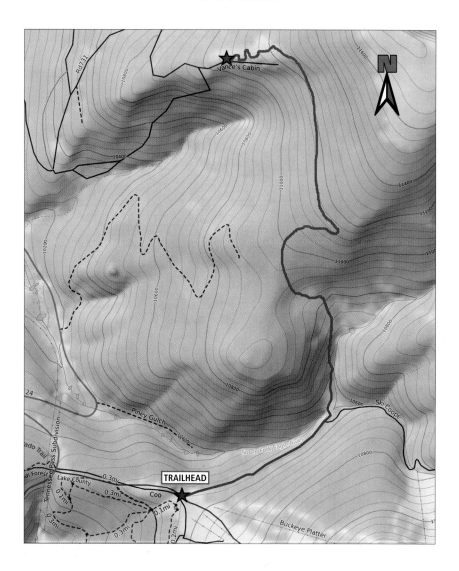

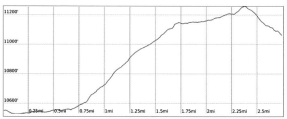

88. Mayflower Gulch

DISTANCE	5.6 miles roundtrip
DIFFICULTY	Easy
SKILL LEVEL	Novice to intermediate
HIGH POINT	12,472 feet
ELEVATION GAIN	1,428 feet
AVALANCHE DANGER	Low to moderate, increasing past the cabins
MAP	Trails Illustrated Breckenridge Tennessee Pass
CONTACT	Dillon Ranger District, White River National Forest, 970-468-5400

COMMENT: The Mayflower Gulch Trail is a relatively easy trail into a basin surrounded by impressive ragged peaks. The remains of the mining town of Boston offer opportunities to explore Colorado's silver and gold mining past, and the spot is one of the most photogenic in the state. The first part of the trail crosses property owned by Climax Molybdenum Company, which graciously allows access for the public. Please respect their property and be aware that you may encounter some mining activity. Skinny skis are adequate, but the descent is more fun on mid-width skis.

GETTING THERE: From Frisco/Dillon/Silverthorne, take I-70 west to Exit 195 at Copper Mountain. Travel south on Highway 91 toward Leadville. The parking area will be at 5.3 miles on the left side. It is usually plowed all winter.

THE ROUTE: From the parking area, begin skiing up the old mining road that runs parallel to Mayflower Creek. After about 1 mile, you break out of the trees, and will start to see some mining artifacts and cabin ruins on both sides of the road. In another 0.6 mile, you will arrive at the ruins of the Boston Mine. Just before the mine, there is a gate beyond which motor vehicles are not allowed. The structures are all that remain of the old mining camp's cabins and a boarding house, and it's hard to imagine being able to work surrounded by these stunning views. Please respect these historic artifacts and treat them as living pieces of history. This is a fine spot to stop, eat a snack or lunch, explore a little, take some photos, and turn around for a satisfying 3.2-mile adventure. As you descend you get a good view of 13,205-foot Jacque Peak and the top of one of the lifts at Copper Mountain.

If you want to continue, ski up the open snowfield on the south side of the gulch and continue on the old mining road, contouring around the hills on a gradual climb.

The remains of a once-thriving mining camp for the Boston Mine.

Be aware of the possibility of avalanches as the terrain gets steeper. After about 1mile, the trail descends toward Mayflower Amphitheater and a magnificent view of Mayflower Hill, Pacific Peak, and Fletcher Mountain sitting squarely in the middle. Turn around here and head back to the trailhead.

DOGS: Do's and Don'ts

Author Alan Apt's dogs have loved skiing and he has loved having them with him, but there are some written and unwritten rules that you need to pay attention to. In this book you will see a restriction comment that usually talks about leash laws for dogs. There are good reasons for leash laws that often have to do with preventing injury to wildlife, ranch stock, or your dog. In these areas, keep your dog on a leash. In busy areas where there are a lot of skiers, it can be dangerous for the dog and the skier when the skier is coming downhill and the dog is on the trail. Dogs have been injured when a skier is trapped between a dog and a tree—they will have to choose running into the dog for self-preservation.

In most areas your dog must be under voice command. If he or she doesn't respond to voice command, don't bring him or her. Most of us love dogs, but there are people who are really afraid of dogs. Make sure your dog stays with you and doesn't approach other snowshoers or skiers without an invitation.

Let's talk a bit about dog poop. Pick it up and put it in a bag. Pack it out with you. Period. Please don't bag it up and leave it next to the trail—in winter or summer. There is no poop patrol ranger who collects these packages. Take it along with you and dispose of it properly.

Be careful with your dog's footpads. Often hard snowballs form in the creases of the footpad and are painful. Limping or stopping and licking his feet is a sure sign of snowballs. You can try strap-on booties, but some dogs may not wear them comfortably.

MAYFLOWER GULCH

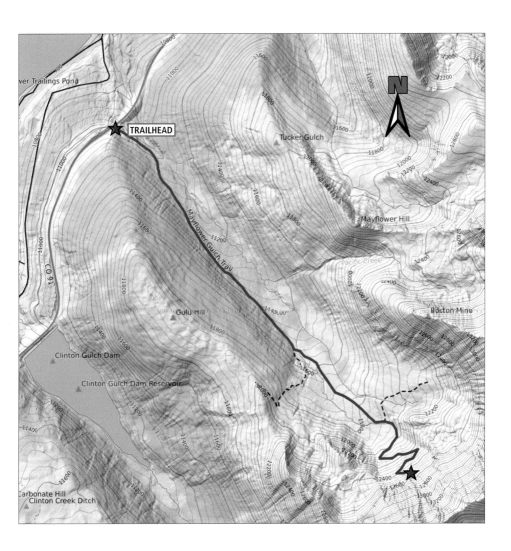

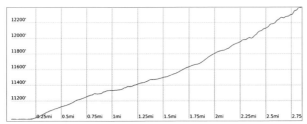

89. **Taylor Hill**

ROUND TRIP	6 miles
DIFFICULTY	Challenging
SKILL LEVEL	Intermediate to expert
HIGH POINT	11,725 feet
ELEVATION GAIN	1,325 feet
AVALANCHE DANGER	Moderate to considerable; can be avoided
MAP	Trails Illustrated #109, Breckenridge, Tennessee Pass
CONTACT	Holy Cross Ranger District, White River National Forest, 970-827-5715

COMMENT: Climbing Taylor Hill gives a panorama of the Tennessee Pass area, with 360 degrees of great views. You get a close-up look at Chicago Ridge to the east, the spectacle of the Holy Cross Wilderness to the west, and the Sawatch Range to the south. It is not a good route to attempt at times of high avalanche danger. Most of the route is low-angle, but there is avalanche potential toward the top. Winter mountaineering skills are preferred for this route. Backcountry skiers love this hill for earning turns through the trees, so you are likely to have company. There are lots of options for skiing through well-spaced trees. This route is more fun with AT or telemark skis.

GETTING THERE: Leadville is on US 24, 23 miles south of I-70. From Denver, drive west on I-70 about 80 miles to Copper Mountain and take Exit 195, before Vail Pass, to Highway 91. Drive southwest about 23 miles to Leadville. Turn right on Highway 24 and go north 7 miles to Ski Cooper and Tennessee Pass. The Ski Cooper ski area is on the right/east side of the road. Pull into the parking lot and as you near the main lodge, look for a small one-story building on the right/south side of the road and the west side of the parking lot. It is the Nordic ski and snowshoe rental hut where you can get information about trail conditions and permission to park overnight.

THE ROUTE: The trailhead is a cat-tracked road across the road from the Nordic building, 100 yards from the main lodge, on the left/north edge of the ski area. The route leaves the road in less than 0.5 mile; you will go downhill to cross the irrigation ditch and then the road continues uphill. Watch for a trail sign near the ditch.

Follow the road, Piney Gulch/Cooper Loop Nordic trail, downhill into the drainage toward Chicago Ridge, crossing Burton Ditch at about 0.3 mile. Bear right after crossing the ditch, as the trail climbs higher, going along the edge of a

View of Taylor Hill and the trailhead.

meadow and then entering trees. The trail reaches the intersection with the turnoff for Vance's Cabin at about 0.6 mile. The 10th Mountain Trail is marked with some blue diamonds but is not signed for the hut. At the junction where the trails separate (the trail to Vance's Cabin tracks to the left, northwest), stay to the right/northeast for Taylor Hill, and continue toward the Piney Gulch drainage heading northeast. The trail for Taylor Hill is not well marked and is often hard to identify. Watch for tree blazes. If you miss it, consult your topographic map and compass and head for a saddle that is northeast from the Vance's Cabin trail.

When you reach a secondary drainage coming in from the left/north at about 2 miles, turn north, and shoot for the saddle on the northeast side of Taylor Hill. Avoid open slopes that are more than 30 degrees, which are farther northeast than you want to go; make your own switchbacks to the saddle. This is the steepest section of the trek, and requires patience, given the elevation. You will be gaining 600 feet in this short stretch and ending up on a saddle that is around 10,900 feet. From the top of the saddle at about 2.75 miles follow the ridgeline north/northeast to the summit of Taylor Hill for a real treat. You will have a much more gradual trek on the saddle as you slowly climb another 800 feet to reach the summit. You will have nice views before actually reaching the summit, so you can reverse course at any point and feel satisfied. Snow conditions can vary widely.

Decide how far to go based on the difficulty level of the snowpack. Enjoy the panorama and have a nice snack and water break before retracing your steps through the powder to the trailhead. There are lots of opportunities for romping through the powder on the return, but stay off the steepest slopes and weave your way through the trees to the west where possible in order to avoid avalanche danger.

TAYLOR HILL

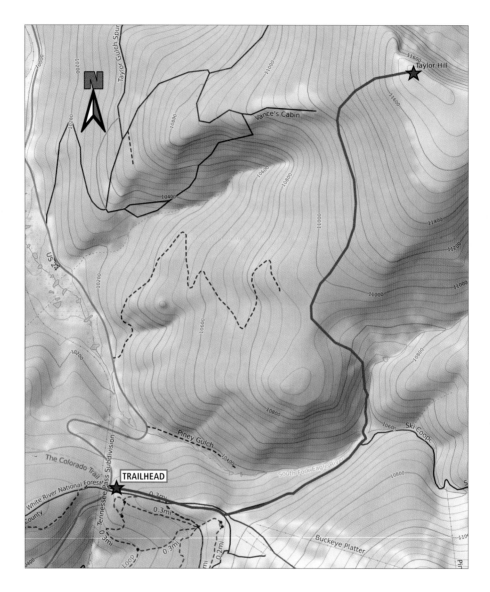

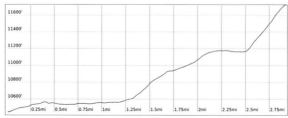

90. Mitchell Creek Loop

ROUND TRIP	6.5 miles
DIFFICULTY	Easy to moderate
SKILL LEVEL	Novice
HIGH POINT	10,600 feet
ELEVATION GAIN	200 feet
AVALANCHE DANGER	Low
MAP	Trails Illustrated #109, Breckenridge, Tennessee Pass
CONTACT	Leadville Ranger District, San Isabel National Forest, 719-486-0749

COMMENT: The Mitchell Creek Loop follows the Tennessee Pass portion of the Colorado Trail, part of which is a former railroad bed, which rolls gently across the interesting terrain. The trailhead is across the road from the Cooper Ski area. There are facilities and a coffee shop with tasty snacks in the Nordic area. The loop offers great views of the Holy Cross Wilderness and Homestake Peak to the west. It is a good trail for beginners but interesting enough in location and terrain to be fun for skiers of all skill levels. Even though it is on Tennessee Pass, there is no avalanche terrain in spite of the fact that you are starting off at 10,000 feet. Keep the elevation in mind for visitors from flatlands. You generally will have excellent snow because of the elevation. Experienced skiers can use any type of ski on this route.

GETTING THERE: Leadville is on US 24, 23 miles south of I-70. From Denver, drive west on I-70 about 80 miles to Copper Mountain and take Exit 195, before Vail Pass, to Highway 91. Drive southwest about 23 miles to reach Leadville. From Leadville drive north on US 24 approximately 8 miles to Tennessee Pass. The Ski Cooper ski area is on the right/east side of the road. The loop trailhead is on the west side of Tennessee Pass across the road from Ski Cooper at the end of a large parking lot.

THE ROUTE: The loop starts on the Colorado Trail, an old railroad grade that descends gradually, traveling to the northwest. After you climb back up a bit, at approximately 0.25 mile, you pass old picturesque charcoal kilns and then the trail gradually descends about 200 feet over the next 1.0 mile. For the first 0.6 mile, you enjoy great views of Homestake Peak, a good place for photos. When you come to the Powderhound Trail junction at about 0.7 mile (it goes uphill to the left), stay to the

An old kiln on the Mitchell Creek Loop.

right. The trail then turns right, to the north. At about 1.5 miles, it levels out at 10,200 feet, then turns left to round the toe of the ridge, heading west.

At a junction just before 2 miles, the Colorado Trail turns off to the right and goes west, then north; stay left on the Mitchell Creek Loop Trail as it travels southwest into the Mitchell Creek drainage, where it bottoms out at around 10,110 feet at 2.5 miles. (You can add in a quick out-and-back on the Colorado Trail if you wish. If you do that, you will soon come to an intersection where a trail on the right goes down Mitchell Creek to the highway; stay to the left to continue on the Colorado Trail.) Continuing left on the Mitchell Creek Loop, the railroad grade ends and the terrain becomes more difficult as the trail begins to climb again for about 1.5 miles. The trail climbs steadily up to 10,600 feet and intersects the Wurts Ditch Road at a saddle at about 4 miles.

Shortly after, the trail crosses over the drainage and enters the trees, traveling downhill and dropping about 200 feet in 0.25 mile, following the road for approximately 0.25 mile to an intersection with the Colorado Trail again. The road continues to the right. Turn sharply left onto the Colorado Trail as it starts to go back to the east and north. You then cross the stream again and another trail goes off to the right; stay straight/left. The Colorado Trail then goes gradually up, and then downhill 2 miles to the pass. Along the way you will have excellent views of mountains to the south for photo opportunities on clear days.

MITCHELL CREEK LOOP

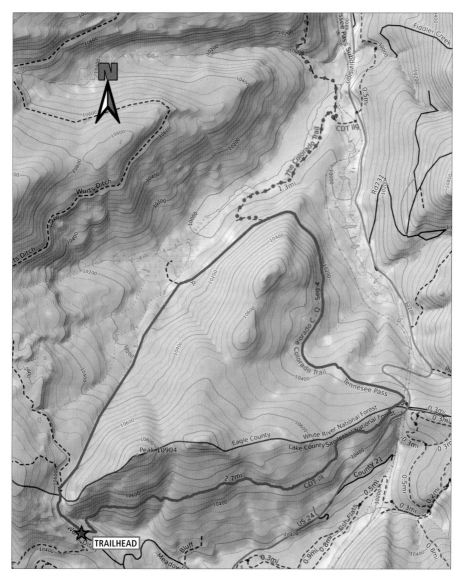

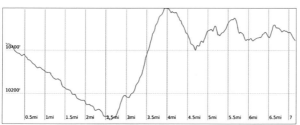

91. Twin Lakes

ROUND TRIP	12 miles
DIFFICULTY	Easy
SKILL LEVEL	Novice
HIGH POINT	9,400 feet
ELEVATION GAIN	200 feet
AVALANCHE DANGER	None
MAP	Trails Illustrated #127, Aspen, Independence Pass
CONTACT	Leadville Ranger District, San Isabel National Forest, 719-486-0749

COMMENT: This route along the road that leads to Independence Pass is surrounded by superb views of Mount Elbert, the highest peak in the state; Parry Peak; 13,000-foot Rinker and Twin peaks; and 13,461-foot Quail Mountain. It is an easy out-and-back, or a suitable one-way with a vehicle shuttle, in a great setting that is ideal for families or for a quick workout. It is not a good place for skiing early or late in the season because of unpredictable snow. Parking can sometimes be challenging immediately after a storm because of snowplowing. Allow time for the plows to work their magic after a storm. An out-and-back trek is probably the best option for families with young children. Skinny skis are the best choice for this fairly flat but highly scenic route.

GETTING THERE: Leadville is on US 24, 23 miles south of I-70. From Denver, drive west on I-70 about 80 miles to Copper Mountain and take Exit 195, before Vail Pass, to Highway 91. Drive southwest about 23 miles to reach Leadville. From Leadville, continue south on US 24 and turn west toward Independence Pass on Highway 82. In a few miles, you reach the eastern edge of Twin Lakes Reservoir. After about 3 miles from US 24, just before a bridge over Lake Creek, watch for a gravel road to the left that goes south below the dam. Take the gravel road around a wetlands area about 0.5 mile to the Twin Lakes trailhead. You might need a four-wheel-drive vehicle to navigate this road after a major storm. For a vehicle shuttle, go back out to the highway, turn left, and drive west about 8 miles through the town of Twin Lakes to the Willis Gulch trailhead on the left/south.

THE ROUTE: From the Twin Lakes trailhead, take the Colorado Trail to the left (south, then west). The rolling trail takes you around the southern edge of Twin Lakes

Twin Lakes adventure.

Reservoir with immediate spectacular mountain views to the west. At about 1.7 miles, the Main Range Trail comes in from the left; stay straight, unless you want to do some climbing to get your heart rate up even higher. In that case, do a quick out-and-back on the Main Range Trail. That is not to say that the Twin Lakes Trail doesn't offer some hilly terrain, too. The trail rolls as it travels along the lakeshore. Cross Flume Creek at about 2.3 miles; shortly after you can enjoy the ruins of the ghost town of Interlaken Historical Site between the Twin Lakes. It is a spectacular setting with views of the southern flank of the Mount Elbert massif and Mount Hope to the north; west and south are Twin Peaks and Quail Mountain. If you choose to go only as far as the ghost town, it is around a 5-mile out-and-back.

Continuing farther on the trail, you pass a wetlands area and then climb 200 feet to the 3-mile point. The trail now stays on the hillside above the second of the Twin Lakes, going southwest toward the western end of the lake. At about 4.4 miles, you will cross Boswell Gulch past the western end of the upper Twin Lake. There is a trail intersection at 5 miles; stay straight and then cross another stream. In another 1 mile, reach the Willis Gulch Trailhead on Highway 82.

OTHER OPTIONS: Independence Pass is closed in the winter and offers skiing opportunities. An easy one is to drive until you reach the road closure, put on your skis, and continue on the Independence Pass road.

TWIN LAKES

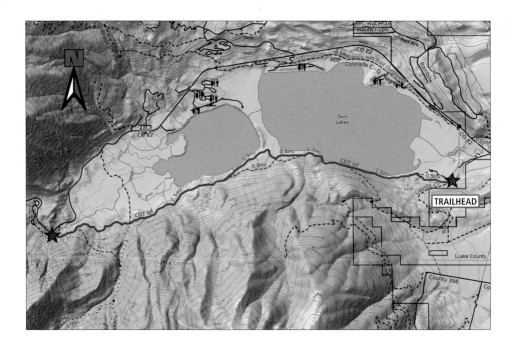

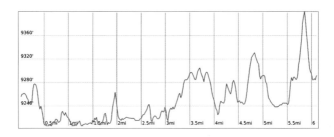

Chapter 17

COLORADO SPRINGS AREA

*"Nature we have always with us, an inexhaustible storehouse of that which
moves the heart, appeals to the mind, and fires the imagination."*

—John Burroughs, *The Writings of John Burroughs,
Volume XV: Leaf and Tendril*

Colorado Springs provides a jumping off point for numerous ski routes. Rampart
Reservoir in Pike National Forest is perfect for beginners, and the Mueller State
Park and Wildlife Area and the nearby Crags in the Pikes Peak foothills are real jewels.

Just 26 miles from Colorado Springs, Mueller State Park looks out on the western
slopes of the Pikes Peak massif from its east-oriented trails. The snowcapped Sangre de Cristo Mountains are the majestic backdrop for its westerly trails. Views from
park trails are 360 degrees because the park is essentially draped over the top of a
10,000-foot mountain, with all trails going downhill from the top. There is enough
tree cover—a colorful tapestry of aspen, pine, fir, and spruce trees—to protect the
snow, but most of the trails open up for good views and sunshine. A look at the map
for this state park and wildlife area will show you that there are a seemingly infinite
number of possibilities for combining trails. It simply depends on the conditions and
your ambitions. Note that the large number of intersecting trails can make routefinding a bit tricky because some of the trails are not well marked.

The park's campground makes a good starting point because it is on the highest
point along the access road. The campground has a limited number of RV and tent
sites available throughout the winter. Though the showers and flush toilets are not
open, vault toilets are available. In winter the visitor center is open only on weekends.
There is a self-service entry station near the campground. A short distance across the
highway is The Crags, northwest of the long Pikes Peak ridge.

92. School Pond & Preacher's Hollow Loops

SCHOOL POND LOOP	1.75 miles
PREACHERS HOLLOW LOOP	1.6 miles
DIFFICULTY	Easy
SKILL LEVEL	Intermediate
HIGH POINT	9,500 feet at trailhead
ELEVATION GAIN	100 feet
AVALANCHE DANGER	None to low
MAP	Mueller State Park and Wildlife Area
CONTACT	Mueller State Park, 719-687-2366

COMMENT: These two loop trails originate near the Mueller State Park Visitor Center, located just south of the Revenuer's Ridge Trailhead. The visitor center is open only on weekends during the winter. Both loops stay on the ridgeline and don't descend as steeply as some of the other trails. They drop down to ponds at their far ends. They can be done singly or together for a 3.2-mile combined loop. Skinny/Nordic skis work well for most of the route.

GETTING THERE: For Mueller State Park, take US 24 From Colorado Springs west 25 miles to the town of Divide. Go west through Divide until you reach the intersection with Highway 67 and then turn left to take it south 4 miles. The entrance to Mueller State Park is on the right/west side of the road. The signed turnoff for The Crags Campground/Rocky Mountain Camp is in another 0.5 mile, on the left/east.

From the Mueller State Park entrance, drive Wapiti Road (the park road) west/southwest about 1.25 miles. Find the trailhead on the south side of the road.

THE ROUTE: The School Pond Loop Trail heads south through heavy tree cover of aspen and pines, which preserves snow when other trails have thinned and offers protection from any wind. The trees are uniquely beautiful spectacles among the whites of winter. In 0.25 mile at a trail junction, the other leg of the loop is to the left, and Stoner Mill Trail is to the right; continue straight. At 0.5 mile when the other end of the Stoner Mill Trail comes in from the right, stay straight/left. Just before 0.75 mile, School Pond itself is to the right; the trail then curves left/north. A little before 1 mile, reach a T-intersection. To the right is the Aspen Trail; go left to continue the loop, now heading west. At about 1.3 miles the other end of the Aspen Trail comes in from the right; continue straight/left. In a short distance, close the loop at 1.5 miles; turn right to return to the trailhead.

From the trailhead, the Preacher's Hollow Loop Trail is a short distance west of the School Pond Loop Trail. There is a nice overlook at the beginning of the Preacher's Hollow Loop Trail. Go to the left to do this loop clockwise, heading south. In 0.3 mile, the trail forks with the Ranger Trail to the left, stay straight/right as the Preacher's Hollow Loop Trail curves west and then south again. Just before 0.5 mile, the trail passes Never-Never Pond and curves west then northwest a short way. At 0.9 mile, you intersect the Rock Pond Trail; go hard to the right to continue the loop, now heading northeast. At 1.25 miles, the trail goes north to curve a couple of times in the last 0.4 mile. The Revenuer's Ridge Trail is on the left shortly before you close the loop.

SEE MAP ON PAGE 321

93. Peak View, Elk Meadow, Livery Loop, & Revenuer's Ridge Trails

ROUND TRIP	2.2 miles
DIFFICULTY	Easy to moderate
SKILL LEVEL	Intermediate
HIGH POINT	9,600 feet at trailhead
ELEVATION GAIN	300 feet
AVALANCHE DANGER	None to low
MAP	Mueller State Park and Wildlife Area
CONTACT	Mueller State Park, 719-687-2366

COMMENT: This delightful route features peak views, aspens, meadows, and a pond. The route consists of a partial loop on the east side of the road, connected by a one-way stretch alongside the road combining four different trails. Skinny/Nordic skis work well for most of the route.

GETTING THERE: For Mueller State Park, take US 24 From Colorado Springs west 25 miles to the town of Divide. Go west through Divide until you reach the intersection with Highway 67 and then turn left to take it south 4 miles. The entrance to Mueller State Park is on the right/west side of the road. From the Mueller State Park entrance, drive Wapiti Road (the park road) west and then north 2.25 miles to the campground area. Peak View Trail is near a campground that is popular because of the great views of the western slopes of Pikes Peak. The well-marked trailhead on the right is easy to locate, about 0.25 mile past the campground entry station.

THE ROUTE: The Peak View Trail heads southeast on a nice, open trail. Peak View Pond is on the right as you descend through the colorful mixture of aspen and pine trees. It is worth a short detour to get some close-up shots of the pond. Take the ridge down the gentle slope to a T-intersection with the Elk Meadow Trail in a little past 0.25 mile. For an easy out-and-back, return to the trailhead.

For the loop, turn right onto the Elk Meadow Trail heading south. It rolls gently along the ridge, with good views to the east. At about 0.75 mile, the trail curves west and eventually climbs back uphill toward the road, intersecting with the Livery Loop Trail at about 1.0 mile. Stay left on the Livery Loop Trail as it meanders across the ridge to the Livery Loop Trailhead at approximately 1.4 miles.

Directly across the road from the Livery Loop Trailhead is the Geer Pond Trailhead; cross to this entry point to the Revenuer's Ridge Trail, and take it to the right/north. This trail parallels the road and the ridgeline, dipping down the ridge somewhat along the way. It features nice views to the west all along the way. This is one of the few trails that does not go downhill on the way out and uphill on the way back, so it is ideal for families with small children or group members who are less ambitious. At 1.5 miles, the Geer Pond Trail comes in from the left; stay straight/right. Reach the Homestead Loop Trailhead in 0.4 mile, at 1.9 miles from the start. Continue north on the road about 0.3 mile back to the Peak View Trailhead to close the loop.

SEE MAP ON PAGE 321

MUELLER STATE PARK

West of Colorado Springs, on the west side of Pikes Peak, Mueller State Park features 55 miles of trails, over 5,000 acres of terrain, and abundant wildlife. The average elevation is 9,500 feet, so snow conditions are good by mid-winter. The park is home to elk, deer, hawks, and black bears. The black bears hibernate in the winter, so they aren't likely to be seen during ski season except during early spring adventures. If you encounter a black bear, speak softly and back away slowly. Do not run. Don't get too close to bull elks, as they have been known to charge people who invade their space.

94. **Homestead & Black Bear Loop**

ROUND TRIP	2.2 miles
DIFFICULTY	Easy to moderate
SKILL LEVEL	Intermediate
HIGH POINT	9,650 feet at trailhead
ELEVATION GAIN	300 feet
AVALANCHE DANGER	None to low
MAP	Mueller State Park and Wildlife Area
CONTACT	Mueller State Park, 719-687-2366

COMMENT: This easy route offers expansive views of the magnificent Sangre de Cristo Mountains as well as beautiful meadows, and is an ideal family excursion. Skinny/Nordic skis work well for most of the route.

GETTING THERE: For Mueller State Park, take US 24 From Colorado Springs west 25 miles to the town of Divide. Go west through Divide until you reach the intersection with Highway 67 and then turn left to take it south 4 miles. The entrance to Mueller State Park is on the right/west side of the road.

From the Mueller State Park entrance, drive Wapiti Road (the park road) west and then north 2.25 miles to the campground area. Homestead Trail is near the campground entry station, on the left/west side of the road.

THE ROUTE: Begin the Homestead Trail near the campground entry station. The trailhead is well marked, with the statistics listed for more than one trail. You start off on a gradual downhill and immediately you will see the Revenuer's Ridge Trail to the left. It looks like a hiking trail, whereas the Homestead Loop Trail is as wide as a service road. After 100 yards or so you can see the Sangre de Cristo Mountains in the distance between the trees.

The trail then plunges more steeply to the wetland valley through a mixture of stately pine and aspen trees. You cross the wetlands and go downhill for a bit and then climb up to the top of a short ridge. The trail then goes downhill again, curving right/north, and intersects with the Beaver Ponds Trail on the left at just past 0.75 mile; stay right on the Homestead Trail. It travels through a delightful aspen grove and tops out on a flat spot that is a good place for a snack or lunch. You then enter another aspen-lined valley and at just past 1 mile, intersect the Black Bear Trail. The Homestead Trail continues straight ahead; instead, go right onto the Black Bear Trail.

This is a fairly hilly trail that rolls and goes uphill on the return. The last 0.5 mile or so climbs back up to Wapiti Road at about 1.6 miles. Walk south alongside the road for about 0.6 mile to connect the loop, or use a vehicle shuttle.

OTHER TRAILS TO EXPLORE: From the intersection of the Homestead and Black Bear Trails at about 1 mile, you could continue straight on the Homestead Trail to intersect the Mountain Logger Trail in a short 0.7 mile, and then follow the Homestead Trail's pine-tree tunnel to get close to Grouse Mountain in another 0.75 mile. Then it is a somewhat steep uphill to the end of the campground road and the Cheesman Trailhead.

MUELLER STATE PARK LOOPS

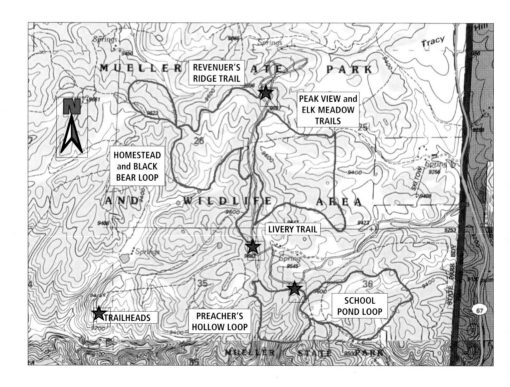

95. The Crags

ROUND TRIP	3 miles
DIFFICULTY	Easy to moderate
SKILL LEVEL	Novice to intermediate
HIGH POINT	10,900 feet
ELEVATION GAIN	800 feet
AVALANCHE DANGER	Low to moderate
MAP	Trails Illustrated #137, Pikes Peak, Cañon City
CONTACT	Pikes Peak Ranger District, Pike National Forest, 719-636-1602

COMMENT: The rock formations of the Crags area are worth a visit any time of the year, but they are starkly and magically backlit by sun and snow in the winter months. The view from the top of The Crags pinnacles is worth the effort, and the trail through the pretty valley is also worthwhile even if you don't want to summit. You can see the Sangre de Cristo Mountains in the distance as well as the backside of Pikes Peak and the interesting landscape of Mueller State Park and Wildlife Area.

Winter makes climbing the actual pinnacles much trickier because of slick rock and ice. Rambling around up to their base is just as much fun and also very scenic. This is one of the summer approaches to climbing Pikes Peak for those who don't want to go up the Barr Trail. You can use this trail as an approach to the summit in the winter too, since avalanche danger is minimal. The trail eventually intersects with the road to the summit.

Skinny skis work well for most of the route. Mid-width will be better if you plan to ski all the way to the summit since the descent will be steep.

GETTING THERE: For Mueller State Park, take US 24 From Colorado Springs west 25 miles to the town of Divide. Go west through Divide until you reach the intersection with Highway 67 and then turn left to take it south 4 miles. The entrance to Mueller State Park is on the right/west side of the road. The signed turnoff for The Crags Campground/Rocky Mountain Camp is in another 0.5 mile, on the left/east.

From the turnoff 0.5 mile south of the park entrance, follow Forest Service Road 383, a narrow, slippery dirt- or snow-packed road in winter that can be challenging because it is only plowed sporadically. Four-wheel-drive is recommended. At the minimum you need good snow tires. The road curves north and around to the south to The Crags Campground in about 3 miles. You might have to park outside the campground and begin your trek from there. Go to the end of the campground road and you will see the trailhead.

THE ROUTE: The trail goes gradually uphill from the trailhead, and you will initially be in tree cover. The trail is very obvious. Follow the Four Mile creek drainage to the east, and then northeast. There is a tributary that goes southeast; ignore it. There are eventually trails on both sides of the stream and both will take you to The Crags. There is a footbridge for crossing to the other side that might not be necessary with deep snow and a frozen stream, but be cautious if and when you attempt to cross. The right fork is a bit more

The view of Pikes Peak from The Crags trail on a bright day.

tree-sheltered, so it is a better choice if the snow cover is thin and it is early or late in the season. However, it does have a short stretch of boulders that might require you to remove your skis.

The left branch is a bit more open and not as rocky, and features a pretty meadow area about 1 mile from the trailhead. From the meadow you will have an impressive view of The Crags pinnacles that might convince you that summiting in the winter is not wise.

When you reach the meadow area, you might also see multiple trails wandering off. You could go up on one branch and back on the other for variety if you don't ascend up to near the top of the pinnacles but stay lower. Just achieving the meadow and then the ridgeline in 1 mile is a rewarding experience because of the views. From the end of the meadow area, the trail that goes to the left/north, climbs gradually, then more steeply, gaining 300 feet in less than 0.5 mile. The trail that stays in the creek bottom gains 100 feet in the same distance.

There is a trail on the right/east side of Four Mile Creek that climbs very steeply, gaining 800 feet in less than a mile. Use your own judgment on the snow and ice conditions and whether to go the additional 0.5 mile to the pinnacles. You really don't have to stand on top of one of the rocks to have great views and a wonderful excursion.

PHOTO BY EVA LIGHT

Pangborns Pinnacle separates the valley from Fourmile Creek drainage on The Crags route.

THE CRAGS

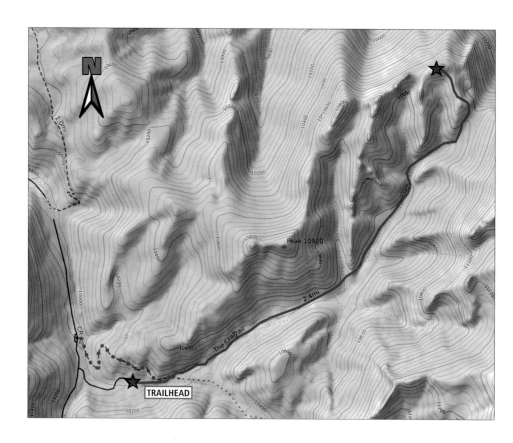

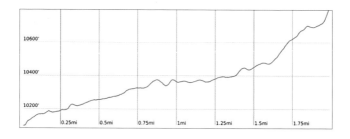

APPENDIX

CONTACT INFORMATION

Colorado Avalanche Information Center (CAIC)

With the Center's mobile app you can get avalanche forecasts and upload your own observations about avalanche danger. 303-499-9650; avalanche.state.co.us

Colorado State Parks and Forests

cpw.state.co.us/placestogo/Parks

Rocky Mountain National Park

970-586-1206; www.nps.gov/romo/
Up-to-date information available on Twitter or Facebook

U.S. Forest Service

https://www.fs.usda.gov/

Forest Service National Avalanche Center
www.fsavalanche.org/

CONSERVATION, OUTINGS, VOLUNTEER ORGANIZATIONS

Backcountry Snowsports Initiative
www.cmc.org/Conservation/BackcountrySnowsportsInitiative

Colorado Mountain Club
www.cmc.org

Special Olympics Colorado
720-359-3100; www.specialolympicsco.org

Ignite Adaptive Sports at Eldora Mountain Resort
igniteadaptivesports.org

Rocky Mountain Conservancy
Field Institute: 970-586-0108
Information about books and seminars: 970-586-0121; www.RMConservancy.org

Rocky Mountain Sierra Club
303-454-3362; www.coloradosierraclub.org

HUTS AND YURTS

Colorado Mountain Club Boulder Group Arestua Hut
cmcboulder.org/cabin-arestua.html

Never Summer Nordic, Inc.
970-723-4070; www.neversummernordic.com

Tenth Mountain Division Huts Association
970-925-5775 ; www.huts.org

AVALANCHE AWARENESS RECOMMENDED READING AND REFERENCE

Books

Custer, Tony. *Backcountry Avalanche Safety: Skiers, Climbers, Boarders, Snowshoers* Daffern, WA: Rocky Mountain Books, 2009.

Ferguson, Sue A. and Edward R. Lachapelle. *The ABCs of Avalanche Safety.* Seattle, WA: Mountaineers Books, 2003.

Fredston, Jill and Doug Fesler. *Snow Sense: A Guide to Evaluating Snow Avalanche Hazard, 5th Edition*, Alaska Mountain Safety Center, Inc., 2011.

McClung, David and Peter Schaerer. *The Avalanche Handbook, 3rd Ed.,* Seattle, WA: Mountaineers Books, 2006.

Tremper, Bruce. *Avalanche Essentials: A Step by Step System for Safety and Survival,* Seattle, WA: Mountaineers Books, 2013.

Films

Switchback: Trigger Your Senses
A feature-length documentary about Colorado's unique avalanche problem

Backcountry Access: video series for avalanche safety; www.backcountryaccess.com

ACKNOWLEDGMENTS

Thanks to the family members who have accompanied me on some of these trails: my children Amy, Kate, Laura, and Ryan; their spouses Adam and Kevin; my grandchildren Jeremiah, Lylah, Milo, Max, Seamus and Barrett; and especially my partner Nancy Olsen, who accompanied me on many fun outings.

I also had many friends over the years who endured varying degrees of good and bad weather and snow: Bill Black, David Bye, Dan Bowers, John Gascoyne, Bill Jacobi, Joseph Piesman, John Madsen, Laming Paine, Eric Kallgren, Jim Welch, Larry Caswell, Alan Garten, Andre Mallinger, John Leventhal, Alan Stark, Bill Ikler, and my co-author Kay Turnbaugh, and many of my fellow members of the Diamond Peaks and Bryan Mountain Ski Patrols.

Thanks to John Bartholow, Daniel Bowers, Eva Light, Russ Brinkman, and Dave Cooper for their photos used either in my slideshows or books.

Thanks to Tom and Barbara Humphrey for providing historical maps that were valuable references.

Thanks to my co-author Kay Turnbaugh for producing the excellent maps, designing the layout, checking for errors, and producing the final files, in addition to contributing trails and photos to the book. This book would not have happened without her.

Thanks to Jeff Golden and the Colorado Mountain Club Press team.

Thanks to the Colorado Mountain Club, Neptune Mountaineering, REI, Avogardos Number and Save the Poudre, and the Sierra Club for hosting slideshows to support this and my other books.

—*Alan Apt*

My thanks go out to all my ski companions through the years, including Bill Ikler, Phil Dougan, Lee Tillotson, Nancy Olsen, Alan Apt, and all the others too numerous to name who have shared adventures and chocolate with me. I also thank Jeff Golden and the Colorado Mountain Club Press team.

This book began with Alan's awesomely informative trail descriptions, and they were the inspiration to create what we hope will be an indispensable resource for your outdoor adventures.

We sincerely appreciate every one of our readers—this book is for you. Be safe and have fun out there as you create your own memories that will last a lifetime.

—*Kay Turnbaugh*

ABOUT THE AUTHORS

Alan Apt has snowshoed, skied, hiked, climbed, and backpacked in Colorado for fifty years. He is a reformed peak bagger who has climbed many of Colorado's highest mountains. Apt is also the author of the guidebook *Afoot and Afield in Denver, Boulder and Colorado's Front Range, 184 Spectacular Outings in the Colorado Rockies* (Wilderness Press) and *Snowshoe Routes: Colorado's Front Range* (Colorado Mountain Club Press). He is a former local columnist for the Fort Collins Coloradoan and has contributed to the Denver Post and Boulder Weekly.

Alan volunteers with with Special Olympics and is an Ignite Adaptive Sports ski instructor at Eldora Mountain Resort. He is a certified member of the Professional Ski Instructors Association and a former member of the Bryan Mountain and Diamond Peak Nordic Ski Patrols. He is a member of the Colorado Mountain Club and resides in Nederland.

Kay Turnbaugh is an avid skier, snowshoer, hiker, mountain biker, and road biker. She's been skiing in Colorado's backcountry for more than sixty years and still looks forward to every new ski season. She is the author of the Willa Award-winning *The Last of the Wild West Cowgirls;* children's book *The Mountain Pine Beetle—Tiny but Mighty* (Westwinds Press); *Around Nederland* (Arcadia Publishing Images of America Series); and *Rocky Mountain National Park Dining Room Girl: The Summer of 1926 at the Horseshoe Inn* (with co-author Lee Tillotson).

She co-authored *Afoot and Afield in Denver, Boulder and Colorado's Front Range, 184 Spectacular Outings in the Colorado Rockies* (Wilderness Press) with Alan Apt. Her latest book is a history of some of Colorado's favorite hiking trails: *Following In Their Footsteps: Historical Hikes of the Northern Front Range* with co-author Lee Tillotson.

Join Today.
Adventure Tomorrow

The Colorado Mountain Club helps you maximize living in an outdoor playground and connects you with other adventure-loving mountaineers. We summit 14ers, climb rock faces, work to protect the mountain experience and educate generations of Coloradans.

cmc.org